Taxcafe.co.uk Tax Guides

Salary versus Dividends

& Other Tax Efficient
Profit Extraction Strategies

By Carl Bayley BSc FCA
and
Nick Braun PhD

Important Legal Notices:

Published by:
Taxcafe UK Limited
67 Milton Road
Kirkcaldy KY1 1TL

Email: team@taxcafe.co.uk

ISBN 978-1-911020-97-4

Twenty-fifth edition, September 2024

Trademarks
Taxcafe® is a registered trademark of Taxcafe UK Limited. All other trademarks, names and logos in this tax guide may be trademarks of their respective owners.

Disclaimer
Before reading or relying on the content of this tax guide please read the disclaimer.

Disclaimer

1. This guide is intended as **general guidance** only and does NOT constitute accountancy, tax, investment or other professional advice.

2. The authors and Taxcafe UK Limited make no representations or warranties with respect to the accuracy or completeness of this publication and cannot accept any responsibility or liability for any loss or risk, personal or otherwise, which may arise, directly or indirectly, from reliance on information contained in this publication.

3. Please note that tax legislation, the law and practices of Government and regulatory authorities (e.g. HM Revenue & Customs) are constantly changing. We therefore recommend that for accountancy, tax, investment or other professional advice, you consult a suitably qualified accountant, tax adviser, financial adviser, or other professional adviser.

4. Please also note that your personal circumstances may vary from the general examples provided in this guide and your professional adviser will be able to provide specific advice based on your personal circumstances.

5. This guide covers UK taxation only and any references to 'tax' or 'taxation', unless the contrary is expressly stated, refer to UK taxation only. Please note that references to the 'UK' do not include the Channel Islands or the Isle of Man. Foreign tax implications are beyond the scope of this guide.

6. All persons described in the examples in this guide are entirely fictional. Any similarities to actual persons, living or dead, or to fictional characters created by any other author, are entirely coincidental.

About the Authors & Taxcafe

Carl Bayley is the author of over twenty Taxcafe guides designed specifically for the layperson and the non-specialist. Carl's particular speciality is his ability to take the weird, complex, and inexplicable world of taxation and set it out in the kind of clear, straightforward language taxpayers themselves can understand. As he often says himself, "My job is to translate 'tax' into English."

In addition to being a recognised author, Carl has often spoken on taxation on radio and television, including the BBC's It's Your Money programme and the Jeremy Vine Show on Radio 2.

A chartered accountant by training, Carl is a past Chairman of the Tax Faculty of the Institute of Chartered Accountants in England and Wales and was a member of the Institute's governing Council between 2003 and 2023.

Nick Braun founded Taxcafe.co.uk in 1999, along with his partner, Aileen Smith. As the driving force behind the company, their aim is to provide affordable plain-English tax information for private individuals and investors, business owners, accountants and other advisers.

Since then Taxcafe has become one of the best-known tax publishers in the UK and has won several business awards.

Nick has been involved in the tax publishing world since 1989 as a writer, editor and publisher. He holds a doctorate in economics from the University of Glasgow, where he was awarded the prestigious William Glen Scholarship and later became a Research Fellow. Prior to that, he graduated with distinction from the University of South Africa, the country's oldest university, earning the highest results in economics in the university's history.

Contents

Introduction

This guide answers one of the most common questions asked by company owners: "What's the best way to take money out of my company if I want to pay less tax?"

In Part 1 we kick off with a plain English guide to how *companies* are taxed.

Corporation Tax rates increased on 1st April 2023. Calculating your company's tax bill also became more complicated. As a result, new tax planning opportunities have arisen.

The Corporation Tax changes are covered in detail in this part of the guide and, throughout the guide, we explain how the changes affect your profit extraction decisions this year and in the years ahead.

In Part 1 we also explain how *company owners* are taxed. As a director/shareholder you can choose the best **mix** of salary and dividends. We examine the pros and cons of each type of income.

Company owners can also choose the most tax efficient **level** of income. We will see how, by smoothing your income or varying it significantly from year to year, you may be able to cut your tax bill considerably.

Tax-Free Salaries & Dividends

In Part 2 we reveal how much tax-free salary and dividend income you can withdraw from your company this year. You'll discover how to calculate the 'optimal' tax-efficient salary and how couples in business together can receive £26,140 this year without paying any Income Tax.

In Part 3 we explain how much dividend income you can take taxed at just 8.75% and how to avoid paying tax at 33.75%.

This part of the guide also contains important tax saving strategies for parents who want to avoid the Child Benefit Charge. This now kicks in when your income exceeds £60,000 (previously £50,000) but many company owners will be able to avoid it completely or in part.

There is also important tax planning information for high income earners (those with income over £100,000) and for *really big* earners, who may actually benefit from reversing the strategy that usually benefits everyone else.

Income from Other Sources

In Part 4 we turn to company owners who have income from other sources (e.g. pensions, rental income, interest income, income from another business and stock market dividends).

We explain why you may need to adjust your company salary or dividends to avoid the higher tax rates that kick in when your income reaches certain key thresholds (£50,270, £60,000 and £100,000).

We also examine some tax planning techniques that can be used to reduce or eliminate the tax payable on your income from other sources.

Company owners who are also landlords need to be aware of the restriction to tax relief on mortgage interest. Fortunately, company owners have more flexibility than other landlords when it comes to avoiding some of the worst effects of this additional tax charge.

Company owners can also enjoy much more tax-free interest than most other taxpayers (up to £6,000 per year).

Splitting Income with Family Members

Part 5 explains how company owners can gift shares in the business to their spouses, partners or children and save over £10,000 in tax this year, with similar savings every year.

We also show how additional savings can be achieved by paying tax-free salaries to family members, including your minor children.

There are, however, many traps to avoid when it comes to splitting income with family members and these are fully covered in this part of the guide. For example, we examine the danger of gifting shares that have fewer rights than ordinary shares and the danger of using dividend waivers to divert income to your spouse/partner.

Alternative Profit Extraction Strategies

Part 6 looks at alternative profit extraction strategies:

- **Directors' loans:** How they can be used to reduce or postpone tax.

- **Rent:** Why getting your company to pay you rent is more tax efficient than a dividend in many circumstances.

- **Interest:** How to receive up to £6,000 of tax-free interest from your company.

- **Charity:** Who should donate: you or the company?

- **Pension contributions:** Why they're better than dividends, who should make them (you or the company), plus a chapter on putting property into a pension.

- **Capital gains:** How to pay 10% tax when you sell or wind up your company; How to pay 0% tax when you sell your company to an employee ownership trust.

In Part 7 we turn to some of the practical issues and dangers that may be experienced when extracting money from your company:

- How to avoid the minimum wage regulations
- How to make sure your salary is a tax-deductible expense
- Making sure your company has sufficient distributable profits to declare dividends
- How to declare dividends properly and avoid an HMRC challenge
- When HMRC might try to tax your dividends as earnings

Finally, in Part 8, we look at some other tax saving strategies for company owners, including how they may be able to reduce the amount of Capital Gains Tax payable when assets like rental properties are sold.

In this part we also explain how you may be able to completely avoid tax by emigrating.

Using This Guide & Limitations

This tax guide deals primarily with the 2024/25 tax year, starting on 6th April 2024 and finishing on 5th April 2025. Unless expressly stated to the contrary, all references, examples etc, are based on the tax rates, thresholds, and allowances applying for 2024/25.

Nonetheless, there are some references to other tax years, for example when discussing the advantages and disadvantages of postponing income to a future tax year.

Following various Budgets in recent times, we know the expected Income Tax and National Insurance rates and thresholds for each tax year until 2027/28. Furthermore, the new Government has pledged: *"Labour will not increase taxes on working people, which is why we will not increase National Insurance, the basic, higher, or additional rates of Income Tax, or VAT"*.

However, it's important to emphasise that the new Government could make various changes to these and other taxes that do not break this pledge. Thus, the tax rules that will apply in future years are not known with any degree of certainty: and the further one strays into the future, the more uncertain the position becomes!

The reader must bear in mind that tax laws (and HMRC's interpretation of them) are continually changing.

Please note that, although small company owners are this book's main target audience, this is NOT supposed to be a do-it-yourself (DIY) tax planning guide. Our purpose in writing this guide is to explain in plain English how companies and company owners are taxed and provide some tax planning ideas that can be taken to an accountant or other professional adviser for further discussion.

We do not recommend 'going it alone' when it comes to this type of tax planning and there are several reasons for our cautious approach. Firstly, although the guide covers a fair amount of ground, it does not cover every possible scenario: that would be impossible without making the guide much longer and possibly much more difficult to digest.

In other words, in places we have had to sacrifice definitiveness in favour of making the guide a manageable and hopefully enjoyable read for the average small company owner.

Companies come in many different shapes and sizes, as do their owners, so it is possible the information contained in this guide will not be relevant to your circumstances.

In particular, please note this guide is aimed mainly at UK resident director/shareholders who own and work for UK resident companies.

Secondly, the main focus of this tax guide is *Income Tax* planning: helping company owners pay less tax on their salaries, dividends and other income. There are, however, other taxes that often have to be considered, including Capital Gains Tax (CGT) and Inheritance Tax.

Steps that you take to reduce one type of tax can have an adverse impact on your liability to pay other taxes. While some mention is made of other taxes in this guide, we cannot guarantee that all interactions are covered.

Thirdly, there are potential risks involved when it comes to structuring your affairs to reduce the tax payable on salaries, dividends and other payments made by your company.

While most of the tax planning ideas contained in this book are widely used by many accountants and other professional advisers, and have been for many years, this does not mean they have the blessing of HM Revenue & Customs!

There are some grey areas when it comes to this area of tax planning and some tax savings may not always be guaranteed. In other words, we cannot be certain that some of the tax planning ideas contained in this book will not be subject to some sort of attack from HMRC, even if only at some point in the future.

For example, in the chapters that follow, we will show that the most tax-efficient mix of income for most company owners is a small salary coupled with a larger dividend. While this is a well-established, reasonable form of tax planning which, if carried out correctly, is generally accepted, even if grudgingly, by HMRC, there are circumstances under which they might seek to tax dividends as earnings.

We'll look at this potential threat further in Chapter 42, but it's also worth pointing out that, *at present*, such attacks are rare and generally only occur where aggressive tax avoidance schemes are involved. For the vast majority of small company owners, the danger is remote and lies firmly in the future.

Fourthly, there are also *non-tax* factors that have to be considered when deciding how much money you withdraw from your company and in what form. In some instances, other considerations will outweigh any potential tax savings.

For all of these reasons, it is vital that you obtain professional advice before taking any action based on information contained in this guide. The authors and Taxcafe UK Ltd cannot accept any responsibility for any loss that may arise as a consequence of any action taken, or any decision to refrain from taking action, as a result of reading this guide

Corporation Tax Rates

Much of the planning and analysis in this guide is dependent on the company's Corporation Tax rate. As we will see in Chapter 1, under the new Corporation Tax regime, a company's overall tax rate could be anything between 19% and 25%.

However, it is generally a company's *marginal* Corporation Tax rate that matters for the purposes of this guide, rather than its *overall* tax rate. A company's marginal Corporation Tax rate will be either 19%, 26.5%, or 25%. It is these three rates we will use in our illustrations, examples, etc, throughout most of this guide.

Matching Up Company and Personal Tax Rates

It is *most likely* that a company owner who is a basic rate taxpayer will have a company paying Corporation Tax at 19%, while higher or additional rate taxpayers will have companies paying Corporation Tax at higher rates. We will generally follow these principles for our main examples throughout this guide.

However, we will also cater for the possibility that higher or additional rate taxpayers may have companies paying Corporation Tax at only 19%, while basic rate taxpayers may have a company paying Corporation Tax at a higher rate as, for various reasons, all these combinations are possible.

Scottish Taxpayers

The Scottish Parliament can set the Income Tax rates applying to most types of income received by Scottish taxpayers, but not interest or dividends. The vast majority of the information contained in this guide is relevant to Scottish taxpayers. However, unless stated to the contrary, all examples, tables and calculations assume the individual concerned is not a Scottish taxpayer.

Despite this general assumption, there is a great deal of extra information in this guide specific to Scottish taxpayers, as we want to include them as much as we can without making the guide too complicated (we are Scottish taxpayers ourselves, after all.)

It's also worth pointing out that, where a director needs to be a basic rate taxpayer for a particular strategy to work (see Chapters 10 and 11, for example), a Scottish intermediate rate taxpayer can be included.

To be a basic or intermediate rate taxpayer for 2024/25, a Scottish taxpayer needs taxable income excluding dividends, interest, and savings income, of no more than £43,662 *and* total taxable income of no more than £50,270.

Spouses and Civil Partners

Under UK tax law, all legally married spouses and registered civil partners are treated the same. Hence, when we refer to a 'spouse' in this guide, it includes a civil partner. For tax purposes, a spouse does not include a common-law partner or co-habitee. Where we are discussing a partner who may either be a legally married spouse or a common-law partner, we will use the term 'spouse/partner'.

Furnished Holiday Letting

At present, for the 2024/25 tax year, furnished holiday letting businesses meeting specific qualifying criteria (see the Taxcafe guide *Using a Property Company to Save Tax* for details) are treated as trading businesses for the purpose of a number of key tax reliefs, including business asset disposal relief and holdover relief, which we will discuss in Chapters 1, 27, 28, and 36.

Profits from furnished holiday letting are also currently treated as earnings for pension purposes, and mortgage interest and other finance costs can be properly deducted in full, just as when the world was sane before George Osborne ruined it.

Under current Government proposals, however, from 6th April 2025, furnished holiday letting will be treated as an investment activity for all tax purposes, in the same way as other property letting. The key CGT reliefs discussed in Chapters 1, 27, 28, and 36 will generally no longer be available, profits will not be classed as earnings, and mortgage interest and other finance costs will only attract basic rate tax relief in the same was as other residential lettings (as discussed in Chapter 26).

For more information on these forthcoming changes and how to plan for them, see the Taxcafe guide *Furnished Holiday Lets: Big Tax Changes Ahead*.

Some Assumptions
Unless stated to the contrary, we will assume throughout this guide that directors and company owners are:

i)   UK resident individuals
ii)   Not subject to the 'off payroll working' rules (sometimes known as 'IR35': see Chapter 43)
iii)   Not subject to the Child Benefit Charge (we will look at this in Chapter 17 however)
iv)   Not Scottish taxpayers (see above)
v)   Not claiming the marriage allowance (see Chapter 4)
vi)   Not subject to the minimum wage rules (see Chapter 38)

We will also assume, again unless stated to the contrary, that companies:

i)   Have no associated companies
ii)   Are UK resident
iii)   Have a twelve-month accounting period
iv)   Are not close investment holding companies

The relevance of these assumptions is explained in Chapters 1 to 3.

In this edition, we will also ignore the possibility, which may still exist in a few circumstances, that payments to directors will attract Corporation Tax relief in an accounting period commencing before 1st April 2023. For guidance on this issue, see the previous edition of this guide.

Part 1

How Companies & Company Owners Are Taxed

Chapter 1

How Companies Are Taxed

Companies pay Corporation Tax on both their income and capital gains.

On 1st April 2023 the main rate of Corporation Tax increased from 19% to 25%.

But not all companies pay Corporation Tax at the new rate. In fact, most of the small companies this guide is aimed at will be paying tax at a different rate.

Calculating the Company's Effective Tax Rate

Not only has Corporation Tax increased, it has also become more complicated, just like it was a few years ago. From 1st April 2023, there are two official Corporation Tax rates:

- Small profits rate   19%
- Main rate   25%

The practical effect is that companies pay tax as follows:

- **Profits £50,000 or less** – Company continues to pay 19% tax on all its profits

- **Profits between £50,000 and £250,000** – Company pays 19% tax on the first £50,000 and 26.5% on the remainder

- **Profits greater than £250,000** – Company pays 25% tax on all its profits

Some sample Corporation Tax bills and overall Corporation Tax rates are shown in Table 1.

TABLE 1
Overall Corporation Tax Rates

Profits	Corporation Tax	Corporation Tax Rate
£50,000	£9,500	19.00%
£60,000	£12,150	20.25%
£70,000	£14,800	21.14%
£80,000	£17,450	21.81%
£90,000	£20,100	22.33%
£100,000	£22,750	22.75%
£110,000	£25,400	23.09%
£120,000	£28,050	23.38%
£130,000	£30,700	23.62%
£140,000	£33,350	23.82%
£150,000	£36,000	24.00%
£160,000	£38,650	24.16%
£170,000	£41,300	24.29%
£180,000	£43,950	24.42%
£190,000	£46,600	24.53%
£200,000	£49,250	24.63%
£210,000	£51,900	24.71%
£220,000	£54,550	24.80%
£230,000	£57,200	24.87%
£240,000	£59,850	24.94%
£250,000	£62,500	25.00%

A company with profits of £100,000 will pay 19% on the first £50,000 and 26.5% on the final £50,000. The total tax bill will be £22,750 which means the company will have an overall tax rate of 22.75% (£22,750/£100,000).

A company with profits of £150,000 will pay 19% on the first £50,000 and 26.5% on the remaining £100,000. The total tax bill will be £36,000 which means the company will have an overall tax rate of 24% (£36,000/£150,000).

A company with profits of £20,000 (i.e. less than £50,000) will simply pay £3,800 (19%). A company with profits of £300,000 (i.e. more than £250,000) will simply pay £75,000 (25%).

Non-Resident Companies

Only UK resident companies are able to benefit from the 19% small profits rate. A non-resident company that earns rental income from UK properties, for example, has to pay 25% Corporation Tax on all its UK rental profits.

Accounting Periods vs Financial Years

A company's own tax year (also known as its accounting period) can end on any date, for example 31st December, 31st March, etc.

Corporation Tax, on the other hand, is calculated according to financial years. Financial years run from 1st April to 31st March. The 2024 financial year is the year starting on 1st April 2024 and ending on 31st March 2025.

This doesn't matter most of the time, but does when Corporation Tax rates change. For example, on 1st April 2023, the main rate of Corporation Tax increased from 19% to 25%. A company with profits of more than £250,000 whose accounting period ran from 1st January 2023 to 31st December 2023 will therefore pay Corporation Tax as follows:

- 3 months to 31st March 2023   19%
- 9 months to 31st December 2023   25%

The company will therefore pay 19% Corporation Tax on roughly one quarter of its profits (3/12) and 25% tax on roughly three quarters of its profits (9/12). (It doesn't generally matter at what point during the year the profits are actually made.)

This means the company's overall Corporation Tax rate for this year will be 23.5%. (In practice, Corporation Tax is calculated using days not months and this will result in a small difference.)

Because the Corporation Tax increase is now in full force, the above calculations are no longer necessary for current accounting periods. For example, the above company will simply pay 25% Corporation Tax on all its profits for the accounting period running from 1st January 2024 to 31st December 2024.

However, if Corporation Tax rates change again in the future, these split-year calculations will become relevant once more.

Marginal Tax Rate Planning

The Corporation Tax increase means many companies are paying more tax on their profits. The good news is many companies are also enjoying more Corporation Tax relief on their spending.

Before the increase companies enjoyed 19% Corporation Tax relief no matter how much profit they made or when they spent their money. A company incurring an additional £1,000 of tax-deductible spending would reduce its taxable profits by £1,000, saving it £190 in Corporation Tax.

The Corporation Tax increase means the amount of tax relief a company enjoys now depends on its profits. The position is as follows:

- A company with profits of £50,000 or less has a marginal tax rate of 19% and continues to enjoy 19% tax relief on its spending.

- A company with profits of between £50,000 and £250,000 has a marginal tax rate of 26.5% and enjoys 26.5% tax relief on its spending. (However, if the company's spending pushes its profits below £50,000 it will start to receive just 19% tax relief on any additional spending.)

- A company with profits of more than £250,000 has a marginal tax rate of 25% and enjoys 25% tax relief on its spending. (However, if the company's spending pushes its profits below £250,000 it will start to receive 26.5% tax relief on any additional spending.)

In Table 1 we listed the new *overall* tax rates companies face. For example, a company that makes a profit of £100,000 has an overall tax rate of 22.75%.

However, this overall rate is NOT used for most tax planning purposes, for example calculating the amount of tax a company will save if it spends some more money. Instead it is the company's marginal tax rate.

This makes sense when you consider a simple example. A company that anticipates making a profit of £100,000 and incurs an additional £10,000 of tax-deductible expenditure will reduce its taxable profits by £10,000. This will reduce its tax bill by £2,650 (26.5%). The company's overall tax rate of 22.75% does not tell us how much tax the company will save.

The Marginal Tax Rate Bands

To summarise, companies now effectively have three marginal tax rate bands:

Profits up to £50,000	19%
Profits between £50,000 and £250,000	26.5%
Profits over £250,000	25%

These bands apply in the majority of cases, but can be affected by factors such as whether the company has any associated companies, which we will examine in Chapter 2. They are an important concept in tax planning for companies, so watch out for references to the company's 'marginal tax rate band' later in this guide: it is these bands we are referring to.

(A director also has his or her own marginal tax rate band for Income Tax purposes. We'll get onto those later but, for now, it's important to emphasise that the ***director's*** marginal rate band and the ***company's*** marginal rate band are different things: although both of them are critically important for the purposes of this guide.)

Should My Company Postpone or Accelerate Spending?

Where a company's profit level changes from one year to the next, it may be able to save more Corporation Tax by postponing or accelerating some of its spending. For example, a company with profits not exceeding £50,000 in the current year will be taxed at 19% on those profits but, if it expects to make profits between £50,000 and £250,000 next year, its marginal tax rate will increase to 26.5%.

A company expecting this sort of increase in its marginal tax rate would enjoy an additional 7.5 percentage points of tax relief on spending it is able to postpone, saving £750 for every £10,000 it postpones.

In other cases, where the company expects its marginal tax rate to *decrease* next year, accelerating expenditure could produce similar savings.

But not all types of expenditure are suitable to be postponed or accelerated. Furthermore, in many cases, the timing of the tax relief is not dependent on the date the money is spent. For more information on this type of planning, which can yield almost 40% greater tax savings on deductible expenditure, see the Taxcafe guide *Putting it Through the Company*. Naturally, the commercial implications of postponing or accelerating business expenditure always need to be considered.

As far as most of the issues covered in this guide are concerned, it is generally the *director's* marginal tax rate that is far more important (as this can vary by a great deal more than 7.5%). For example, you might save 7.5% more Corporation Tax by postponing your 2024/25 salary to next year, but what use is that if it costs you an extra 28% in Income Tax and National Insurance?

Nonetheless, there are exceptions where the company's marginal tax rate alone is the key factor in determining the optimal time for it to spend money: pension contributions on the director's behalf are a prime example (see Chapter 33).

Tax Relief on Salaries etc

If your company pays you a salary, rent, interest, or makes pension contributions on your behalf, these are generally tax-deductible expenses for the company.

As we shall see in the chapters that follow, when deciding how much salary or other income to pay yourself, the amount of Corporation Tax relief your company receives on these payments is an important factor.

If your company's marginal Corporation Tax rate doesn't change, the amount of tax relief it gets is clear. Assuming the payment does not itself alter the company's marginal Corporation Tax rate, it will provide relief at 19%, 26.5%, or 25%, depending on which of the three marginal tax rate bands set out above your company's profits fall into.

In the vast majority of cases, it's as simple as that, and you can safely ignore the rest of this chapter.

In fact, we're going to ignore it for the majority of the guide ourselves and, unless stated to the contrary, will assume the company obtains Corporation Tax relief at 19%, 26.5%, or 25% on all its tax-deductible expenses, including payments made to, or on behalf of, directors.

Example: Angela takes a salary of £12,570 out of her company, which makes an annual profit of around £80,000 and thus has a marginal Corporation Tax rate of 26.5%. Her salary produces a Corporation Tax saving of £3,331 (£12,570 x 26.5%).

One quirk to watch out for though, is that the expense itself can sometimes lead to the company's profits dropping into a different marginal tax rate band.

Example: Belinda also takes a salary of £12,570 out of her company, but its annual profit before paying her salary is just £60,000. The Corporation Tax saving produced by Belinda's salary is thus:

£10,000 @ 26.5%	£2,650
£2,570 @ 19%	£488
Total	£3,138

For the sake of illustration, we've ignored employer's National Insurance in these simple examples, but we will, of course look at that later in the guide, as well as examining whether £12,570 was the best salary for these directors to take.

Changing Marginal Corporation Tax Rates

Things can get a little more complicated when a company's marginal Corporation Tax rate changes during the course of the *Income Tax* year.

Last year (2023/24), most companies that did not have a 31st March accounting date suffered an increase in their marginal Corporation Tax rate during the course of the *Income Tax* year. This year (2024/25), only some companies will see a change in their marginal Corporation Tax rate during the course of the *Income Tax* year (for example, if profits go from less than £50,000 to more than £50,000).

Where the company's marginal Corporation Tax rate changes from one accounting period to the next, the exact amount of tax relief it will enjoy in respect of payments made during the *Income*

Tax year will depend on its accounting date and profit level, on whether the payments are made monthly, annually, or as a 'one off', and on how the payment is recognised in the company's accounts.

Companies must operate the accruals basis of accounting, which means any periodic cost must be spread over the period to which it relates. For example, a company with a 31st December accounting date may make a single annual rental payment of £20,000 to its owner/director, who owns the company's trading premises personally. Whenever the payment is made, the director (who we will assume, for the time being, is not using the cash basis) will have taxable rental income of £20,000 for 2024/25.

But the payment that suffers Income Tax in the director's hands in 2024/25 will need to be recognised on a time apportionment basis in the company's accounts. Hence £15,000 (9/12ths) of the rent will fall into the company's accounting period ending 31st December 2024 and attract Corporation Tax relief at its marginal rate for that year; and £5,000 (3/12ths) will fall into the accounting period ending 31st December 2025 and attract Corporation Tax relief at its marginal rate for that year.

Let's say the company's profits turn out to be £200,000 for 2024 and £300,000 for 2025. Hence, it will have a marginal Corporation Tax rate of 26.5% for the year ending 31st December 2024, and 25% for the year ending 31st December 2025. The Corporation Tax relief for the rent on which the director pays Income Tax in 2024/25 will therefore be:

£15,000 @ 26.5%	£3,975
£5,000 @ 25%	£1,250
Total	£5,225

The overall effective rate of relief is thus 26.125%.

Sometimes periodic costs are apportioned on a daily, rather than monthly basis, which gives a slightly different result. Either approach is equally acceptable for both accounting and tax purposes, but we'll stick with monthly apportionment in this guide to keep life simple (or as simple as possible anyway).

The rent of £20,000 in our example might be either a single payment in respect of the twelve months to 31st March 2025, or it might be made up of the appropriate portions of annual payments made in respect of the twelve months to 31st December 2024 and twelve months to 31st December 2025. Either way, the director will pay Income Tax on £20,000 of rental income in 2024/25, and the company will enjoy Corporation Tax relief of £5,225.

Where something is a periodic cost, it's important to appreciate that, for Corporation Tax purposes, it is generally spread over the period to which it relates, regardless of when it is actually paid. Hence, the rent payment above would attract the same amount of Corporation Tax relief, and in the same accounting periods, even if it was not paid until after 5th April 2025.

There are some exceptions to this rule, however. Companies cannot claim Corporation Tax relief on:

- Salaries or bonuses that are still unpaid nine months after the end of the accounting period
- Interest charged by the company's owner that is still unpaid twelve months after the end of the accounting period

In these cases, relief can only be claimed when payment is actually made: credits made to the director's loan account count as payment though.

On the other side of the equation, directors are generally only taxed on payments from their company when they receive them (again, a credit to the director's loan account counts as receipt).

This applies to salary, bonuses, and interest paid to the director (as well as dividends, although these do not attract Corporation Tax relief). The only potential exception is rent, where the position depends on whether the director is taxed on their property income under the cash basis, or under traditional accruals basis accounting (see the Taxcafe guide *How to Save Property Tax* for detailed explanations of both methods and when they are available).

So, where does all this leave us with the effective rate of Corporation Tax relief for payments made to, or on behalf of, directors in 2024/25?

Generally, if something is paid monthly, it will be a periodic cost. Some things are always a periodic cost, even if paid annually.

Rent and interest are always periodic costs and thus will generally attract Corporation Tax relief at the rates for the relevant accounting period or periods, as in our example above.

Salaries and pension contributions paid monthly will usually also be periodic costs, attracting Corporation Tax relief at the rates for the relevant accounting period or periods.

Salaries or bonuses, and pension contributions, paid annually, or as a one-off, may not be periodic costs, but this depends on the circumstances. The position for salaries is discussed further below, pension contributions are discussed in Chapter 33.

Where payments are not periodic costs, they will generally attract Corporation Tax relief at the company's marginal rate for the accounting period in which they are paid: although, as we shall see later, there are exceptions to this.

What about Dividends?

Dividends are paid out of a company's *after-tax profits*. Thus, the total amount of tax paid on dividend income, including the Corporation Tax suffered by the company, will change if the company's Corporation Tax rate changes.

However, the effective rate of tax applying depends on what we are comparing the dividend with. For example, if a director takes a dividend instead of a monthly salary, the effective Corporation Tax rate applying to that dividend will change if the company's Corporation Tax rate changes during the course of the *Income Tax* year, and needs to be calculated like a periodic cost (see below).

Alternatively, if the director takes a dividend instead of a bonus, the effective Corporation Tax rate applying will be the company's marginal rate for the accounting period in which the bonus would have attracted Corporation Tax relief if it had been paid.

Salaries in the Current 2024/25 Tax Year

The current tax year for *individuals* runs from 6th April 2024 to 5th April 2025. As discussed above, for most companies, whose marginal tax rate does not change, it will be simple to calculate the amount of Corporation Tax relief the company will enjoy on salaries and other regular payments made to directors: it will generally be at 19%, 26.5%, or 25%.

Where the company's marginal Corporation Tax rate changes during the course of the 2024/25 Income Tax year, however, the calculation becomes more complex.

Example: Average Company Ltd has an accounting period that runs from January to December. It makes monthly salary payments to the directors. For the accounting period ending 31st December 2024, the company makes a profit of just £50,000 and hence will enjoy Corporation Tax relief at just 19% on the salary payments it makes.

For the accounting period ending 31st December 2025, the company makes a profit of £100,000, and hence will enjoy 26.5% Corporation Tax relief on any additional salary payments.

The 2024/25 tax year falls into both of these years, so the company will enjoy the following tax relief on its salary payments:

April to December 2024	*9/12 x 19%*	*14.250%*
January to March 2025	*3/12 x 26.5%*	*6.625%*
Total Corporation Tax relief		*20.875%*

The company will enjoy a total of 20.875% Corporation Tax relief on salary payments made during the current 2024/25 tax year.

Note this assumes the payment of the salary does not itself alter the company's marginal Corporation Tax rate for either accounting period.

The outcome may be different where the director's salary is paid in a single annual lump sum, rather than monthly.

Example: Annpay Ltd has an accounting period that runs from January to December. In the year ending 31st December 2024, it makes a profit of just £50,000, but in the year ending 31st December 2025, its profits increase to £100,000.

The company's director, Anne, takes her salary in a single lump sum in March each year. The salary she takes in March 2025 is accounted for as an expense in the company's accounts for the year ending 31st December 2025 and will thus provide Corporation Tax relief at 26.5%.

If we compare the results in the last two examples, we can see that a single lump sum payment (as for Annpay Ltd) may produce a different overall rate of tax relief to regular monthly payments:

Average Company Ltd (monthly pay): Relief at 20.875% on average
Annpay Ltd (lump sum):   Relief at 26.5%

In both cases, we are talking about salary falling into the same *Income Tax* year, 2024/25.

However, such single annual lump sum payments are not always accounted for as an expense of the company accounting period in which they are paid.

It would have been equally acceptable for Annpay Ltd to have accrued part of the cost of the salary paid to Anne in March 2025 as an expense of its accounting period ending 31st December 2024, with the remainder treated as an expense of the accounting period ending 31st December 2025. The split would be done on a time apportionment basis, with the end result being that the overall average rate of Corporation Tax relief for Anne's 2024/25 salary would be the same as for the monthly payments made by Average Company Ltd.

The proper accounting treatment of a lump sum payment like this is really a question of whether Anne's lump sum salary paid in March 2025 is seen as a reward for her efforts as company director over the period from April 2024 to March 2025, or as a bonus paid in recognition of her continuing service to the company.

In many cases, the decision on how to treat the director's annual lump sum salary in the company's accounts will have been made some years ago. If so, it could be difficult to argue for a different treatment this year just because the company's marginal Corporation Tax rate is changing.

There is, however, a way to control the timing of relief for a director's salary (when paid as a lump sum), which may be beneficial where the company's marginal Corporation Tax rate fluctuates from one accounting period to the next.

Securing Optimal Corporation Tax Relief for a Director's Salary or Bonus

For tax purposes, a director's bonus is effectively the same as a lump sum salary payment. For the purposes of this technique, it is better to refer to it as a bonus, however.

It is possible to secure Corporation Tax relief for a director's bonus in an accounting period that has already ended before the director is paid (or deemed to be paid: see Chapter 4).

The first step is to hold a directors' board meeting before the end of the old accounting period and minute the fact that the directors have agreed to pay themselves a bonus in respect of their performance during that accounting period. The amount of the bonus is not specified at this time (as we will see in Chapter 4, this could trigger an immediate Income Tax liability, which the company would have to put through the payroll and pay via the PAYE system).

However, while no Income Tax liability or payroll reporting obligation under PAYE has been created yet, the company now has a commitment to pay the bonus in respect of that accounting period.

As long as the director is then paid (or deemed to be paid: see Chapter 4) within nine months after the accounting date, the company can accrue the cost in its accounts and secure Corporation Tax relief in the earlier period.

Let's say, for example, a director's optimal salary (or bonus) for 2024/25 is £12,570 and they plan to take this as a single lump sum in March 2025. The company has a 31st December accounting date and usually makes profits somewhere between £45,000 and £75,000 before taking account of the director's salary.

Once the company's profits for the year ending 31st December 2024 are known, it can decide how much bonus to pay. In the scenarios that follow, 'profit' means the company's profit before taking account of the director's bonus or salary (for 2024/25). We'll also ignore employer's National Insurance for the sake of illustration.

Scenario 1: The company's profit for the year ending 31st December 2024 turns out to be £50,000 or less. The company pays a bonus of £1 to honour its commitment in respect of that accounting period. A further £12,569 can then be paid, as a separate, routine lump sum salary payment, later (but by 5th April 2025) and this will obtain Corporation Tax relief in the year ending 31st December 2025, possibly at 26.5%.

Scenario 2: The company's profit for the year ending 31st December 2024 is between £50,001 and £62,569. The company pays a bonus equal to the amount of profit in excess of £50,000, thus obtaining Corporation Tax relief at 26.5% on this amount. A further sum to bring the director's total salary and bonus (combined) for 2024/25 up to £12,570 can then be paid, as a separate, routine lump sum salary payment, later (but by 5th April 2025), which will obtain Corporation Tax relief in the year ending 31st December 2025, possibly also at 26.5%.

Scenario 3: The company's profit for the year ending 31st December 2024 is £62,570 or more. The company pays a bonus of £12,570 and obtains Corporation Tax relief at 26.5%.

Again, all these actions should be minuted as part of a directors' board meeting: this technique requires formality to succeed!

Under scenarios 1 and 2, the company could, instead, choose to go ahead and pay the full bonus of £12,570. This would mean some or all of the bonus only attracts Corporation Tax relief at 19% but, if the company is not confident of making profits in excess of £50,000 in the year ending 31st December 2025, it may be better to get Corporation Tax relief in the earlier period as at least this provides a cashflow benefit.

Under scenario 3, there may be instances where a salary of more than £12,570 becomes optimal for the director (we'll see these later in the guide). This technique can again be used to pay the optimal salary by way of a bonus.

The technique can also be used to fix the director's salary at the optimal level in other scenarios, such as when following the large salary strategy covered in Chapter 21.

Salary versus Bonus
Many directors prefer the simplicity and certainty of a regular monthly salary. However, as we have seen, when it comes to maximising Corporation Tax relief, it will often be better to take an annual lump sum as a bonus. But it's up to you!

Chapter 2

Multiple Companies

Company owners often think about setting up a second company, to keep a new venture separate from an existing business. Often there are sound commercial reasons for using more than one company, including to:

- Reduce risk (limit liability)
- Involve different shareholders
- Enable a stand-alone sale of each business
- Make it easier to borrow money

Using more than one company allows you to reduce your risk: if one business goes bankrupt, the other venture housed in a separate company should be protected because each company has limited liability status.

Using more than one company is also ideal when you want each business to have different shareholders. It's not uncommon for business owners to engage in different projects with different people.

Using separate companies may also make it easier to exit each business. For example, someone who owns an ecommerce business and a restaurant chain may wish to keep them in separate companies to make it easier to sell each business to a different buyer in the future.

When it comes to borrowing money, it's not uncommon for property investors to put their properties in a separate, stand-alone company and lenders often insist on this. Mortgage lenders tend not to like companies that have 'trading' activities, which are perceived as being more risky than property investment.

Saving Tax
Using separate companies may also be attractive when it comes to saving CGT and Inheritance Tax: in particular when one business is a trading business and the other is not. Companies that own too many non-trading assets, like rental property, can lose important

tax reliefs, including business asset disposal relief, holdover relief, and business property relief.

For example, someone who owns a software company and a property rental business may wish to keep them in separate companies so that the trading business (the software company) is not 'contaminated' by the non-trading business (the property rental business).

Conversely, under certain circumstances, keeping all your assets in one company can actually save Inheritance Tax (see the Taxcafe guide *How to Save Inheritance Tax* for more information).

Using separate companies has drawbacks too. For example, if you initially expect losses from a new trading activity, those losses can usually be set off against the profits from an existing activity, if both businesses are in the same company. This is generally not possible if the businesses are in separate companies (unless you form a group: see the Taxcafe guide *Putting it Through the Company* for details).

With the increase in Corporation Tax, some people may also be asking whether they can benefit from more than one company each enjoying up to £50,000 of profit taxed at just 19%.

The answer is generally no if the companies are controlled by the same people.

Associated Company Rules

To prevent people artificially spreading their business activities across multiple companies, the £50,000 lower limit and £250,000 upper limit are divided up if there are any 'associated companies'.

A company is associated with another company if:

- One company controls the other company
- Both are under the control of the same person or persons

For example, if you own all the shares in two companies, these companies will be associated. Each company will start paying Corporation Tax at 26.5% when its profits exceed £25,000 (i.e. £50,000/2). Each company will pay 25% tax on all its profits if its profits are greater than £125,000 (£250,000/2).

If there are three associated companies, each company will start paying Corporation Tax at 26.5% when its profits exceed £16,667 (£50,000/3)... and so on.

Example: *Jamie owns Company 1, which has annual profits of £100,000. He then decides to start a second business and is trying to decide whether to house it in Company 1 or set up Company 2. Let's say the new business makes a profit of £30,000. If he keeps it in Company 1, the additional profit will be taxed at 26.5% producing a total tax bill of £30,700.*

If Jamie decides to house the new business in Company 2, the two companies will be associated (if we assume he controls them both). The companies will pay Corporation Tax as follows:

Company 1: £25,000 x 19% + £75,000 x 26.5% = £24,625
Company 2: £25,000 x 19% + £5,000 x 26.5% = £6,075
Combined tax bill: £30,700

The total Corporation Tax bill will be the same whether Jamie uses one company or two. Jamie will still benefit from having £50,000 of profits taxed at 19% (£25,000 in each company).

However, if Company 2 has profits of less than £25,000, Jamie will effectively be penalised for running two companies. For example, if Company 2 breaks even (i.e. has a profit of exactly £0) he will pay £1,875 more tax with two companies. This is because Company 1 will have just £25,000 instead of £50,000 taxed at 19%.

For further details on the associated company rules, including situations where company shareholdings owned by your spouse, another close family member, or a business partner, may have to be counted when applying these rules, see the Taxcafe guide *Putting It Through the Company*.

Corporation Tax Quarterly Instalments

The associated company rules will also be relevant in deciding whether a company has to pay Corporation Tax in quarterly instalments. Instalments are generally payable by companies whose profits exceed £1.5 million but this amount will be divided up if there are any associated companies. Whereas most companies only have to pay Corporation Tax nine months after the end of their accounting period, companies subject to instalments have to start paying tax half way through the year.

Chapter 3

Investment Companies

In tax jargon, a 'trading' company is one involved in, for want of a better word, 'regular' business activities, e.g. a company that sells goods online, a catering company, or a firm of garden landscapers.

Common types of *non-trading* company include those that hold substantial investments in property or financial securities or earn substantial royalty income.

Corporation Tax
Before 1st April 2023, companies engaged mainly in non-trading activities paid Corporation Tax at the same 19% rate as most other companies.

However, the increase in Corporation Tax will see some of these companies having to pay Corporation Tax at the main rate of 25% on all their profits.

This is because a company classed as a close investment holding company (CIC) cannot benefit from the small profits rate. It has to pay Corporation Tax at the main rate on all its profits.

For example, a company that is set up to hold stock market investments will pay Corporation Tax at 25%, even if it only makes a small amount of profit. (Having said that, companies do not pay Corporation Tax on dividend income: but they do on capital gains or other forms of investment income.)

Fortunately, companies that mainly derive their profits from renting property to unconnected third parties (i.e. not to family members, etc) are excluded from the CIC provisions. Hence, the vast majority of property investment companies will enjoy the 19% small profits rate where appropriate.

Capital Gains Tax
If a company has too many non-trading activities (including most property investment and property letting) it may lose its trading status for CGT purposes.

This will result in the loss of two important CGT reliefs:

- Business asset disposal relief
- Holdover relief

Business asset disposal relief allows you to pay CGT at just 10% (instead of 20%) when you sell your company or wind it up.

Holdover relief allows you to give shares in the business to your children, common-law unmarried partner, or other individuals and postpone CGT. (You don't usually need holdover relief to transfer shares to your spouse because such transfers are generally exempt.)

Clearly, if the company's only business is property investment or property letting (or any other form of investment activity) then it will not be classed as a trading company and the relevant CGT reliefs will not be available.

Where a company has both trading and non-trading activities, it will only lose its trading status for CGT purposes if its non-trading activities are 'substantial'. HMRC generally accepts the non-trading activities are not substantial where neither non-trading income nor non-trading assets exceed 20% of the totals for the company as a whole. However, this test is only a yardstick and is not conclusive. In a recent tax case, it was held that non-trading activities would only be regarded as substantial where they were of material or real importance in the context of the company's activities as a whole.

Nonetheless, to avoid any argument over the issue, it is wise to keep both non-trading income and non-trading assets below 20% to safely preserve the company's trading status wherever possible.

Inheritance Tax
Shares in trading companies generally qualify for business property relief, which means they can be passed on free from Inheritance Tax. However, if the company holds investments (including rental property) this could result in the loss of business property relief. The qualification criteria are more generous than for CGT purposes and a company generally only loses its trading status for Inheritance Tax purposes if it is 'wholly or mainly' involved in investment related activities. For more information see the Taxcafe guide *How to Save Inheritance Tax*.

Chapter 4

How Directors Are Taxed: Employment Income

When HMRC and tax professionals talk about 'employment income', they are referring to salaries and bonuses.

Salaries and bonuses are subject to Income Tax and National Insurance. They are also generally a tax-deductible expense for the company.

Income Tax

For the 2024/25 tax year, starting on 6th April 2024, most individuals pay Income Tax as follows on their salaries:

- 0% on the first £12,570 Personal allowance
- 20% on the next £37,700 Basic rate band
- 40% above £50,270 Higher rate threshold

If you earn more than £50,270 you are a higher rate taxpayer; if you earn less you are a basic rate taxpayer.

The number £50,270 is important to remember because it will be mentioned repeatedly in the chapters that follow.

Using the Personal Allowance
It is worth mentioning that the personal allowance can be allocated to any income the taxpayer receives, and this rule takes precedence over any other rules governing the order in which income must be taxed.

In the vast majority of cases, however, for a small company owner with both salary and dividend income, it will be most beneficial to allocate the personal allowance to their salary first. There are some occasional exceptions to this (for example see Chapter 26) but, throughout the rest of this guide, we will operate on the basis that the personal allowance is allocated to salary first, other income such as rental income, interest, or pensions next, and dividends last: this is usually the best approach.

Transferable Personal Allowance

It is possible to transfer 10% of your personal allowance to your spouse or civil partner (£1,260 during the current tax year).

Only basic rate taxpayers can benefit from this tax break, known as the 'marriage allowance', so the maximum potential tax saving is £252 (£1,260 x 20%).

Unmarried couples are excluded: this was the rather feeble attempt by David Cameron to use the tax system to reward marriage. Married couples can only benefit from the maximum potential saving of £252 if:

- One person earns less than £11,310 (not including savings interest of up to £6,000 or dividends of up to £500) and is therefore wasting at least £1,260 of their personal allowance,
- The other person earns no more than £50,270 (£43,662 in Scotland), but at least £13,830, and
- Both individuals were born after 5th April 1935.

You have to register to use it at: www.gov.uk/marriageallowance

Potential winners are married couples where one person does not work (e.g. full-time parents) or only has a part-time job.

Example: *During the current tax year Bill earns a salary of £30,000 and his wife Daphne earns £6,000 working part time. Daphne has £6,570 of unused personal allowance. She can transfer £1,260 of this to Bill, which means Bill no longer has to pay tax on £1,260 of his income. This will save him £252 in tax (£1,260 x 20%).*

The saving is, in fact, given to the transferee by way of a £252 non-refundable tax credit. And, provided the couple qualify, it's always £252 (unless the transferee is a Scottish taxpayer, when it may be up to £265).

This means married couples running a company together can sometimes benefit, even if they both have income in excess of the personal allowance (but they must both be basic rate taxpayers).

Example: *Claire and Debbie are a married couple running a company together. They have no other income from outside the company. They each take a salary of £9,100 and dividends of £30,000. If they did this*

in 2024/25, they would usually each pay Income Tax at 8.75% on £26,030 of their dividends.

Instead, Claire transfers £1,260 of her personal allowance to Debbie. This means Claire suffers an additional £110 in Income Tax on her dividend income (£1,260 x 8.75%).

Debbie, however, gets a tax credit of £252 meaning that, overall, the couple are £142 better off.

It's a nice little tax saving under the right circumstances. However, both of the couple have to be basic rate taxpayers and this, in turn, will usually mean salaries of £12,570 are preferable (as we will see later).

Dropping one salary to £11,310 might enable the £142 Income Tax saving to be achieved, but this means forgoing Corporation Tax relief on £1,260. If the company's Corporation Tax rate is only 19% and dropping the salary leads to an employer's National Insurance saving it might, just about, be worthwhile. But with a maximum overall net saving of just £44, it's not really worth the effort.

So, it's an interesting quirk, but I think we'll ignore it for the rest of the guide.

Income over £100,000
When your taxable income exceeds £100,000, your personal allowance is gradually withdrawn. For every additional £1 you earn, 50p is taken away. When your income reaches £125,140, your personal allowance will have completely disappeared. It also means that those who earn salary income between £100,000 and £125,140 face a marginal Income Tax rate of 60%.

Example: Caroline, a company director, has received salary income of £100,000 so far during the current tax year. If she receives an extra £100 of salary, she will pay an extra £40 of Income Tax. She will also lose £50 of her Income Tax personal allowance, so £50 of previously tax-free salary will be taxed at 40%, adding £20 to her tax bill. All in all, she pays £60 tax on her extra £100 of salary, so her marginal Income Tax rate is 60%.

Income above £125,140

Once your taxable income exceeds £125,140, you pay 45% Income Tax on any extra employment income. This is known as the additional rate of tax. The threshold was previously £150,000, but was reduced to £125,140 for 2023/24 and subsequent years, aligning it with the point where your personal allowance is completely withdrawn.

National Insurance

In recent times the main rate of Class 1 National Insurance paid by directors and other employees has been reduced from 12% to 8%.

From 6th April 2024 National Insurance is payable as follows on employment income:

- 0%   on the first £12,570   Primary threshold
- 8%   on the next £37,700
- 2%   above   £50,270   Upper earnings limit

The way National Insurance is calculated is different if you're a company director.

For regular salaried employees paid monthly, National Insurance is calculated using monthly thresholds. So, although the thresholds for the whole year are £12,570 and £50,270, it is the monthly thresholds of £1,048 and £4,189 that are used to calculate how much National Insurance is payable in any specific month.

If a regular salaried employee received a salary payment of £12,570 at the start of the tax year in April, they would pay 0% on the first £1,048, 8% on the amount between £1,048 and £4,189 and 2% on the amount over £4,189: £419 in total.

By contrast, for company directors, National Insurance is calculated on a *cumulative annual basis*. Thus, a director who receives a salary payment of £12,570 at the start of the tax year in April will pay no National Insurance at all because his or her total pay for the year will not yet exceed the £12,570 primary threshold.

If the director receives any additional salary payments in the months that follow, they will pay 8% National Insurance on the whole amount (up to an additional £37,700). After that they will pay 2%.

As we can see, these thresholds and bands are the same as those for Income Tax: perhaps one of the few pieces of genuine tax simplification the Government has ever managed to achieve.

However, for many directors, things are not as simple as they may seem, as the National Insurance thresholds apply purely to their salary, whereas the Income Tax thresholds apply to **all** their income. For example, a director who also has rental income of £5,000 can receive a salary of £12,570 free from employee's National Insurance, but only £7,570 free from Income Tax.

Combined Tax Rates
The combined marginal rates of Income Tax and National Insurance applying to director's salaries in 2024/25 are as follows:

Up to £12,570	0%
£12,570 to £50,270	28%
£50,270 to £100,000	42%
£100,000 to £125,140	62%
Over £125,140	47%

Employer's National Insurance

Most employees don't lose sleep over their employer's National Insurance bill. However, for company owners this extra tax is an important consideration.

For salaries that exceed the 'secondary threshold' of £9,100, the rate of employer's National Insurance is 13.8%. The threshold has been frozen until April 2028, which means employers will pay more National Insurance, even if salaries paid to employees only increase because of inflation.

Employer's National Insurance is a tax-deductible expense. So, if a company pays £100 of National Insurance, this will reduce its taxable profits by £100, saving the company between £19 and £26.50 in Corporation Tax. Thus, the overall net cost is actually somewhere between £73.50 and £81.

There is no employer's National Insurance on salaries of up to £50,270 paid to under 21s, or apprentices under 25. The exemption is not lost if the employee earns more than £50,270: employer's National Insurance is then simply payable on the excess.

There is also a National Insurance holiday for employers taking on military veterans. The holiday is for the employee's first year of civilian employment. The exemption again applies to salary up to the higher rate threshold of £50,270.

The Employment Allowance

Most businesses qualify for the £5,000 employment allowance. There are, however, two exclusions, one of which will not concern many readers of this guide, but one of which will!

We will come onto the more important exclusion shortly. First, however, to dispense with the exclusion that will not bother many of us: the allowance is not available to employers whose National Insurance bill was £100,000 or more in the previous tax year. You'd have to employ 35 people at a salary of £30,000 each to reach this level, so most small businesses are unaffected.

The reason for covering the employment allowance in this guide is because it may affect some company owners' own salary choice. For example, two company owners who have no other employees can pay themselves a salary of £27,216 each this year without having to pay any employer's National Insurance.

But is it a good idea to take this much salary to avoid wasting the employment allowance? We'll answer this question in Chapter 9. In this section, we'll take a brief look at some of the employment allowance rules.

One Man Band Companies

Unfortunately, the exclusion that does really hurt small businesses is that the employment allowance is not available to 'one man band' companies where there is just one director who is the only employee.

According to HMRC guidance, the employment allowance also cannot be claimed if there are other employees BUT the director's salary is the only one on which employer's National Insurance is payable. This is to prevent directors of one-man band companies employing friends or family and paying them a token amount in order to claim the employment allowance for their own salaries.

At least one of the additional employees must be paid more than the secondary threshold. For example, a company that employs a seasonal worker who earns above the secondary threshold in a week (£175 for 2024/25) will be eligible for the employment allowance for the whole tax year.

The second employee can be another director (e.g. your spouse/partner) provided both directors' salaries exceed the *annual* secondary threshold (£9,100 for 2024/25 or pro rata if the directorship begins after the tax year has started).

If circumstances change during the tax year and the director becomes the only employee paid above the secondary threshold, the employment allowance can still be claimed for that tax year.

If a company with just one director who earns less than the National Insurance threshold employs just one other person (not a director), the company can claim the employment allowance if the employee earns more than the National Insurance secondary threshold.

It should be pointed out that several expert commentators, including the Institute of Chartered Accountants, believe HMRC has not interpreted the law correctly and that it should be possible to claim the employment allowance even if the second employee receives a small salary on which no employer's National Insurance is payable.

However, to play it safe it would be advisable to pay any second employee a salary slightly higher than the secondary threshold.

Other Employment Allowance Rules
The employment allowance can only be used against Class 1 National Insurance and not against Class 1A National Insurance. Class 1A is due on most taxable benefits in kind provided to employees, e.g. company cars.

If your company belongs to a group of companies, only one can claim the allowance. If your business runs multiple PAYE schemes, the allowance can only be claimed against one scheme.

The allowance is claimed as part of the payroll process. The full £5,000 can be claimed in month one of the tax year if your employer's Class 1 National Insurance exceeds £5,000 per month.

You can start claiming the allowance after the tax year has started and make a catch-up claim which can also be offset against your other PAYE costs.

If you claim the allowance at the end of the tax year and your remaining PAYE costs are not sufficient to use the entire allowance, the unclaimed balance can be carried forward to the next tax year.

Naturally, the amount claimed can never exceed the amount of employer's National Insurance which would otherwise arise in the tax year.

Connected Companies
A company cannot claim the employment allowance if a connected company already claims it.

Companies are connected if one company has control of the other company, or both companies are controlled by the same person or persons.

A person is generally considered to have control of a company if they hold more than 50% of the company's share capital or voting power, or if they are entitled to more than 50% of the company's distributable income or assets if the company is wound up.

For example, if you own all the shares in two companies, you will only be entitled to one employment allowance, even if the two companies are completely separate businesses with, for example, separate premises and staff.

If the company that claims the employment allowance has employer's Class 1 National Insurance of less than £5,000, the balance cannot be claimed by the other company.

Under certain circumstances, the shareholdings of close relatives and other 'associates' may have to be added together to determine whether two or more companies are controlled by the same person or group of persons.

For example, if you own all the shares in company X and your spouse owns all the shares in company Y, your spouse's holding in company Y could be attributed to you, so that you are treated as controlling both companies, as is your spouse.

However, this treatment is only applied where there is 'substantial commercial interdependence' between two or more companies (see the Taxcafe guide *Putting It Through the Company* for details of what this means and how this rule is applied in practice).

If the two companies are completely unrelated, then two employment allowances can be claimed. If there is substantial commercial interdependence between the companies then only one allowance can be claimed.

How Far Does the Employment Allowance Go?

The full £5,000 allowance is enough to cover £36,232 worth of salaries in excess of the £9,100 employer's National Insurance threshold. As mentioned above, that would cover two directors' salaries of £27,216 each.

It could also cover a single director's salary of up to around £45,300 but, as explained above, there needs to be at least one other employee, so the full £5,000 allowance will not generally be available.

Each employee uses up £138 of the employment allowance for every £1,000 of salary in excess of £9,100. So, an employee with a salary of £21,100 (£12,000 over the threshold) would use up £1,656 of the allowance (12 x £138), leaving £3,344 available to cover a director's salary.

The amount of director's salary that could be covered is then calculated as follows:

$$£3,344/0.138 = £24,232 + £9,100 = £33,332$$

As we will see in Chapter 11, this does not necessarily mean it is a good idea to pay this salary. However, there are some exceptions, which we will come across later in the guide.

Case Study: Total Tax Payable on Salary

Jane, a director, earns a salary of £60,000. Her Income Tax for 2024/25 can be calculated as follows:

- 0% on the first £12,570 = £0
- 20% on the next £37,700 = £7,540
- 40% on the final £9,730 = £3,892

Total Income Tax bill: £11,432

Her National Insurance for 2024/25 can be calculated as follows:

- 0% on the first £12,570 = £0
- 8% on the next £37,700 = £3,016
- 2% on the final £9,730 = £195

Jane's National Insurance bill: £3,211.

Her company claims the £5,000 employment allowance, but this is used up paying salaries to other employees. Her company's National Insurance bill on her salary is therefore:

- 0% on the first   £9,100 = £0
- 13.8% on the next £50,900 = £7,024

The company's National Insurance bill is £7,024. The company will enjoy Corporation Tax relief at up to 26.5%, so its National Insurance bill, net of Corporation Tax relief, will be £5,163 at best, and possibly a bit higher (see Chapter 1).

The total tax paid by Jane and her company is as follows:

Income Tax	£11,432
Employee's National Insurance	£3,211
Employer's National Insurance	£5,163
Total taxes	£19,806

When you include employer's National Insurance, it's startling how much tax is paid on Jane's income. Her £60,000 salary is not low by any standards, but you wouldn't describe her as a high income earner either. Nevertheless, an amount equivalent to at least 33% of her salary is paid in direct taxes on her *whole* income.

TABLE 2
Total Tax Payable on Salary 2024/25

Salary	Income Tax	Employee NI	Employer NI	Total	%
£10,000	£0	£0	£93	£93	1
£20,000	£1,486	£594	£1,128	£3,209	16
£30,000	£3,486	£1,394	£2,163	£7,044	23
£40,000	£5,486	£2,194	£3,198	£10,879	27
£50,000	£7,486	£2,994	£4,233	£14,714	29
£60,000	£11,432	£3,211	£5,268	£19,911	33
£70,000	£15,432	£3,411	£6,303	£25,146	36
£80,000	£19,432	£3,611	£7,338	£30,381	38
£90,000	£23,432	£3,811	£8,373	£35,616	40
£100,000	£27,432	£4,011	£9,408	£40,851	41
£110,000	£33,432	£4,211	£10,443	£48,086	44
£120,000	£39,432	£4,411	£11,478	£55,321	46
£130,000	£44,703	£4,611	£12,513	£61,827	48
£140,000	£49,203	£4,811	£13,548	£67,562	48
£150,000	£53,703	£5,011	£14,583	£73,297	49
£160,000	£58,203	£5,211	£15,618	£79,032	49
£170,000	£62,703	£5,411	£16,653	£84,767	50
£180,000	£67,203	£5,611	£17,688	£90,502	50
£190,000	£71,703	£5,811	£18,723	£96,237	51
£200,000	£76,203	£6,011	£19,758	£101,972	51
£225,000	£87,453	£6,511	£22,346	£116,309	52
£250,000	£98,703	£7,011	£24,933	£130,647	52
£275,000	£109,953	£7,511	£27,521	£144,984	53
£300,000	£121,203	£8,011	£30,108	£159,322	53

Once again, it's startling how much tax is paid on salaries, especially when you look at the overall tax rate (the last column).

Table 2 shows the total tax on a range of salaries. We assume the employer's National Insurance attracts 25% Corporation Tax relief and does not benefit from the employment allowance. The employer's National Insurance may instead attract Corporation Tax relief at 19% or 26.5%, the same as the salaries themselves, as discussed in Chapter 1. However, we used the main 25% rate in Table 2 for simplicity and because the company would have to be making substantial profits to be able to afford some of the salaries listed.

Scottish Income Tax

The Scottish Parliament can set Income Tax rates and thresholds for most types of income including salaries, self-employment income, rental income and pensions.

It does NOT have the power to tax interest and dividend income (including small company dividends). These types of income continue to be taxed using UK rates and thresholds. The Scottish Parliament also does not have the power to set the personal allowance. National Insurance and most other taxes, including Corporation Tax, CGT and Inheritance Tax, also remain the preserve of the UK Government.

Scottish Income Tax 2024/25
The following Income Tax rates apply:

£0 - £12,570	0%	Personal allowance (PA)
£12,570 - £14,876	19%	Starter rate
£14,876 - £26,561	20%	Basic rate
£26,561 - £43,662	21%	Intermediate rate
£43,662 - £75,000	42%	Higher rate
£75,000 - £100,000	45%	Advanced rate
£100,000 - £125,140	67.5%	PA withdrawal
£125,140 +	48%	Top rate

The top rate has been increased to 48% and a new 45% 'advanced rate' has been introduced for those earning over £75,000.

Coupled with National Insurance (set by the UK Government), the combined tax rates on salary income for directors are as follows:

£0 - £12,570	0%
£12,570 - £14,876	27%
£14,876 - £26,561	28%
£26,561 - £43,662	29%
£43,662 - £50,270	50%
£50,270 - £75,000	44%
£75,000 - £100,000	47%
£100,000 - £125,140	69.5%
£125,140 +	50%

Table 3 compares Scottish Income Tax with the rest of the UK. 'Income' does not include dividends or interest.

Table 3
Income Tax: Scotland vs Rest of UK
2024/25

Income	Scottish Taxpayer	Rest of UK	Difference
£20,000	£1,463	£1,486	-£23
£30,000	£3,497	£3,486	£11
£40,000	£5,597	£5,486	£111
£50,000	£9,028	£7,486	£1,542
£60,000	£13,228	£11,432	£1,796
£70,000	£17,428	£15,432	£1,996
£80,000	£21,778	£19,432	£2,346
£100,000	£30,778	£27,432	£3,346
£125,000	£47,653	£42,432	£5,221
£150,000	£59,681	£53,703	£5,978
£175,000	£71,681	£64,953	£6,728
£200,000	£83,681	£76,203	£7,478

Many Scottish taxpayers pay more tax than those in the rest of the UK. For example, someone earning £50,000 in Scotland will pay £1,542 more tax than someone living elsewhere in the UK, someone earning £100,000 will pay £3,346 more tax.

Those with income below £28,867 pay slightly less than their counterparts elsewhere in the UK, with a maximum saving of £23.06, or about 44p per week!

Who is a Scottish Taxpayer?
Someone is a Scottish taxpayer if their sole or main place of residence is in Scotland. For example, someone who rents a flat in London where they work during the week will probably be treated as a Scottish taxpayer if their spouse/partner and children live in the family home in Edinburgh and most of their friends and other social links are also in Edinburgh.

In some cases, however, it may be difficult to establish where the main residence is located.

Where no close connection to Scotland can be identified (for example, because it is not possible to establish the person's main place of residence), Scottish taxpayer status will be determined through day counting. You will then be a Scottish taxpayer if you spend more days during the tax year in Scotland than you spend in England, Wales, or Northern Ireland (taking each country separately).

Throughout this guide, where we refer to a Scottish taxpayer, or a Scottish company owner, we are using this definition. As far as tax is concerned, it doesn't matter where you were born or who you support in the Six Nations (apart from Inheritance Tax perhaps).

Scottish Company Owners
Scottish company owners who pay themselves a small tax-efficient salary (see Chapter 9) and take the rest of their income as dividends are completely immune from Scottish Income Tax. They pay exactly the same amount of tax as company owners living in the rest of the UK.

This is because the Scottish Parliament cannot change the Income Tax personal allowance or National Insurance thresholds and cannot tax dividend income.

This assumes the company owner does not have any other income subject to Scottish Income Tax, for example rental income.

Being subject to Scottish Income Tax is not necessarily a bad thing for company owners. It's only when Scottish company owners have salary income and other income subject to Scottish tax of more than £28,867 that they will pay more tax than those living elsewhere in the UK.

Welsh Income Tax

Since April 2019, the Welsh Parliament (Senedd Cymru) has been able to vary the Income Tax rates payable by Welsh taxpayers.

However, this year (2024/25) Welsh taxpayers will pay exactly the same Income Tax as those in England and Northern Ireland.

As in Scotland, the Welsh powers are limited with the UK Government retaining responsibility for the Income Tax personal allowance and the taxation of savings and dividend income. The UK Government also retains control of most other taxes such as National Insurance, VAT, Corporation Tax, CGT and Inheritance Tax.

Timing Directors' Salary Payments

Directors' salaries, like any other employee's pay, are subject to all the rules, regulations, and reporting obligations of the PAYE system. This can cause cashflow issues sometimes as payments made earlier in the tax year could trigger an Income Tax liability that can only be recovered when another payment is made later in the tax year, or even later, via the self-assessment system.

Assuming the director has a 'normal' PAYE code, these irritations can generally be avoided by either paying the salary in equal monthly instalments or in a single lump sum paid between 6th March and 5th April (assuming the company is using monthly pay periods for payroll purposes).

Generally, any salary or bonus payment is treated as paid for tax purposes when it is either paid in cash or posted as a credit to the director's loan account. However, it is important to be aware that, as soon as the **amount** of a payment is established and recorded anywhere in the company's records (e.g. in the minutes of a director's board meeting) this is deemed to represent payment for tax purposes and, if done too soon, can trigger unwanted tax liabilities.

Chapter 5

How Directors Are Taxed: Dividend Income

Dividends are subject to Income Tax but not National Insurance. Also, the Income Tax rates on dividends are lower than the Income Tax rates on salaries because dividends are paid out of a company's *after-tax* profits: the money has already been taxed in the company's hands, whereas salaries are a tax-deductible expense.

Starting this year (2024/25) the first £500 of dividend income you receive is tax free thanks to the 'dividend nil rate band', also known as the 'dividend allowance' (£1,000 last year).

For those receiving dividends in excess of the dividend allowance, the following tax rates apply:

Basic rate taxpayers	8.75%
Higher rate taxpayers	33.75%
Additional rate taxpayers	39.35%

Overall Tax Rates on Dividend Income
Because income paid out as dividends is taxed twice (first in the hands of the company and second in the hands of the shareholder) it's easy to lose sight of how much tax is being paid overall.

As a company owner, you are likely to be equally concerned about your company's tax bill as your own, so it's worth showing the overall combined tax rates on dividend income.

As we saw in Chapter 1, each company's overall Corporation Tax rate is now somewhere between 19% and 25%. The resultant total tax rates on dividend income are now in the following ranges:

Total Tax Rate

Basic rate taxpayers	26.1% to 31.6%
Higher rate taxpayers	46.3% to 50.3%
Additional rate taxpayers	50.9% to 54.5%

Company owners whose companies have profits of £50,000 or less will face the lowest total tax rates. For example, a company with total profits below £50,000 will pay £19 Corporation Tax on each £100 of profit, leaving £81 to pay out as dividends. Ignoring the dividend allowance, a basic rate taxpayer will pay just over £7 tax on this income (£81 x 8.75%), so the total tax bill on each £100 of profit is just over £26, which is 26.1%.

For companies with profits over £50,000, the combined tax rates on dividend income will vary according to the amount of profit the company makes. For example, a company with profits of £100,000 will face a total Corporation Tax bill of £22,750 (see Table 1), leaving £77,250 to pay out as dividends. If higher rate tax at 33.75% is payable on all of this income, the total tax bill on the £100,000 profit will be £48,822, which is 48.8%.

Owners of companies with profits of £250,000 or more will face the highest total tax rates. For example, a company with total profits of £250,000 will pay £25 Corporation Tax on each £100 of profit, leaving £75 to pay out as dividends. An additional rate taxpayer will pay £29.50 tax on this income (£75 x 39.35%), so the total tax bill on each £100 of profit is £54.50, which is 54.5%.

The combined total tax rates on dividend income are higher than the regular Income Tax rates that apply to most types of income (20% for basic rate taxpayers, 40% for higher rate taxpayers and 45% for additional rate taxpayers).

This is because the Government has been levelling the playing field between company owners (who often don't pay any National Insurance) and self-employed business owners and regular employees, who pay National Insurance on most of their earnings.

From a tax planning perspective, once a company owner has used up the £500 dividend allowance, they are usually better off paying themselves income that is taxed at the 'regular' Income Tax rates in preference to dividends, wherever possible.

Examples include rental income and interest income. Salary also fits the bill whenever there is no National Insurance cost (or where the cost is outweighed by Corporation Tax relief: see Chapters 9, 10, and 21).

Table 4 contains the total tax rates that apply at different profit levels and different Income Tax rates. In all of these calculations, we ignore the dividend allowance.

Some of these tax rates are unrealistically low if we assume that all of the company's profits are paid out in a single year to a single director.

For example, if a company has pre-tax profits of £200,000, it would be impossible for its after-tax profits of £150,750 to be paid out to just one director in one tax year with just 8.75% basic rate Income Tax payable (resulting in a total tax rate of just 31.22%).

However, this tax rate could be payable if dividends are paid to several directors who are all basic rate taxpayers, or if the profits are paid out over a number of years.

Similarly, some of the total tax rates are unrealistically high if the director does not have income from other sources. For example, if a company has pre-tax profits of just £50,000 this would never result in additional rate tax at 39.35% being payable if the director has no other sources of income.

If, however, the director does have a significant amount of income from other sources, it is possible the total tax rate on some or all of their dividend income will be 50.87%.

TABLE 4
Total Tax Rates on Dividend Income

Profits	Tax Rate @ 8.75%	Tax Rate @ 33.75%	Tax Rate @ 39.35%
£50,000	26.09%	46.34%	50.87%
£60,000	27.23%	47.17%	51.63%
£70,000	28.04%	47.76%	52.17%
£80,000	28.65%	48.20%	52.58%
£90,000	29.13%	48.55%	52.90%
£100,000	29.51%	48.82%	53.15%
£110,000	29.82%	49.05%	53.35%
£120,000	30.08%	49.24%	53.53%
£130,000	30.30%	49.40%	53.67%
£140,000	30.49%	49.53%	53.80%
£150,000	30.65%	49.65%	53.91%
£160,000	30.79%	49.75%	54.00%
£170,000	30.92%	49.84%	54.08%
£180,000	31.03%	49.93%	54.16%
£190,000	31.13%	50.00%	54.23%
£200,000	31.22%	50.06%	54.29%
£210,000	31.30%	50.12%	54.34%
£220,000	31.38%	50.18%	54.39%
£230,000	31.44%	50.23%	54.43%
£240,000	31.51%	50.27%	54.47%
£250,000	31.56%	50.31%	54.51%

Marginal Tax Rates

The total tax rates listed in Table 4 are calculated using the total Corporation Tax and Income Tax payable if all of the company's after-tax profits are paid out as dividends.

However, for companies with profits between £50,000 and £250,000 these are not the ones we would typically use to make tax planning decisions. For these purposes we would use the company's *marginal tax rate*.

Remember, companies with profits between £50,000 and £250,000 pay 19% on the first £50,000 and 26.5% on the rest. 26.5% is the company's marginal tax rate. Its total (average) tax rate will be lower because some of its profits will be taxed at 19%.

For companies with profits of £50,000 or less, the total tax rate and the marginal tax rate are the same: 19%. Similarly, for companies with profits of £250,000 or more, the total tax rate and the marginal tax rate are also the same: 25%. (However, if the company spends enough money to take its profits below £250,000, it will start to have a marginal tax rate of 26.5%)

Marginal Tax Rate Planning and Dividends
Take a company owner who is a higher rate taxpayer and anticipates that, as things stand, their company will make a profit of £60,000. Let's say the company already pays them rent to use an office property they own personally and they want to know whether they'll be better off paying themselves an additional £1,000 of rent, or taking the money as a dividend.

If they pay themselves rent this will be a tax-deductible expense for the company, so the whole £1,000 will be paid out and after paying 40% Income Tax they will be left with £600.

Alternatively, the company will pay 26.5% Corporation Tax on this final £1,000 of profit, leaving £735 to pay out as dividend income. After paying Income Tax at 33.75% they will be left with £487.

The total tax payable on the additional dividend income is £513, which is 51.3%. Clearly in this case additional rental income is more attractive.

Note, 51.3% is higher than the 47.17% rate in Table 4 for a company with profits of £60,000. That total tax rate is calculated using the company's total Corporation Tax rate. Most of its profits are taxed at just 19%, so the total tax rate in the table is lower.

The rate we've used in this example, however, is the company's 26.5% marginal tax rate, the rate which applies to the final £1,000 of profit we are looking at.

In summary, the total tax rates listed in Table 4 give you some idea of the total amount of Corporation Tax and Income Tax that will be payable if all of a company's after-tax profits are paid out as dividends. But, when it comes to choosing between a dividend and some other type of income, the marginal tax rate is more relevant.

For company owners whose companies have profits between £50,000 and £250,000 the combined marginal tax rate (Corporation Tax and Income Tax) on dividend income will be as follows:

	Combined Marginal Tax Rate
Basic rate taxpayers	32.93%
Higher rate taxpayers	51.31%
Additional rate taxpayers	55.42%

The Dividend Allowance

Company owners do not enjoy an additional standalone amount of £500 tax free. Instead, the dividend allowance typically uses up some of your basic rate band.

The dividend allowance only uses up your basic rate band if, like many company owners, you have dividend income subject to basic rate tax. It works differently if you have a lot of other income and all your dividends are subject to higher rate tax.

Dividend Taxation Examples

Let's take a look at some sample dividend tax calculations for the current 2024/25 tax year. To keep things simple, we'll assume the company owners take a small salary of £12,570 and the rest of their income as dividends.

There may be £479 of employer's National Insurance payable by the company on this salary. See Chapter 9 for a discussion as to why this amount of salary may nevertheless be the most tax efficient.

We'll also assume the company owners have no other taxable income. The examples apply equally to Scottish company owners.

Example – Basic-Rate Taxpayer

Stuart is a company owner with a salary of £12,570 and cash dividend of £20,000. His total income is thus £32,570.

His salary is tax-free because it is covered by his personal allowance. The first £500 of his dividend income is tax free thanks to the dividend allowance. The remaining £19,500 of his dividend income is taxed at 8.75%, producing a total tax bill of £1,706.

Example – Higher-Rate Taxpayer

Robert is a company owner with a salary of £12,570 and dividend of £50,000. His total income is thus £62,570.

His salary is tax-free, covered by his personal allowance. The first £500 of his dividend is also tax-free thanks to the dividend allowance. The dividend allowance uses up £500 of his £37,700 basic rate band so just £37,200 of his dividend income is taxed at 8.75%, producing a tax bill of £3,255. The final £12,300 of his dividend takes him over the higher rate threshold and is taxed at 33.75%, producing a tax bill of £4,151.

Robert's total tax bill is £7,406

Example – Personal Allowance Withdrawal

Alpesh is a company owner with a salary of £12,570 and dividend of £97,430. His total taxable income is £110,000. His personal allowance is reduced from £12,570 to £7,570. Thus £5,000 of his salary is taxed at 20% (£12,570 – £7,570), producing a tax bill of £1,000.

The first £500 of his dividend income is tax free, being covered by the dividend allowance. The next £32,200 of his dividend income is covered by his remaining basic rate band (£37,700 – £5,000 – £500) and taxed at 8.75%, producing a tax bill of £2,818.

The remaining £64,730 of his dividend income is taxed at 33.75%, producing a tax bill of £21,846.

His total tax bill is therefore £25,664.

Example – Additional-Rate Taxpayer

Maeve is a company owner with a salary of £12,570 and dividend of £200,000. Her total income is thus £212,570. Because her income exceeds £125,140, she is an additional rate taxpayer.

The first £500 of her dividend income is tax free but her Income Tax personal allowance is completely withdrawn. This means she will pay 20% Income Tax on her salary, £2,514; and her remaining basic rate band will be reduced to just £24,630 (£37,700 – £12,570 salary – £500 dividend allowance). She will thus pay 8.75% tax on £24,630 of her dividend income (£2,155).

The next £87,440 of her dividend (£125,140 less £37,700) is subject to higher rate tax at 33.75%, resulting in additional tax of £29,511. The remaining £87,430 of dividend income takes her over the £125,140 *additional rate tax threshold and is taxed at 39.35%, resulting in additional tax of £34,404.*

Maeve's total tax bill is £68,584.

Taxpayers with Significant Non-Dividend Income

The dividend allowance only forms part of your basic rate band if you have dividend income that falls into the basic rate band. It works differently if your basic rate band is completely used up by other income, e.g. salary or rental income.

The way to think about it is like this: dividends are always treated as the top slice of your income and taxed at your highest marginal rate. The dividend allowance exempts the *bottom* £500 of that income from tax. So, if you have dividend income taxed at both 8.75% and 33.75%, the dividend allowance will exempt some of the income taxed at 8.75%.

But if ALL your dividend income is taxed at 33.75% (because you have a lot of other income, e.g. rental income) the dividend allowance will be part of your higher rate band and you'll pay 0% tax instead of 33.75% tax on £500 of your dividend income.

Example: *In 2024/25 Julia has £60,000 of salary and rental income and £30,000 of dividend income. Her salary and rental income uses up her personal allowance and basic rate band, taking her over the higher rate tax threshold. The first £500 of her dividend is tax free; £29,500 is taxed at the 33.75% higher rate.*

The dividend allowance does not form part of her basic rate band as none of her dividend income falls into the basic rate band.

Example: *In 2024/25 Leon has £90,000 of salary and rental income and £50,000 of dividend income. With this much income his personal allowance is completely withdrawn.*

The first £500 of his dividend income is covered by the dividend allowance, leaving £34,640 taxed at the 33.75% higher rate. Along with his salary this takes Leon up to the £125,140 additional rate threshold. The final £14,860 of his dividend is taxed at 39.35%.

Leon has dividend income taxed at both the higher rate and additional rate. The dividend allowance reduces the amount of his dividend income taxed at the 33.75% higher rate.

Tax Charges on Tax-Free Dividends

Dividends covered by the dividend allowance are still taxable income, even if they are taxed at a rate of 0%. This means these supposedly tax-free dividends can give rise to tax or other similar costs as they are counted for the purposes of:

- The Child Benefit Charge
- Withdrawal of the personal allowance (income over £100,000)
- Whether any of the basic rate band is still available to reduce the rate of CGT payable on capital gains
- Reductions in the personal savings allowance where income exceeds the higher rate tax threshold or the additional rate tax threshold (see Chapter 26)
- The pension annual allowance taper (see Chapter 22)
- Student loan repayments ('student persecution payments' as my children call them)
- Tax-free childcare (withdrawn if income exceeds £100,000)

Use It or Lose It

Subject to the points above (especially the last one), and although it is now just a pathetic £500, it generally makes sense to ensure you use your dividend allowance every year, as it does not carry forward. Hence, for the rest of this guide, unless stated to the contrary, we'll be assuming you always pay yourself at least enough dividends to use your dividend allowance.

Taxpayers with Other Dividend Income

Each individual gets one dividend allowance to cover all their dividend income each tax year. If you also have dividends from stock market investments, you will not be able to use the full dividend allowance against dividends from your own company.

Scottish Taxpayers

The Scottish Government can tax most types of income but not dividends or interest. It also cannot change the personal allowance or National Insurance. This means:

- Scottish company owners pay exactly the same amount of tax on their dividend income as company owners living in the rest of the UK.

- Scottish company owners who also pay themselves a small tax-efficient salary (no higher than the £12,570 personal allowance) are completely immune from Scottish Income Tax, assuming they do not have any other income subject to Scottish tax.

- Scottish company owners whose salary income, rental income and other income (except interest and dividends) exceeds £12,570 will pay Scottish Income Tax.

  However, if this income is less than £28,867, they will pay less tax on this income than people living elsewhere in the UK. If this income exceeds £28,867, they will pay more tax.

  They will pay the same amount of tax on their dividend income as company owners living in the rest of the UK.

(See Chapter 18 for more information for high income earners.)

Example: *Alan is a company owner living in Scotland. He has salary and rental income of £30,000 and dividend income of £25,000.*

He is subject to Scottish Income Tax on his salary and rental income. As we saw in Table 3 in Chapter 4, this means he will pay £11 more tax on this income than someone living elsewhere in the UK; but what about his dividend income?

Although the higher rate threshold is £43,662 in Scotland, it is the UK higher rate threshold (£50,270) that applies to his dividend income.

The first £500 is tax free thanks to the dividend allowance. This leaves him with £19,770 of basic rate band (£50,270 – £30,000 – £500). This income will be taxed at 8.75%.

The remaining £4,730 of his dividend income takes him over the £50,270 higher rate threshold and will be taxed at 33.75%.

Dividend Tax Terminology
The 0% tax rate applying to the dividend allowance or dividend nil rate band is known officially as the 'dividend nil rate'. The 8.75% rate is known as the 'ordinary rate', the 33.75% rate is known as the 'upper rate' and the 39.35% rate as the 'additional rate'. We do not use these terms much in this guide, preferring the terms basic rate, higher rate, and additional rate.

Will Dividend Tax Rates be Increased Again?

Dividend tax rates were increased by 1.25% on 6th April 2022. This increase was designed to match an identical increase in National Insurance rates (because many company owners take most of their income as dividends and do not pay much National Insurance).

Unfortunately, dividend tax rates were not reduced when the National Insurance increase was later scrapped. And they were also not reduced when the previous Government cut the main rate of Class 1 National Insurance from 12% to 8%.

It must also be remembered that the increase in Corporation Tax from April 2023 has resulted in a further increase in the total combined tax rates on dividend income.

Will dividend rates be increased again? The new Government stated in its election manifesto that: *"Labour will not increase taxes on working people, which is why we will not increase National Insurance, the basic, higher, or additional rates of Income Tax, or VAT."*

We at Taxcafe think there could potentially be a further increase in dividend tax rates under the new Labour Government. In their eyes, we suspect, dividends are not paid to 'working people', instead they're viewed as investment income.

Furthermore, the election manifesto mentions the basic and higher rates of Income Tax, but the tax legislation relating to dividends uses the terms 'ordinary rate' and 'upper rate', so the Government arguably wouldn't even be breaking its manifesto pledge by increasing these rates... and most voters wouldn't care anyway.

Chapter 6

Don't Forget Payments on Account

Payments on account are made twice a year and allow HMRC to collect some of the tax you owe early. Common victims include sole traders and landlords, i.e. those whose Income Tax is not collected at source. Payments on account are not extra tax but they do affect your cashflow.

Most salary earners do not have to make payments on account because their tax is collected almost immediately through PAYE.

However, many company owners have to make payments on account as dividend income is not taxed at source and tax has to be paid through the self-assessment system.

How Payments on Account Are Calculated
If you paid yourself a dividend during the previous tax year, which started on 6th April 2023 and ended on 5th April 2024, the Income Tax is normally payable by 31st January 2025: almost ten months after the tax year ended.

For example, let's say a company owner paid themselves a salary of £12,570 and dividend of £21,000 and had no other taxable income. To keep the example simple, let's also assume they have never had to make any payments on account in the past.

No Income Tax was payable on their salary because it was fully covered by their personal allowance and the first £1,000 of their dividend income was tax free thanks to the dividend allowance for 2023/24.

The remaining £20,000 of their dividend income for 2023/24 is taxed at 8.75%, producing a total Income Tax bill of £1,750, which is due to be paid by 31st January 2025.

2024/25 Tax Year

Now let's move forward to the current 2024/25 tax year, which started on 6th April 2024 and ends on 5th April 2025.

We will assume our company owner pays themselves a tax-free salary of £12,570 and a dividend of £24,000. Their Income Tax bill will be £2,056 (the first £500 of dividend income is tax free, the rest is taxed at 8.75%). However, this time they cannot wait until 31st January 2026 to pay the tax.

On 31st January 2025, when they pay their 2023/24 tax bill, they will also have to make a payment on account of £875 for 2024/25. They must also make another payment on account of the same amount on 31st July 2025. Thus, their total tax payments will be as follows:

- 31st January 2025   £1,750 + £875 = £2,625
- 31st July 2025   £875

Each payment on account is normally half the previous year's self-assessment tax.

In January 2026, they will have to make a final tax payment for 2024/25, but will be able to deduct the two payments on account.

In this example, the company owner will have an additional £306 to pay in respect of 2024/25 (£2,056 – £1,750 payments on account) because their payments on account will not fully cover their tax bill.

Furthermore, they will usually also be paying their first payment on account for 2025/26 at the same time, so the total amount payable by 31st January 2026 would generally be £1,334 (£306 + £2,056/2).

Where the final self-assessment tax liability for the year turns out to be less than the payments on account, the excess payment can either be refunded or set against the first payment on account for the following year. This might happen, for example, if a company owner takes a much smaller dividend in 2024/25 than they took in 2023/24.

Postponing Tax

Making payments on account is still much better than paying tax through the PAYE system. Take a look at our company owner's tax payments for 2024/25.

The first payment is due around *ten months* after the start of the tax year (January 2025), the second payment is due around *16 months* after the start of the tax year (July 2025) and the third payment is due around *22 months* after the tax year has started (January 2026).

This means that if you pay yourself a dividend at the start of the tax year, you will have free use of the taxman's money for well over a year.

That money could be invested in a cash ISA or some other low-risk investment. The returns are likely to be better than those available from your company's bank account.

Who Has to Make Payments on Account?

Payments on account are all about the tax you paid for the *previous tax year*. You only have to make payments on account if your self-assessment tax (i.e. ignoring tax deducted at source) for the previous tax year was more than £1,000.

For example, if during the current 2024/25 tax year, you pay yourself a salary of £12,570 and a dividend of £11,000, your total Income Tax bill will be £919 and you will not have to make any payments on account in January and July 2026.

Of course, if you have income from other sources (e.g. rental income from property) this will have to be factored into the equation too.

You do not have to make payments on account, however, if more than 80% of your total tax from the previous year was covered by tax deducted at source.

How to Reduce Payments on Account

Where your self-assessment liability for the current year can reasonably be expected to be less than that for the previous year, you can apply to reduce your payments on account to the appropriate level (i.e. half of the anticipated liability for the current year).

For example, if you take a much smaller dividend in 2024/25 than you took in 2023/24, you can apply to reduce your payments on account due on 31st January and 31st July 2025. You can do this when you submit your 2023/24 tax return.

You have to be careful when doing this, however. If you claim a reduction in your payments on account and then find you have more tax to pay than you expected, you will have to pay interest on the underpayment. There could also potentially be a penalty if there is a significant underpayment and you had no reasonable grounds for having reduced your payments on account by so much.

Chapter 7

Salary versus Dividends:
The Basics

Unlike self-employed business owners (sole traders and partnerships), company owners are in the fortunate position of wearing two caps.

On the one hand, you can reward your work as a director; on the other hand, you can reward your entrepreneurship as a shareholder.

As a company director and shareholder you can split your income into salary and dividends and this can generate Income Tax and National Insurance savings.

For example, while National Insurance is payable on salaries, it is not payable on shareholder dividends.

By structuring distributions from your company carefully and taking the 'optimum' amount of salary and dividends, you could end up with a significantly higher after-tax income than a regular salaried employee who earns a higher income before tax.

However, while saving Income Tax will be an important consideration, other factors are important too. The major differences between a salary and dividend are:

Salaries Are Tax Deductible
Salaries usually qualify for Corporation Tax relief, dividends do not. If the company pays you a salary, its taxable profits will be reduced and it will pay less Corporation Tax.

Dividends are paid out of a company's after-tax profits, so paying a dividend does not reduce the *company's* tax bill.

This is an important point to remember because most company owners are concerned about both their own and their company's tax bill.

For example, if a company has a taxable profit of £10,000, it will pay £1,900 Corporation Tax (19%), leaving only £8,100 to distribute as dividends. This Corporation Tax must be added to any Income Tax paid by the shareholder on their dividend income when calculating the total tax suffered.

Dividends Require Profits

Only companies that have made profits can pay dividends. Profits are usually calculated when the company's annual accounts are drawn up (often many months after the end of the company's accounting period).

So dividends will usually be paid out of profits made in a previous accounting period. It is, however, possible to pay dividends out of profits made during the current year, for example if accurate management accounts are drawn up to determine the level of the company's distributable profits (see Chapter 41).

Salaries can be paid even if the company is making losses.

Income Tax and National Insurance

Salaries and dividends are subject to different rates of Income Tax.

Salaries are generally subject to National Insurance, dividends are not. Both the director and the company may be subject to National Insurance.

Tax Payment Dates

The Income Tax and National Insurance payable on salaries is collected almost immediately via PAYE. The Income Tax on dividends is collected via self-assessment: generally at a later date.

Earnings

Salaries are classed as 'earnings', which is important if you want to make significant pension contributions personally. Dividends are not classed as earnings.

Chapter 8

Company Owners Can Control Their Income Tax Bills

In Chapter 7 we mentioned that a company owner can often decide whether any distribution of the company's money is classified as salary or dividend.

Another advantage of being a company owner is that you have control over *how much* income you withdraw in total. This gives you significant control over your Income Tax bill.

Unlike sole traders, who pay tax each year on ALL the profits of the business, company owners only pay tax on the income they decide to pay themselves. This allows company owners to reduce their Income Tax bills by adopting the following strategies:

- 'Smooth income'
- 'Roller-coaster income'

Smooth Income

With smooth income, the company owner withdraws roughly the same amount of money each year, even though the company's profits may fluctuate considerably.

Smooth income allows the company owner to stay below the key Income Tax thresholds that could result in a higher tax bill:

- £50,270   Higher rate tax
- £60,000   Child Benefit Charge
- £100,000   Personal allowance withdrawal

We will return to how you can plan your salary and dividend withdrawals around these key Income Tax thresholds in the chapters that follow.

The higher rate threshold generally increases each year with inflation, but has been frozen until 5th April 2028.

The Child Benefit Charge used to kick in when the highest earner in the household had income over £50,000. However, starting with the current 2024/25 tax year the charge is now only payable when the highest earner's income exceeds **£60,000**. Furthermore, the charge is now levied more gradually. The full charge will only be payable when the highest earner's income reaches **£80,000**.

The £100,000 threshold was introduced in April 2010 and has *never* been increased. If it had gone up with inflation you would only start losing your personal allowance with an income of around £175,000 today.

By freezing various thresholds the Government has decided to deploy 'fiscal drag' to raise taxes. Fiscal drag occurs when an increase in your income, which is purely down to inflation, pushes up your tax rate. At Taxcafe we call fiscal drag the Silent Killer.

Less silent, but more deadly, was the decision to reduce the additional rate threshold to £125,140. The original £150,000 threshold was introduced in 2010. If it had gone up with inflation, you would only start paying 45% tax with an income of around £260,000 today. Yet instead it is now less than half what it should have been by this time.

With the reduction in the additional rate threshold to align it with the point where the personal allowance is completely withdrawn, this threshold is no longer relevant for the smooth income strategy; but it plays an important role in our next strategy.

Roller-Coaster Income

With 'roller-coaster income', the company owners take a bigger or smaller salary or dividend than would normally be required to fund their lifestyles. Roller-coaster income could save you tax in the following circumstances:

Avoiding Additional Tax Costs
There are two parts of the Income Tax system that create an additional tax cost for a limited band of taxable income:

- The Child Benefit Charge where income is between £60,000 and £80,000
- Withdrawal of the personal allowance where income is between £100,000 and £125,140

Where a company owner needs income above the key threshold of £60,000 or £100,000 each year *on average*, they can still avoid these additional charges in some years by using a roller-coaster income strategy. We will look at this planning technique and the potential savings available in more detail in Chapters 17 to 19.

Income Tax Rates Are Going Up or Down
If the Government announces that Income Tax rates will *rise* during a future tax year, you may wish to pay yourself more income now and less income later on. And if your tax rate will *fall* during a future tax year, you may wish to pay yourself less income now and more income later on.

You Want to Save Capital Gains Tax
It may also make sense for company owners to pay themselves less income during tax years in which they sell assets subject to CGT such as rental properties.

Why? This may allow some of your basic rate band (£37,700 this year) to be freed up, which means some of your capital gains will be taxed at 10% or 18% instead of 20% or 24% (see Chapter 44).

Cashflow Savings
In Chapter 6 we looked at how payments on account work and how these affect the timing of your tax payments.

For example, let's say you need to extract £30,000 of after-tax income from your company every year. In 2024/25, you do this by taking a salary of £12,570 and dividends of £19,054, leading to an Income Tax bill of £1,624. From this you deduct the payments on account you made in January and July 2025, to give you the final payment in respect of 2024/25 due by 31st January 2026.

Ordinarily, you would also need to make payments on account in respect of 2025/26 of £812 each on both 31st January and 31st July 2026. You would again get your usual after-tax income of £30,000 for 2025/26 by taking a salary of £12,570 and dividends of £19,054, giving you an Income Tax bill for the year of £1,624. After setting off your payments on account, you would have no final payment in respect of 2025/26 to make by 31st January 2027. You would then have payments on account of £812 each to make in January and July 2027 in respect of 2026/27.

But let's now suppose you decide, and are able, to break that pattern by postponing £18,000 of the dividend you would normally take in 2025/26 and taking it early in 2026/27 instead. This will reduce your Income Tax bill for 2025/26 to just £48, meaning you can apply to reduce your payments on account due in January and July 2026 to just £24 each and no payments on account will be due at all in January and July 2027.

In 2026/27, your income will be increased by the extra £18,000 of dividends you postponed from 2025/26. But this will not mean any payments on account are due in respect of that year, as these are based, in the first instance, on your tax bill for 2025/26: which was just £48.

Then, if you are able, you could again postpone £18,000 of the dividends you would normally take in 2027/28, and take them as extra income early in 2028/29… and so on.

The table below compares the cashflow position of either taking your usual after-tax income of £30,000 every year, or using the roller-coaster strategy to dramatically reduce your payments on account while still maintaining the same after-tax income each year *on average*.

Tax Due	Usual Income	Roller-Coaster	Cumulative Saving
31st January 2026*	£812	£24	£788
31st July 2026	£812	£24	£1,576
31st January 2027	£812	£0	£2,388
31st July 2027	£812	£0	£3,200
31st January 2028	£812	£3,224	£788
31st July 2028	£812	£24	£1,576
31st January 2029	£812	£0	£2,388
31st July 2029	£812	£0	£3,200
31st January 2030	£812	£3,224	£788

* Ignoring the final balancing payment in respect of 2024/25, which would be the same whether or not the roller-coaster strategy is adopted.

Assuming no changes in tax rates or thresholds, the pattern then continues repeating. When changes in tax rates or thresholds do occur, the pattern will be slightly disrupted, but the fundamental principles remain unaltered.

The same tax is paid in the end, and the director receives the same amount of after-tax income overall: but the timing of the tax payments is altered significantly.

As we can see, in cashflow terms, the roller-coaster strategy provides considerable savings. At any given point in the two-year cycle, the cumulative tax paid is reduced by between around six months and two years' worth of the tax arising on the regular, annual after-tax income of £30,000.

Note that, in order to illustrate the cashflow advantages of the roller-coaster strategy, the figures in this example were chosen to ensure the director remained a basic rate taxpayer throughout the period covered. In later chapters, we will look at how the roller-coaster strategy can be used to save tax in other circumstances; or where the 'smooth income' strategy might be more appropriate.

Living Abroad
If you intend to move abroad and become non-UK resident in the future, you could consider withdrawing less income from your company while you are UK resident and more income after you become non-resident.

Providing you move to a country with favourable Income Tax rates, this strategy could potentially save you significant amounts of UK Income Tax (but see Chapter 45 for potential dangers).

Pension Income
When you reach age 55 you may decide to start withdrawing money from any private pension plan you have, for example a self-invested personal pension (SIPP). Any amount you withdraw over and above your 25% tax-free lump sum will be subject to Income Tax.

Fortunately, with a drawdown arrangement you can vary the amount of income you withdraw from your pension scheme every year and there are no limits placed on the amount of income you can withdraw.

Coupled with the fact you can vary the amount of income you withdraw from your company, this could allow you to minimise your Income Tax bill by staying below any of the key Income Tax thresholds listed earlier.

Part 2

Tax-Free Salaries & Dividends

Chapter 9

Tax-Free Salaries

After reading the preceding chapters you should have a good understanding of how salaries and dividends are taxed. The next question is: What is the most tax-efficient mix of salary and dividends for directors who want to extract money from their companies?

In this chapter, we will look at the 'optimal' amount of salary you should withdraw from your company this year.

All amounts are for the current 2024/25 tax year, which ends on 5th April 2025. The answer changes almost every year, so it's important to stay up to date.

Assumption: No Other Taxable Income
We will assume for now that the company owner has no taxable income from other sources (just their company salary and dividends). This keeps the number crunching as simple as possible.

It's not a totally unrealistic assumption either. Although most company owners will have at least some other taxable income, for example bank account interest or stock market dividends, many will have no more than a few hundred pounds. In fact, if the company owner's only income from outside the company is interest income up to £5,500 and/or dividend income up to £500, this will not alter the conclusions drawn in this chapter.

For those company owners who do have significant amounts of other taxable income, for example rental profits from a portfolio of properties, more information is provided in Part 4.

Why a Small Salary is Tax Efficient
The first point to make is that most company owners should pay themselves a small salary. They should not take all their income as dividends.

The first few thousand pounds of either salary or dividend income you receive are tax free thanks to your personal allowance. However, a dividend is not as tax efficient for the *company*.

This is because dividends are paid out of the company's *after-tax* profits, once Corporation Tax has been paid. So, every dividend has a Corporation Tax bill attached.

And as a company owner you should be equally concerned about your company's tax position as your own personal tax position.

A salary, by contrast, is a tax-deductible expense for the company.

In summary, a small salary is usually more tax efficient than a dividend. It's potentially tax free in the hands of the company owner and provides a Corporation Tax saving for the company.

What if You Don't Need the Money?
Because a small salary is so tax efficient most company owners should take one, even if they don't need the income. The money can always be left inside the company until a decision is made to withdraw it.

The general rule is that remuneration cannot be deducted from a company's current taxable profits unless it is 'paid' within nine months of the company's accounting date. However, HMRC will generally accept that remuneration is paid when it is credited to the director's loan account. So, if you don't need the cash, there's nothing to stop you running your salary through the monthly payroll as normal and crediting the amounts to your director's loan account.

The fact that small salaries are so tax efficient is also why company owners should consider paying a salary to their spouse/partner and children (including minor children) wherever possible (see Part 5).

How Much Salary this Year?

There are three relevant thresholds for the 2024/25 tax year:

- Employer's National Insurance   £9,100
- Employee's National Insurance   £12,570
- Income Tax   £12,570

The sharp-eyed among you will have immediately spotted that two of these thresholds are the same amount. For the moment, while we are operating under our key assumption that the director has no other taxable income from outside the company, this means we can effectively treat them as being the same thing.

Later in the guide we will need to remember the primary threshold for employee's National Insurance and the Income Tax personal allowance, while they are the same amount, operate in different ways. In a nutshell, the primary threshold for National Insurance relates only to the director's salary, whereas the Income Tax personal allowance can be used up by any of the director's income.

Nonetheless, while we are keeping things simple, we can quickly answer the 'optimal' salary question:

The 'optimal' salary for many directors is £12,570

The word 'optimal' is in inverted commas because every company and company owner is different. A salary of £12,570 will not be optimal for every single company owner in the land. There are many factors that may influence a salary decision.

Where the company has enough of its £5,000 employment allowance (see Chapter 4) remaining to pay the directors' own salaries, a salary of £12,570 will be completely tax free: no Income Tax and no employee's or employer's National Insurance.

Where the company's employment allowance is already used up paying salaries to other employees, a salary of £12,570 will result in an employer's National Insurance bill of £479:

$$£12,570 - £9,100 = £3,470 \times 13.8\% = £479$$

However, the extra salary and employer's National Insurance will attract Corporation Tax relief at a rate of at least 19%:

Corporation Tax relief on extra salary: £3,470 x 19% = £659
Corporation Tax relief on employer's NI: £479   x 19% = £91

The extra Corporation Tax relief (£750) outweighs the National Insurance cost (£479) by £271. At a marginal Corporation Tax rate of 26.5%, this overall net saving would be increased to £568.

That's not the end of the story. To get their hands on this additional sum of between £271 and £568 in the company's bank account, the director will have to pay additional Income Tax.

If the director is a basic rate taxpayer, additional Income Tax of between £24 and £50 will be payable (assuming the money is taken as a dividend taxed at 8.75%). If the director is a higher rate taxpayer, additional Income Tax of between £91 and £192 will be payable (at 33.75%).

The net effect is that basic rate taxpayers will typically be between £247 and £518 better off by taking a salary of £12,570 instead of £9,100 and higher rate taxpayers will typically be between £180 and £376 better off.

This juggling act gets to the heart of the salary/dividend question: as a company owner you have to compare the tax cost to you *personally* with the tax cost and tax relief enjoyed by your *company*. It can get complicated, but our aim is to guide you through all the factors involved and, hopefully, provide simple conclusions that are easy to follow.

And the key conclusion at this stage is, even when there is a National Insurance cost, it is generally still tax efficient to pay yourself a salary of £12,570 instead of £9,100, because the Corporation Tax relief on the extra salary always outweighs the National Insurance cost.

Despite this, some company owners may prefer to take a salary of £9,100 to avoid the hassle of having to make any National Insurance payments. This would include one-man band companies that don't have any employees, and don't enjoy the benefit of the £5,000 employment allowance.

That's a commercial decision, but with net annual tax savings typically between £247 and £376, it's worth investing a little time and effort (or money: saving £247 in tax makes up for extra pre-tax costs in the company of at least £305). And, if you pay that last £3,470 of salary in a lump sum, you've only got to make one National Insurance payment a year.

Most other company owners have nothing to lose by paying themselves a salary of £12,570. If the company has other employees and is making monthly National Insurance payments anyway, there is no extra effort involved in adding a National Insurance payment on behalf of the directors.

Chapter Conclusion

The optimal salary for most small company owners to take in 2024/25 is £12,570. This remains the case whether there is spare National Insurance employment allowance available or not.

Remember, however, we have assumed so far that the company owner has no taxable income from other sources. We will take a closer look at company owners with other income in Part 4.

As well as those with other income, there are a few other scenarios where a bigger or smaller salary may be more tax efficient, including:

- Directors seeking to grow the company and prepared to restrict their own income in the short-term to achieve this (Chapter 10)
- Older and younger directors (Chapter 11)
- High income earners (Chapters 18 to 21)

There are also a few small company owners who may prefer to take a smaller salary to avoid having to make any National Insurance payments, even if this is not the most tax efficient strategy.

Nonetheless, it is now fair to say we can regard £12,570 as effectively being the 'default' optimal salary for many directors. Hence, **in many of the examples throughout this guide, we will assume directors take a salary of £12,570 during the 2024/25 tax year.**

Chapter 10

Growing the Company

A salary of more than £12,570 may be tax efficient where all three of the following are present:

- There is no employer's National Insurance payable on the director's salary because the company's employment allowance is not used up paying salaries to other employees

- The company has a marginal Corporation Tax rate of 26.5% or 25%: this will be the case where it has taxable profits of more than £50,000 after paying the directors' own salaries

- The director remains a basic-rate taxpayer after taking additional salary income (a basic-rate taxpayer is someone whose income does not exceed £50,270)

To ensure the director remains a basic rate taxpayer, it is important to take account of their increased salary, the dividends they take from the company, and any other taxable income received from outside the company in the same tax year (e.g. pensions, interest, rental income, stock market dividends, etc).

We call this the 'growing the company' scenario because it requires the director to ensure their total taxable income for the year does not exceed £50,270, while the company will generally need to be making profits of more than £62,570 before paying the director's salary.

Example
Sushila and her son Robbie own and run a camper van company that makes profits of around £200,000 per year and therefore faces a marginal Corporation Tax rate of 26.5% (satisfying bullet point two above).

The pair wish to extract income of no more than £50,270 each to avoid paying higher-rate tax and leave enough cash in the company to help it grow. To keep the example simple, we'll also assume they do not have any other taxable income from outside the company. Both these points mean that bullet point three above is satisfied.

We'll also assume the company does not have any other employees, so all of the company's £5,000 National Insurance employment allowance is available for the directors' own salaries.

How much salary income should Sushila and Robbie pay themselves this year?

As explained in Chapter 4, the full £5,000 employment allowance will cover two directors' salaries of £27,216 each. So Sushila and Robbie should pay themselves a salary of no more than £27,216 each (satisfying bullet point one above) and make up the balance with a dividend of £23,054 each:

£50,270 less £27,216 salary = £23,054 dividend

Sushila and Robbie will pay 20% Income Tax and 8% employee's National Insurance on a significant chunk of their salary income but this is better than the 32.93% combined tax rate on dividend income (see Chapter 5).

But if they pay themselves salaries of more than £27,216, the additional salary income will also suffer 13.8% employer's National Insurance, which is why they are better off taking the additional £23,054 as dividend income.

Note, if the company DOES have other employees, those salaries will use up some or all of the company's £5,000 employment allowance. If all of the employment allowance is used up paying salaries to other employees, the directors should pay themselves a salary of £12,570 each.

If only some of the employment allowance is used up paying salaries to other employees, the directors should reduce their salaries accordingly.

For example, if the company has just one employee earning £25,000 this will use up £2,194 of the company's employment allowance:

£25,000 - £9,100 = £15,900 x 13.8% = £2,194

This will leave £2,806 of employment allowance remaining for the directors' own salaries or £1,403 each. This will allow the directors to pay themselves a salary of £19,267 each with no employer's National Insurance (satisfying bullet point one above):

£19,267 - £9,100 = £10,167 x 13.8% = £1,403

They should then take a dividend of £31,003 each to make up the balance of their income:

£19,267 salary + £31,003 dividend = £50,270 higher-rate threshold

But if the company has two employees earning £25,000 each this will use up £4,388 of the company's employment allowance, leaving just £612 of employment allowance remaining for the directors' own salaries or £306 each.

In such a case our 'baseline' salary of £12,570 remains optimal. This amount of salary results in £479 of employer's National Insurance and therefore uses up all of the remaining employment allowance. If the directors pay themselves a bigger salary bullet point one above will no longer be satisfied.

As we can see, there are some cases where paying a salary of more than £12,570 is tax efficient. It will appeal most to profitable, growing companies run by couples with no other employees.

It could also work well where there is a single director/shareholder with one or two low-paid employees (remember, the employment allowance is not available if a single director/shareholder is the only employee). For another illustration of the benefits of this strategy, based on a single director, see Chapter 14.

Chapter 11

Older & Younger Directors

If a company director is over state pension age, there is no employee's National Insurance payable on their salary.

Employer's National Insurance is still payable, however, unless the company has spare employment allowance to cover the directors' own salaries.

A company director can receive a fairly large salary with no National Insurance payable at all if:

- The director is over state pension age, and
- The company has spare employment allowance

For example, where there are two directors over state pension age, and no other employees, it will be possible for the directors to receive salaries of £27,216 each with no National Insurance liability at all.

A larger National Insurance free salary is usually more tax efficient than taking a smaller salary and dividends.

Even larger salaries could be tax efficient for some of these directors when the company is making profits in excess of £62,570: see Chapter 21.

Where employer's National Insurance is payable because the company does not have any spare employment allowance, the position for these older directors depends on two factors:

- The company's marginal Corporation Tax rate

- Whether, taking all their taxable income for the year into account, the director will remain a basic rate taxpayer (income does not exceed £50,270)

If the company's marginal Corporation Tax rate remains either 25% or 26.5% after paying the director's increased salary *and* the director remains a basic rate taxpayer for the year, an increased salary is more tax efficient than extra dividends.

In other cases, for an older director where no spare employment allowance is available, the most tax efficient salary will generally be £9,100.

This is assuming they have income from outside the company of at least £3,470, which will generally be the case when they are in receipt of a state pension.

If they have no income from outside the company, a salary of £12,570 will generally be optimal.

However, for more profitable companies owned by older directors, a larger salary may sometimes be beneficial, even when there is no employment allowance available. See Chapter 21 for details.

Younger Directors
Surprisingly, someone can be a company director from as young as 16. Less surprisingly, they also become subject to *employee's* National Insurance from the same age.

However, for a director (or any employee) under 21, there is no *employer's* National Insurance payable on a salary up to the higher rate threshold (currently £50,270). For a larger salary, employer's National Insurance is only payable on the excess. Hence, a salary of up to £50,270 becomes optimal for a young director aged under 21 in the following scenarios:

• The company has a marginal Corporation Tax rate of 26.5% or 25% after paying the director's salary *and* the director remains a basic rate taxpayer after accounting for all their income for the year, including dividends from the company (this is effectively the 'growing the company' scenario from Chapter 10, except there is no need for any spare employment allowance to be available).

• The director has a salary of at least £50,270 from another job (way to go, kid).

Even greater salaries may sometimes be optimal for young directors under 21 with more profitable companies: see Chapter 21 for details.

Chapter 12

Salaries: Pension Benefits

Apart from being tax efficient a salary confers two extra benefits on the director/shareholder:

- State pension entitlement
- Ability to make private pension contributions

State Pension Entitlement

To protect your state pension entitlement, you should pay yourself a salary that is greater than the National Insurance 'lower earnings limit'.

For 2024/25, the lower earnings limit is £123 per week, which requires a total annual salary of at least £6,396.

If you want to protect your state pension entitlement, a salary of at least £6,396 should be paid in 2024/25 in preference to taking dividends or any other types of income.

Private Pension Contributions

Everyone under the age of 75 can make a pension contribution of £3,600 per year. The actual cash contribution would be £2,880, with the taxman adding £720 to bring the total gross contribution to £3,600.

If you want to make bigger pension contributions, the contributions you make *personally* (as opposed to contributions made by your company) must not exceed your 'relevant UK earnings'. Salaries count as earnings but dividends, rental income, and interest income do not.

For a company director taking the 'optimal' tax-free salary of £12,570, the maximum pension contribution he or she can make is £12,570.

This is the maximum *gross* contribution. The director would personally invest £10,056 (£12,570 x 80%) and the taxman will top this up with £2,514 of basic rate tax relief for a gross contribution of £12,570.

Company owners can also get their companies to make pension contributions, instead of making them personally. As we shall see in Chapter 34, company pension contributions are more tax efficient than contributions made personally in many circumstances.

Chapter 13

Tax-Free Dividends

If a company owner needs more income than the small 'optimal' salary, as most probably do, the most tax-efficient solution is generally to take a dividend rather than a bigger salary.

In this chapter, we'll take a look at how much tax-free dividend income you can take and then, in the next chapter, we'll look at how much dividend income you can take taxed at just 8.75%.

We know from Chapter 5 that dividends attract no National Insurance and are free from Income Tax if they're covered by the director's personal allowance or their dividend allowance.

As we saw in Chapter 9, the 'optimal' salary for most small company owners in 2024/25 is £12,570. This uses up their personal allowance, meaning the only tax-free dividend they can take in 2024/25 is the measly £500 covered by their dividend allowance.

Combined with their salary, this gives the director/shareholder a maximum total 'tax-free' income of £13,070.

However, when we look at the *company's* tax position, we see that this income is not truly tax free.

Firstly, where the company has no spare employment allowance available then, as we saw in Chapter 9, there is £479 of employer's National Insurance payable on this level of salary.

Secondly, although a dividend of £500 can generally be paid with no tax consequences for the director/shareholder, dividends are paid out of a company's profits after paying Corporation Tax.

Nonetheless, despite the tax costs, this is still generally the best way for most director/shareholders to get the first £13,070 they need out of the company.

The fact that dividends always have a Corporation Tax bill attached is an important point to remember, especially if you want to grow your business rather than extract income from it.

If, for example, a company with a marginal Corporation Tax rate of 26.5% incurs £10,000 of tax-deductible expenditure before the end of its accounting period, its Corporation Tax bill will be reduced by £2,650. This will leave less after-tax profit to distribute as dividends but such a strategy may appeal to some business owners who would prefer to re-invest profits and minimise all taxes, including Corporation Tax.

The fact that dividends come with a Corporation Tax bill is also why company owners should consider other profit extraction strategies, for example paying interest or making company pension contributions (Chapters 31 and 33). Some payments like these can be both tax free in the hands of the director and provide Corporation Tax relief. This is the best case scenario when it comes to extracting money from your company.

Lower Salaries

As discussed in Chapter 9, some small company owners may prefer to take a lower salary of £9,100 to avoid the hassle of having to make employer's National Insurance payments, even though this is not the 'optimal' salary level for them.

Assuming the company owner's total taxable income does not exceed £100,000 (see Chapter 18), this means they can take a 'tax-free' dividend of £3,970 covered by the remaining £3,470 of their personal allowance and their £500 dividend allowance.

Although this amount of dividend income will be tax free in the hands of the company owner it's important to remember that the amount paid out will have suffered Corporation Tax and is therefore not truly tax free.

Doubling the Tax-Free Income

Many companies are started and run by married or unmarried couples. The salaries and tax-free dividends outlined above can then be doubled up. So where salaries of £12,570 are taken:

Tax-free salaries	£25,140
Tax-free dividends	£1,000
Total tax-free income	£26,140

Spouses/Partners Brought into the Business
Not all companies are started or managed by couples. In these cases the questions from a tax planning perspective are:

- Can a spouse/partner be employed in the business?
- Can company shares be transferred to a spouse/partner?
- How much tax will these strategies save?

We'll return to these important tax planning issues in Chapter 27.

Company Directors' Tax Returns
Even if you don't have any Income Tax to pay on your salary and dividends, you may still have to complete a tax return. All company directors have this duty where they either have taxable income or have been issued with a notice to file a tax return.

In fact, HMRC seem to be under the impression that all company directors must file a tax return, even if they have no taxable income. In practice, it's probably easier to file a tax return than to get into an argument with them over this point.

The Next Step: Taxable Dividends
The tax-free salaries and dividends listed above will not provide enough income for the vast majority of company owners, even if the amounts are doubled up where the company is owned by a couple. Those that require more income will have to pay Income Tax on any additional dividends withdrawn, as we shall now see.

Part 3

How to Extract More Income Tax Efficiently

Chapter 14

The Next Step:
Dividends Taxed at Just 8.75%

So far, we've shown that a company owner who has no other income and takes a tax-free salary of £12,570 can also take a tax-free dividend of £500 for a total tax-free income of £13,070. These amounts can be doubled up where the company is owned by a couple.

Of course, most company owners will require more income and the most tax-efficient route is normally to take a bigger dividend.

Any additional dividend income you take will be taxed. However, as long as your total income does not exceed the £50,270 higher rate threshold, you will pay just 8.75% Income Tax. If you take any more dividend income, the tax rate jumps to 33.75%!

If you've taken a salary of £12,570 and tax-free dividend of £500, the maximum amount of additional dividend income you can take taxed at just 8.75% is £37,200. The Income Tax payable on this additional dividend income will be £3,255.

In summary, you can take a salary of £12,570 and a total dividend of £37,700 for a total pre-tax income of £50,270. After paying £3,255 tax you'll be left with after-tax income of £47,015.

These amounts can be doubled up if the company is owned by a couple, leaving them with total after-tax income of £94,030 and a total Income Tax bill of £6,510.

Salary vs Dividends
No Employment Allowance Available

Even though the additional dividend income is taxed, it is generally still more tax efficient than taking a bigger salary. To end up with the same after-tax income of £47,015 in 2024/25, a director/shareholder would require an additional salary payment of £49,425, on top of the £12,570 already paid and the maximum tax-free dividend of £500.

The director would end up with the same amount of after-tax income but the company would end up with around £4,000 less cash. This is because the company has to make such a large salary payment to cover all the extra tax, especially National Insurance.

The table below illustrates this effect in two companies: one paying a small salary and dividends, the other paying a big salary plus a £500 tax-free dividend. For the sake of illustration, we will look at companies with sufficient profits to ensure the big salary attracts Corporation Tax relief at the highest possible rate of 26.5%.

In each case, the director ends up with £47,015. The company paying the big salary ends up with £4,140 less cash.

	Small Salary £	Big Salary £
Company's tax		
Company profit	125,000	125,000
Less: Salary	12,570	61,995
Less: Employer's NI	479	7,300
Net Profit	111,951	55,705
Less: Corporation Tax*	25,917	11,012
After-tax profit	86,034	44,694
Less: Dividend	37,700	500
Company cash	48,334	44,194
Director's tax		
Total income	50,270	62,495
Income Tax	3,255	12,230**
National Insurance	0	3,251
After-tax income	47,015	47,015

* 19% on the first £50,000; 26.5% on the remainder (see Chapter 1)
** Higher for Scottish taxpayers

Salary vs Dividends
Spare Employment Allowance Available

The position is less clear-cut where there is spare employment allowance available, as this reduces the cost of a salary in excess of £12,570 considerably.

As we have seen in previous chapters, the £5,000 employment allowance is enough to ensure two directors of a company with no other employees could each be paid a salary of £27,216 with no employer's National Insurance cost arising. In other cases, a single director of a company with one other part-time, low-paid employee might be able to take a salary of around £45,000 without the company having to pay any National Insurance.

None of this means the salary of £61,995 we looked at in the previous section would be worthwhile but, if the company is enjoying a high enough rate of Corporation Tax relief, a salary that uses up the employment allowance might be beneficial: provided the director does not also take enough dividends to make them a higher rate taxpayer.

This proviso naturally limits the benefit of this strategy. For example, with a salary of £45,000, a director/shareholder could only take a dividend of £5,270 before becoming a higher rate taxpayer. After Income Tax and National Insurance of £9,080 on the salary and Income Tax of £417 on the dividend, the director would be left with just £40,773 of after-tax income.

Nonetheless, if the director is willing to limit their income in this way, a higher salary can save the company money.

By way of illustration, let's look at another two companies. One company pays a salary of £45,000 plus dividends of £5,270, the other pays a small salary of £12,570 plus sufficient dividends to give the director the same after-tax income of £40,773.

We will again assume the companies have sufficient profits to ensure the big salary attracts Corporation Tax relief at the highest possible marginal rate of 26.5%. This time, however, we will also assume the companies have sufficient spare employment allowance to allow the larger salary to be paid without incurring any employer's National Insurance liability.

	Small Salary	Big Salary
Company's tax	£	£
Company profit	125,000	125,000
Less: Salary	12,570	45,000
Net Profit	112,430	80,000
Less: Corporation Tax*	26,044	17,450
After-tax profit	86,386	62,550
Less: Dividend	30,859	5,270
Company cash	55,527	57,280
Director's tax		
Total income	43,429	50,270
Income Tax	2,656	6,903**
National Insurance	0	2,594
After-tax income	40,773	40,773

* 19% on the first £50,000; 26.5% on the remainder (see Chapter 1)
** Higher for Scottish taxpayers

The saving produced by following this strategy is £1,753 (£57,280 – £55,527).

However, this strategy is really only for directors who want to grow their companies and are willing to keep their personal income to a lower level to achieve it. For a further analysis of the benefits of this strategy, see Chapter 10.

Bigger Salaries for Other Reasons

Of course, not all company owners take the most tax efficient or 'optimal' salary. Some take a bigger salary because it suits them to do so for other reasons.

For example, a company owner who takes a salary of £30,000 can still take a tax-free dividend of £500 plus additional dividend income of up to £19,770 taxed at 8.75% (£50,270 – £30,000 – £500).

A company owner who takes a salary of £50,000 can still take a tax-free dividend of £500. However, because their total taxable income exceeds the higher rate threshold, any additional dividend income will be subject to tax at the higher rate of 33.75%.

Chapter 15

Making the Most of the 8.75% Tax Rate

So far, we have shown a company owner who takes a salary of £12,570 can receive dividend income of £500 tax free and a further £37,200 taxed at 8.75%.

Company owners who extract more money from their companies will go over the £50,270 higher rate threshold and start paying Income Tax at 33.75% on their dividends, which is a big leap!

(Remember, at this point, to keep things simple, we are assuming the company owner does not have income from other sources.)

An important tax planning question is whether you should pay yourself as much dividend income as you can taxed at 8.75%, even if you don't need the money immediately?

It's impossible to provide a definitive answer because every company owner is different. However, we will attempt to outline the main benefits and drawbacks in this chapter.

One of the main reasons why you may NOT want to pay yourself the maximum amount taxed at 8.75% this year is if you expect to be able to withdraw the same money tax free next year or in another tax year.

We've shown that a couple who take salaries of £12,570 each can also pay themselves tax-free dividends of £500 each: a total tax-free income of £26,140 in 2024/25.

Although some company owners may be able to survive on the tax-free amounts, most will not and will have to withdraw at least some dividend income each year taxed at 8.75%. Arguably you then have fairly little to lose by withdrawing the maximum amount you can have taxed at 8.75% this year (£37,200 each).

The main drawback is you will end up paying Income Tax earlier than may be necessary. In other words, the extra money you pay in Income Tax will earn interest in the taxman's bank account instead of your company's bank account.

So, what are the benefits of paying tax early? By paying the maximum dividend taxed at 8.75%, you stand to protect yourself against:

- Further dividend tax increases
- Business risk
- Becoming a higher rate taxpayer

In previous editions of this guide, we warned that dividend tax rates could be increased. This has now happened. The rates were all increased by 1.25% from April 2022, and the dividend allowance has been slashed to £500.

In our opinion further increases cannot be ruled out under the new Government, as discussed in Chapter 5.

If you are concerned that dividend tax rates could be increased again, it may be better to withdraw as much income as you can taxed at 8.75% in case the rate is increased to, say, 10%.

Of course, it's also possible that dividend tax rates could be reduced at some point, but this seems highly improbable for the foreseeable future in light of recent Government announcements.

Some company owners may wish to remove cash from their companies to protect against business risk (arguably your money is at greater risk in the company's bank account than your own).

But perhaps the best reason to pay yourself the maximum dividend taxed at 8.75% is if you think you may become a higher rate taxpayer in the future. In other words, it may be better to *definitely* pay 8.75% tax this year rather than *possibly* 33.75% in a future tax year.

Why would you expect to become a higher rate taxpayer in the future? Perhaps you expect the profits of your business to grow or you expect to receive more income from other sources, for example an inheritance.

It's likely many basic rate taxpayers will become higher rate taxpayers, even if their income simply increases because of inflation. This is because the higher rate threshold has been fixed at £50,270 for seven years (until 5ᵗʰ April 2028).

Although you might never become a higher rate taxpayer, you arguably have very little to lose by paying yourself the maximum dividend taxed at 8.75%. If you do become a higher rate taxpayer you will save 25% (by paying 8.75% tax this year rather than 33.75% in the future). If you don't become a higher rate taxpayer you will probably lose nothing because you will pay 8.75% tax this year instead of 8.75% in the future.

Reasons to Pay Smaller Dividends

A company owner may decide to not withdraw the maximum dividend taxed at 8.75% for several reasons:

- The company hasn't made enough profit
- The company needs the cash to grow
- The company owner doesn't need the money
- The company is forced to restrict its dividends
- The company owner has taxable capital gains

The Company Hasn't Made Enough Profit

The company doesn't need to have made any profit to pay *salaries* and tax-efficient salaries should be paid wherever possible because they are also a tax-deductible expense and reduce the company's Corporation Tax bill (even if this is only at a later date if the company is currently not making profits). For example, a salary of £12,570 will reduce a company's tax bill by *at least* £2,388.

Dividends, on the other hand, can only be declared if the company has sufficient distributable profits. It is not necessary for the company to actually make a profit in the year the dividend is paid, as long as there are sufficient accumulated profits (after tax) from previous years. (See Chapter 41 for more information on this issue.)

The Company Needs the Cash to Grow

Even if the company has made sufficient profits, the directors may wish to keep the cash in the company to grow the business.

In these circumstances it may be possible for a dividend to be declared but not paid out. The dividend can simply be credited to the director's loan account and withdrawn at a later date when it is more convenient.

This may be more tax efficient than reducing dividends during one year and then declaring bigger dividends taxed at 33.75% in another year.

Note that the director will be subject to Income Tax on any dividend that has been declared, whether it is paid out or not. In practice, this means it may be necessary to pay out a small portion of the dividend to help the director pay their tax bill.

The Company Owner Doesn't Need the Money

A company owner may decide to take a smaller dividend if they have other resources such as inherited money or proceeds from selling another business or from selling other assets like property or shares. The company owner may also have a spouse/partner who earns enough income to support the family.

In these circumstances the company owner may believe it is sensible to limit the amount taken as dividends to avoid paying tax at 8.75%. In reality, however, the company owner may simply be storing up an Income Tax problem for the future. If accumulated profits are eventually paid out as a large dividend, an Income Tax charge of 33.75% or 39.35% could be payable on a significant portion of any dividend declared.

If income is withdrawn on a more regular annual basis, even if not required immediately, Income Tax can be restricted to 8.75%.

There is one important exception. If the company owner has taxable income from other sources, it may be prudent to take a smaller dividend. So far, we have been assuming the company owner has no other taxable income. If there is other taxable income that uses up some or all of the director's basic rate band, it may be necessary to restrict dividends to avoid paying Income Tax at 33.75%. (There is more about directors with other income in Part 4.)

The Company is Forced to Restrict its Dividends

Lenders may place restrictions on dividend payments to protect their interests (i.e. to stop cash leaking out of the company that should be going to them). In these circumstances it may be difficult for the company owners to structure their dividend payments to mitigate tax.

The Company Owner Has Taxable Capital Gains

If you have taxable capital gains you may want to reduce the amount of income you withdraw from your company to free up some of your basic rate band. This may allow you to pay less CGT: see Chapter 44.

Alternatives to Dividends

Although paying tax at 8.75% is a lot better than paying tax at 33.75%, it's important to remember that dividends are paid out of income that has already been subjected to Corporation Tax.

Thus, if you are a basic rate taxpayer, the true effective tax rate on your dividend income is at least 26%, not 8.75% (see Chapter 5).

This means dividends are less tax efficient than certain other types of income that you may be able to extract from your company.

Take rental income for example. If your company pays you rent of £10,000, the amount will be a fully deductible expense (providing the rent is a reasonable market rate for the company's occupation of a property you own personally). If you are a basic rate taxpayer, you will pay 20% tax on the amount received, leaving you with £8,000.

On the other hand, if your company does not pay you rent it will have extra profits of £10,000 on which it will pay at least 19% Corporation Tax, leaving £8,100 at most to distribute as dividends. After paying 8.75% tax you will be left with £7,391 at most.

Clearly, rental income is a fair bit more tax efficient than dividend income in this situation (see Chapter 30 for more information).

Another example is pension contributions. If your company contributes £10,000 to your pension it can claim Corporation Tax relief. Ignoring investment growth, when you retire you will be able to withdraw 25% tax free and the rest could be taxed at just 20% if you are a basic rate taxpayer.

After tax you'll be left with £8,500, compared with £7,391, at most, from a dividend (see Chapter 33 for more on pension contributions).

It's worth bearing all this in mind before you pay yourself any dividends, as these may effectively limit your ability to make other tax efficient payments. We'll take a closer look at this potential conflict in Chapter 41.

Furthermore, paying dividends may also limit the financial resources available to the company to make other tax efficient payments, e.g. rent or pension contributions.

Chapter 16

Making the Most of the 33.75% Tax Rate

So far, we have shown that a company owner who takes a tax-free salary of £12,570 can extract a tax-free dividend of £500 and a dividend of £37,200 taxed at 8.75%, leaving them with an after-tax income of £47,015.

The company owner's gross, taxable income is then £50,270, meaning they are on the cusp of being a higher rate taxpayer.

These amounts can be doubled in the case of companies owned and run by couples.

If you generally do not require more income, you may be able to adopt an 'income smoothing' strategy: taking the maximum tax-free salary and dividend plus the maximum dividend taxed at 8.75% every year where possible, regardless of whether the company has made bigger than normal profits or lower than normal profits.

Taking Bigger Dividends

If you want more income, the optimal strategy is usually to take additional dividends rather than salary, in order to avoid the National Insurance payable on employment income. However, now that you have reached the £50,270 higher rate threshold, you will pay a whopping 33.75% Income Tax on any additional dividend income you take.

You also have to watch out for two further tax stings:

- Child Benefit Charge: income over £60,000
- Personal allowance withdrawal: income over £100,000

In this chapter, we will assume neither the company owner, nor any other member of their household, is claiming any child benefit. We will return to child benefit in the next chapter.

If no child benefit is being claimed, the next threshold to watch out for is £100,000, where your personal allowance starts to be withdrawn. The personal allowance currently saves higher rate taxpayers up to £5,028 in Income Tax, so many company owners will want to keep their income below £100,000 to avoid losing it.

Maximum Income

With total income of £50,270 the director can take additional dividend income of up to £49,730 taxed at 33.75% before the £100,000 threshold is reached.

A director who takes a salary of £12,570 and the rest of their income as dividends will be left with total after-tax income of £79,961:

£12,570 salary + £87,430 dividend – £20,039 tax = £79,961

If the company is owned and managed by a couple this can potentially be doubled up.

Don't Forget the Corporation Tax Bill!

It's tempting to think that company owners who pay themselves any of the above amounts are paying relatively little tax. After all, a total of £100,000 is being extracted from the company with a total Income Tax bill of just £20,039. The effective Income Tax rate is only 20%!

However, it's important to remember that dividends are always paid out of a company's *after-tax* profits.

To pay a dividend of £87,430, the company will have had to make taxable profits of at least £113,850. This would result in a Corporation Tax bill of at least £26,420 (the first £50,000 at 19%, the remainder at 26.5%: see Chapter 1). Coupled with an Income Tax bill of £20,039, the total tax bill attached to the dividend is £46,459.

Alternatives to Dividends

In Chapter 5 we pointed out that, as a higher rate taxpayer, the total tax rate on your dividend income is at least 46%, and sometimes over 50%. With the tax rate at this level, some small company owners may decide to not pay themselves any dividend income which takes them over the higher rate threshold.

They may simply roll up cash inside their companies, possibly until the business is sold or wound up.

At this point it may be possible to pay just 10% CGT on the funds extracted if the company owner qualifies for business asset disposal relief. We'll explore this issue more in Chapter 36.

Other company owners may decide to pay themselves less dividend income and focus on other techniques to extract money from their companies, such as pension contributions.

For example, if your company contributes £10,000 to your pension, the payment will be a tax-deductible expense for the company. Ignoring investment growth, when you retire you can withdraw 25% tax free and the rest will possibly be taxed at just 20% if you are basic rate taxpayer, as many retirees are. After tax you'll be left with £8,500. This compares with at most £5,366 if instead a dividend is taken equal to what is left of that pre-tax profit of £10,000 (after Corporation Tax) and then taxed again in your hands at 33.75%. (See Chapter 33 for more information.)

Following the Corporation Tax increase, many company owners who are higher rate taxpayers now face a combined marginal tax rate on dividend income of over 51% (see Chapter 5). This makes it even more attractive to extract other types of income from your company (for example rental income or interest income), or focus on other profit extraction techniques, such as pension contributions.

Having said this, company owners whose company currently has profits low enough to pay Corporation Tax at just 19%, but who expect to have higher profits in future, and thus a marginal Corporation Tax rate of 25% or 26.5%, may wish to consider postponing certain types of discretionary spending where possible so as to enjoy more Corporation Tax relief in the future.

In most cases, it is not possible to postpone paying yourself things like rent (if your company uses a property you own) or interest (if your company owes you money). For tax purposes these types of expense are generally allocated to the period they relate to. It may, however, be possible to postpone making pension contributions and various other expenses.

Bringing Dividends Forward

In some cases, where you regularly extract dividends taxed at the higher rate, you might want to consider paying yourself additional dividend income taxed at 33.75%; unless you can extract money from your company in a more tax efficient way.

Why? With the public finances in such a poor state, it seems unlikely the 33.75% higher rate will be reduced in the foreseeable future, it may even be increased.

One group who should certainly consider paying themselves as much dividend income as they can taxed at 33.75% are company owners whose taxable income is getting close to £100,000. This is because, once your income rises above £100,000, your marginal Income Tax rate will typically rise from 33.75% to an effective rate of 56.25% (see Chapter 18).

For example, if you expect your taxable income to be, say, £85,000 this year, it may be better to pay yourself an additional £15,000 this year instead of in a future tax year when your income may have already risen to around £100,000.

The £100,000 threshold has not been increased since it was introduced in 2010 and we don't expect it to be increased any time soon. As a result, more and more taxpayers will probably have their personal allowances withdrawn in the years ahead.

Sample Tax Bills

For company owners who want to withdraw more than £50,270 *this year*, Table 5 contains some sample Income Tax bills. It's assumed that a tax-free salary of £12,570 is taken, with the remaining income taken as dividends. The table goes up to £100,000: beyond that your personal allowance is withdrawn.

The numbers are fairly easy to calculate. The first £12,570 is tax free thanks to your personal allowance and the next £500 of dividend income is also tax free thanks to the dividend allowance. The next £37,200 of dividend income is taxed at 8.75%, resulting in tax of £3,255. At this point the company owner has income of £50,270 and is on the higher rate threshold. Any additional dividends will be taxed at 33.75%.

TABLE 5
Income between £50,270 and £100,000

Income	Income Tax	After-tax Income
£50,270	£3,255	£47,015
£55,000	£4,851	£50,149
£60,000	£6,539	£53,461
£65,000	£8,226	£56,774
£70,000	£9,914	£60,086
£75,000	£11,601	£63,399
£80,000	£13,289	£66,711
£85,000	£14,976	£70,024
£90,000	£16,664	£73,336
£95,000	£18,351	£76,649
£100,000	£20,039	£79,961

Someone who extracts £75,000 will pay £3,255 on the first £50,270 and £8,346 on the final £24,730 (£24,730 x 33.75%), resulting in a total tax bill of £11,601.

The amounts listed in Table 5 can be doubled for companies owned and run by couples. For example, a couple can withdraw £150,000 (£75,000 each) with a total Income Tax bill of £23,202 (£11,601 each).

Income Smoothing
If your company makes bigger than normal profits during one accounting period you may be tempted to pay yourself a bigger dividend, even if this results in Income Tax being payable at a higher rate.

Paying a bigger than normal dividend is perfectly acceptable from a tax planning perspective IF you expect the company's profits to remain at a higher level, or continue to grow, AND expect to extract those profits as dividends each year.

If, however, you expect the company's profits to fall back, it may be wiser to 'smooth' your income and withdraw any bumper profits gradually, paying tax at no more than 8.75%.

Chapter 17

How to Protect Your Child Benefit

If you wish to withdraw more than £60,000 income from your company *and* you are the highest earner in a household that receives child benefit, you will be subject to two tax stings:

- 33.75% tax on your dividend income, and
- The Child Benefit Charge

The Child Benefit Charge used to kick in when the highest earner in the household had income over £50,000. Child benefit was fully withdrawn when that person's income reached £60,000.

However, this has all changed starting with the current 2024/25 tax year.

The charge is now only payable when the highest earner's income exceeds **£60,000**. Furthermore, the charge is now levied more gradually. The full charge will only be payable when the highest earner's income reaches **£80,000**.

This is a welcome change and means that, for the first time since the Child Benefit Charge was introduced in 2013, families which have a main breadwinner earning between £60,000 and £80,000 can hold onto at least some of their child benefit payments.

The Child Benefit Charge has important implications for company owners who want to determine how much income to withdraw from their companies during the current and future tax years.

How Much is Child Benefit Worth?
Child benefit is a valuable *tax-free* handout from the Government. Those who qualify receive the following payment in 2024/25:

- £1,331 for the first child
- £881 for each subsequent child

Depending on the number of children, a family can expect to receive the following total child benefit payment in 2024/25:

Children	Total Child Benefit
1	£1,331
2	£2,212
3	£3,093
4	£3,974

Plus £881 for each additional child

Child benefit generally continues to be paid until your children are 16 years old. The payments will continue until age 20, if the child is enrolled in full-time 'non-advanced' education, including:

- GCSEs
- A levels
- Scottish Highers
- NVQ/SVQ level 1, 2 or 3
- BTEC National Diploma, National Certificate, 1st Diploma

So, if your child is aged between 16 and 19, and enrolled in one of the above courses, child benefit will continue to be paid. Once the child is 20 years old, all child benefit payments will cease.

The following courses do NOT qualify:

- Degrees
- Diploma of Higher Education
- NVQ level 4 or above
- HNCs or HNDs
- Teacher training

In other words, if your children are aged 16 or more, and enrolled in any of these courses, you will **not** receive any child benefit.

Total Value of Child Benefit

Child benefit payments continue for between 16 and 20 years. Based on the current child benefit rates applying for 2024/25, the total amount you can expect to receive over the total period your child qualifies is:

- £21,296 to £26,620 tax free for the first child
- At least £14,096 tax free for each additional child

These are very much 'back of the envelope' figures because they are based on the rates applying for a single year, 2024/25, and ignore fluctuations due to inflation and changes of Government policy.

Furthermore, the amount received for second and subsequent children will vary from family to family. When your first child ceases to qualify, your second child will step into their shoes and qualify for the higher payment. In other words, when you stop receiving £1,331 for your first child, the payment for your second child will increase from £881 to £1,331 (at current rates).

Thus, families will receive different overall amounts depending on the age difference between their children and where they study.

The above overall figures nevertheless illustrate how valuable child benefit is over many years and why it's worth protecting.

How the Child Benefit Charge is Calculated
For every £200 of income over £60,000, an Income Tax charge equivalent to 1% of the child benefit is levied on the highest earner in the household.

For example, if the highest earner in the household has income of £65,000, the tax charge will be equivalent to 25% of the child benefit claimed. If the highest earner has income of £75,000, the tax charge will be equivalent to 75% of the child benefit. And if the highest earner has income of £80,000 or more, the tax charge will be equivalent to 100% of the child benefit.

Marginal Tax Rates
Once your income goes above £60,000, you may face the Child Benefit Charge _and_ 33.75% tax on your dividend income.

For the highest earner in the household, the Child Benefit Charge creates the following marginal tax rates on dividend income in the £60,000 to £80,000 tax bracket:

Children	Marginal Tax Rate on Dividends
1	40.4%
2	44.8%
3	49.2%
4	53.6%
5	58.0%

Example: David, a company owner, has taken a salary and dividends totalling £60,000 so far in 2024/25. He is the highest earner in a household claiming child benefit for two children.

David decides to withdraw additional dividend income of £20,000. His total income will be £80,000, so he will face the maximum Child Benefit Charge. The tax payable on the additional dividend is £8,962, calculated as follows:

£20,000 dividend x 33.75%	*£6,750*
£2,212 child benefit x 100%	*£2,212*
Total additional tax	*£8,962*

The overall tax rate on the additional £20,000 dividend is 44.8%.

The dividend tax rates listed above actually understate the total tax payable. When you include Corporation Tax, the total tax rates rise significantly (remember dividends are paid out of a company's profits after Corporation Tax has been paid).

For example, for a company with a marginal Corporation Tax rate of 26.5%, the total tax rates are as follows:

Children	Total Tax Rate
1	56.2%
2	59.4%
3	62.7%
4	65.9%
5	69.2%

Income between £80,000 and £100,000
If you have more than £80,000 of income, you will already be paying the maximum Child Benefit Charge. Hence, dividends falling into the income bracket between £80,000 and £100,000 are simply taxed at 33.75%.

Once your income rises above £100,000, you face a fresh tax sting: withdrawal of your Income Tax personal allowance.

Why You Should Always Claim Child Benefit
Where you regularly have income in excess of £80,000, it may be tempting not to claim child benefit in the first place, since you will only have to pay it back in Income Tax. Think again!

If you claim child benefit in respect of a child aged under 12, you will get a credit for state pension purposes. You can also apply to transfer this credit to your spouse/partner.

If you are getting a state pension credit (or had it transferred from your spouse/partner), this will mean it isn't necessary to take *any* salary from your company for this purpose. We won't always mention this possibility when discussing minimum salaries in the rest of this guide, but it's worth bearing in mind (although a salary of at least £9,100 is generally desirable in any case).

If you don't want to get hit with the CBC, you can claim child benefit but apply to stop the payments. This still provides the state pension credit, where relevant. It also allows you to claim the stopped payments later, any time within two years of the end of the relevant tax year. If you hadn't claimed in the first place, you could only backdate a future claim by a maximum of three months.

But frankly, why not just take the cash, even if you have to pay it back later. Stick it in an ISA in the meantime and earn some tax-free interest!

How to Avoid the Child Benefit Charge

Company owners arguably have the most flexibility when it comes to reducing or avoiding the Child Benefit Charge because they can often adopt the following strategies:

- **Smooth income** – Pay just enough dividend income to stay below the £60,000 threshold every year.

- **Roller-coaster income** – Pay big dividends in some tax years and smaller dividends in other tax years, thereby avoiding the Child Benefit Charge every second year.

- **Income Splitting** – Split your income with your spouse or partner by gifting them shares in the company.

Let's take a company owner who pays themselves a tax-free salary of £12,570 (see Chapter 9) and the rest of their income as dividends.

We'll also assume they have no income from other sources and they are highest earner in a household receiving child benefit.

The Income Tax payable on their income is as follows:

- First £13,070   Tax free (£12,570 + £500 divi allow)
- £13,070-£50,270   8.75%
- £50,270-£60,000   33.75%
- £60,000-£80,000   40.4% to 58.0% (1 to 5 children)
- £80,000-£100,000   33.75%
- £100,000-£125,140   56.25% (PA withdrawal)
- £125,140+   39.35%

Income Smoothing
Where possible, company owners should try to keep their total income below £50,270 to avoid the big jump in Income Tax from 8.75% to 33.75% that occurs when you become a higher-rate taxpayer.

As discussed in Chapter 15, if the income you withdraw is currently somewhere below £50,270 and you expect your company's profits and your own income to continue growing, you should consider extracting approximately £50,270 for several tax years, where possible, even if this is more money than you need.

This is because it's better to pay 8.75% tax now rather than 33.75% in the future.

Similarly, those who already pay themselves £50,270 but expect their company's profits and their own income to continue growing may wish to consider paying themselves an income of up to £60,000 per year, where possible.

They will have to pay 33.75% tax on an additional £9,730 of dividend income but, by doing so, may be able to avoid the Child Benefit Charge in future years.

Roller Coaster Income

With the roller-coaster income strategy, you pay yourself a bigger than normal income one year and a smaller than normal income the next year.

The options to avoid the Child Benefit Charge using this strategy are fairly limited following the recent change to the way the charge is levied.

If you plan to withdraw £80,000 from 2024/25 onwards, you could consider taking £100,000 in year 1 and £60,000 in year 2. Instead of paying the maximum Child Benefit Charge every year you will only have to pay it every second year.

What about someone who plans to withdraw £70,000 per year from their company? Such a person will effectively lose 50% of the family's child benefit every year – over a three-year period they'll lose 3 x 50% = 150%. They could instead consider paying themselves £90,000 in year 1 and £60,000 in years 2 and 3. They'll lose 100% of their child benefit in year 1 but nothing in years 2 and 3. The net saving is 50% which currently equates to £1,106 for a household with two children.

Those thinking about using the roller-coaster strategy to avoid the Child Benefit Charge have to watch out for the £100,000 threshold where the marginal tax rate on dividend income rises to 56.25% as a result of the personal allowance being withdrawn.

For example, if you normally pay yourself income of £90,000, you might instead consider paying yourself £120,000 in year 1 and £60,000 in year 2. You will completely avoid the Child Benefit Charge in year 2. But in year 1 you will also lose most of your Income Tax personal allowance which would usually outweigh any child benefit saving.

Income Splitting

Keeping your income below £50,270 or £60,000 is possibly easier said than done. The higher-rate threshold has been the same since 2021 and many company owners will need to extract much more than £50,270 to pay their bills. Some will also have to extract more than £60,000 which means they may struggle to escape the horrendous tax rates that kick in when the Child Benefit Charge becomes payable.

However, those who own their companies with a spouse or partner are in a more fortunate position because they can effectively double up the amount of income taxed at the lower rates.

For example, where the company is owned equally by a couple a total of £100,540 can be taken out as income (£50,270 each) and tax of just 8.75% will be payable on the dividend income.

If that's not enough income the couple can pays themselves a total of £120,000 (£60,000 each). They'll pay 33.75% on £19,460 of their combined dividend income but will avoid the higher tax rates that kick in when the Child Benefit Charge becomes payable.

Other Issues
When paying yourself dividends that are smaller than normal or bigger than normal there may be lots of other issues to consider.

For example, you can only declare bigger dividends if the company has sufficient distributable profits.

If you postpone taking some of your dividends until a future tax year, you may leave yourself exposed to any future increase in tax on company owners. Remember tax rules are constantly changing.

If you take a smaller than normal dividend this may have other financial repercussions, for example it may affect the size of mortgage you are able to get.

Chapter 18

Income over £100,000

So far, we have shown that a director/shareholder can extract a tax-free salary of £12,570 and a dividend of £87,430 (with £500 tax free, £37,200 taxed at 8.75%, and £49,730 taxed at 33.75%). Total pre-tax income: £100,000. Total after-tax income: £79,961.

The salary may give rise to employer's National Insurance of £479, but this cost can be avoided if the company has sufficient spare employment allowance available. Both the salary and employer's National Insurance will attract Corporation Tax relief at up to 26.5%.

The above amounts can be doubled up if the company is also owned and run by your spouse/partner.

The Child Benefit Charge is payable if the highest earner in the household has income of more than £60,000 (see Chapter 17).

Income between £100,000 and £125,140

Many company owners will be satisfied with a net after tax income of around £80,000.

For those who wish to extract more cash, a dividend is often the best option. However, now you face an additional tax sting: withdrawal of your Income Tax personal allowance.

Once your taxable income rises above £100,000, your personal allowance is gradually withdrawn at the rate of £1 for every £2 of additional income.

In other words, if you have income of £101,000 your personal allowance will be reduced by £500. Once your gross taxable income reaches £125,140, you will have no personal allowance left at all.

Company owners with income in the £100,000 to £125,140 bracket could end up paying Income Tax at an effective rate of over 50% on any additional dividends they withdraw.

Example: Annabel, a company owner, has already taken a salary of £12,570 and dividend of £87,430. Total income: £100,000. She decides to pay herself additional dividend income of £25,140. She will pay 33.75% Income Tax on the additional dividend: £8,485. She will also lose all her personal allowance, which means her salary of £12,570 will now be taxed at 20%. Additional tax: £2,514.

In addition, her salary now uses up £12,570 of her basic rate band, which means £12,570 of dividends will be taxed at 33.75% instead of 8.75%. Additional tax: £3,142.

The total additional Income Tax is £14,141, which is equivalent to 56.25% of the £25,140 dividend.

Don't Forget the Corporation Tax Bill!
As always, it's important to remember that dividends are paid out of a company's *after-tax* profits.

To pay an additional dividend of £25,140, a company with a marginal Corporation Tax rate of 26.5% will have had to make additional profits of £34,204, resulting in Corporation Tax of £9,064. Coupled with an Income Tax bill of £14,141, the total tax bill on the £34,204 of profit is £23,205, or a staggering 68%!

These extortionate tax rates do not apply to all dividend income over £100,000: only income between £100,000 and £125,140. Once your income exceeds £125,140, your personal allowance will have disappeared altogether and any further dividends will simply be taxed at the additional rate of 39.35%.

How to Avoid 56.25% Tax
Unlike regular salaried employees or owners of unincorporated businesses (sole traders and partnerships), company owners can avoid this extortionate tax rate by simply not paying themselves salary and dividends in excess of £100,000 per year. Thus, a company owner taking a salary of £12,570 could extract dividends not exceeding £87,430.

A company owner whose income may fluctuate from year to year, in line with the company's profits, may want to consider smoothing income to avoid the £100,000 threshold. In other words, if possible, try not to pay yourself a salary and dividend of £80,000 in year 1 and £120,000 in year 2. It may be better to pay yourself £100,000 during both tax years, to preserve all your Income Tax personal allowance in year 2.

Bigger Companies

Owners of companies earning substantial profits face a dilemma. While they may choose to extract no more than £100,000 per year, ultimately they may end up with a lot of surplus cash inside their companies.

For example, if you are the only shareholder in a company that is making an after-tax profit of £200,000 per year, you may not wish to extract just £100,000 per year indefinitely, especially if the surplus cash is not needed to help grow the business.

Company owners who wish to pay themselves more than £100,000 per year may be able to keep their personal allowances in some years by using the 'roller-coaster' strategy: paying bigger dividends in some tax years and smaller dividends in other years.

Remember, once your income exceeds £125,140, your personal allowance will have disappeared altogether and the only penalty for taking further dividends is that these will be subject to additional rate tax at 39.35%: far better than the punitive effective rates of up to 56.25% applying to income between £100,000 and £125,140.

For example, let's say you had been planning to withdraw a salary of £12,570 and dividend of £112,430 both this year and next year (total income £125,000 in each year). With this level of income almost all your personal allowance will be withdrawn in both years.

If instead you pay yourself a total of £150,000 this year, but only £100,000 next year, this will allow you to keep all your personal allowance in 2025/26. Potential net tax saving across the two years: £4,201.

For more potential savings based on the roller-coaster strategy, see Chapter 19.

Salary vs Dividends

As we saw in Chapter 9, the optimal salary for most small company owners is £12,570. If you expect to have taxable income of more than £100,000, however, it may sometimes be possible to achieve a small saving by paying yourself a smaller salary.

The potential saving depends on a number of factors, including how much profit the company makes, its marginal Corporation Tax rate, and whether the company has spare National Insurance employment allowance available.

Where the company does not have any spare employment allowance available, and the company owner's taxable income exceeds £100,000, a saving can often be achieved by taking a salary of £9,100: the employer's National Insurance threshold.

The potential tax saving (compared with a salary of £12,570) is not very impressive, however: possibly no more than around £150.

All in all, it's a very small saving for someone with so much income. Nevertheless, this may suit some company owners, for example owners of 'one man band' companies that aren't entitled to the employment allowance and don't want the hassle of making National Insurance payments.

A salary of £12,570 nearly always remains preferable where the company has spare employment allowance available.

Finally, remember our analysis here is based on the assumption the director has no income from outside the company.

When You Should Not Reduce Your Salary

There are also various tax and non-tax reasons why you may not want to reduce your salary too far. In other words, what may be 'mathematically optimal' does not always make for sound tax planning.

In order to protect your state pension entitlement, you should always make sure you receive a salary that exceeds the National Insurance 'lower earnings limit'. For 2024/25, the lower earnings limit is £123 per week which requires a total annual salary of at least £6,396.

Scottish Company Owners

In previous chapters, we have stated that company owners in Scotland who take a small salary and the rest of their income as dividends are completely immune from Scottish Income Tax.

However, those with income over £100,000 will have their personal allowances gradually taken away, which means their salaries will become subject to Scottish Income Tax. Their dividends will continue to be taxed using UK rates and thresholds.

As it happens, this is not necessarily a bad thing. As long as your salary and other income subject to Scottish tax (e.g. rental income) is less than £16,297 this year, you will pay a bit less tax than company owners living elsewhere in the UK, even if you lose your personal allowance.

In this way, the SNP Government has unwittingly handed a tax cut to company owners who have big dividends but only small salaries!

Couples Can Keep One Personal Allowance

Where a couple own a company together, it is usually most beneficial for them to split income equally, in order to make the best use of allowances, their basic rate bands, etc.

However, where the couple's total combined income exceeds £200,000, savings may sometimes be possible by having a non-equal split.

Example: Jack and Gwen own a highly profitable company based in Cardiff. They each take a salary of £9,100 and dividends of £135,000 making them additional rate taxpayers. They also both lose their personal allowance.

Alternatively, if Jack were to transfer some of his shares to Gwen, so that she owned two thirds of the company and he owned one third, his total income would fall to £99,100 (salary of £9,100 plus dividends of £90,000), meaning he retained his personal allowance.

Jack's Income Tax bill would fall by £21,516 (from £41,251 to £19,735). This saving is made up as follows:

Dividends no longer taxed at 39.35% (Note 1)	
£18,960 x 39.35%	*£7,461*
Dividends no longer taxed at 33.75% (Note 2)	
£26,040 x 33.75%	*£8,789*
Personal allowance restored (Note 3)	
Tax saved on salary	
£9,100 x 20%	*£1,820*
Tax saved on dividends	
£3,470 x 33.75%	*£1,171*
£9,100 x 25% (33.75% - 8.75%)	*£2,275*
Total	*£21,516*

Gwen, on the other hand, now has £45,000 more dividends taxed at 39.35%, leading to a £17,708 increase in her Income Tax bill. Nonetheless, by restoring one personal allowance (Jack's in this case, but it could equally have been Gwen's if their roles were reversed), the couple have saved £3,808 overall (£21,516 – £17,708) and, if their total income remains the same in future years, this will be an annual saving!

Notes
1. This doesn't actually save anything, as Gwen is taxed at the same rate on these dividends
2. This gives rise to an overall cost at 5.6% on these dividends as Gwen is taxed at 39.35% instead of Jack's 33.75% BUT it's a price worth paying because…
3. Restoring Jack's personal allowance saves £5,266, far outweighing the additional cost of £1,458 under (2) in this case

The saving achieved by restoring a full personal allowance for one person will always be £5,266 as per Note 3 when the salary taken is £9,100. However, the cost arising under Note 2 will vary and may need to be monitored year on year.

While some savings are possible whenever the couple's total income exceeds £200,000, the best savings can only be achieved when their total income is £250,280 or more. Savings are maximised by keeping the total income of the person with the lower income as close to £100,000 as possible (slightly under is better than slightly over). The best possible saving, where the lower income is exactly £100,000 in total, including a salary of £9,100, is £3,858.

For more on saving tax by transferring shares, and on how and when the transfer itself can be carried out tax free, see Chapter 27.

Chapter 19

Income over £125,140

Once your income rises above £125,140, your personal allowance will have been completely withdrawn, and you will also become an additional rate taxpayer.

Most people are familiar with the 45% tax rate that applies to most types of income above this threshold. If you are a company owner though, it's likely it will be your dividends that take you over the £125,140 threshold (dividends are always treated as the top slice of income: see Chapter 24). Technically, once your dividend income rises above £125,140, the Income Tax rate rises from 33.75% to 39.35%.

However, as we saw in Chapter 18, the *effective* tax rate on dividend income between £100,000 and £125,140 is often 56.25%. So once your dividend income rises above £125,140, the effective Income Tax rate generally *falls* from 56.25% to 39.35%.

Don't Forget the Corporation Tax Bill
Although 39.35% is lower than the 45% rate most people associate with high income levels, we mustn't forget that dividends are paid out of profits that have already been taxed.

For example, a company paying Corporation Tax at 25% will pay £250 tax on every £1,000 of profit. That leaves £750 to distribute as a dividend. If the director/shareholder then pays 39.35% Income Tax on the £750 distribution, the additional tax comes to £295. The total tax paid by the director and the company is £545, which is 54.5%!

Avoiding the 39.35% Tax Rate
The simplest way to avoid paying 39.35% tax on your dividends is to keep your taxable income below £125,140 (e.g. by extracting higher than normal profits over more than one tax year).

But, frankly, this is not really what you should be aiming to do. Since the effective tax rate on dividends actually *falls* once your income exceeds £125,140, it is the punitive rates applying to income between £100,000 and £125,140 you should really be trying to avoid.

In other words, if you're going to keep your income below £125,140, it makes sense to keep it below £100,000: at least in most years, anyway.

Some company owners will be able to do this, and we looked at tax planning for these director/shareholders in Chapter 18.

In Chapter 18, we also looked at tax planning for company owners who can't, or don't wish to, keep their income to a maximum of £100,000 every year, including the savings available by employing the roller-coaster strategy. In effect, that strategy involves using the 39.35% rate in some years in order to avoid punitive effective rates of up to 56.25% in other years.

Owners of more profitable companies (who don't want to roll up profits inside the company indefinitely) should remember that going over the additional rate threshold is very different to going over other key thresholds.

When your income rises above £50,270 the dividend tax rate goes from 8.75% to 33.75% and you start paying an extra £250 tax on every additional £1,000 of dividend income you receive. When your income rises above £100,000, you start to lose your personal allowance and you may end up paying up to £225 extra on every additional £1,000 of dividend income.

But when your income rises above £125,140, the effective tax rate on dividend income generally *reduces* from 56.25% to 39.35% and you pay £169 **LESS** on every additional £1,000 of dividend income.

In short, unlike the other key Income Tax thresholds, the additional rate tax threshold is really nothing to fear. In fact, sometimes it is to be embraced!

When Paying 39.35% is a Good Idea
In many cases, it is better to pay the 39.35% tax rate during one tax year in order to protect your Income Tax personal allowance during another tax year. This is because losing your Income Tax personal allowance is generally more costly than paying the additional rate.

Example: *Sam owns a successful chain of gyms. In 2024/25, she decides to take a salary of £12,570 and a dividend of £137,430. Her total taxable income is £150,000, so she pays the 39.35% additional rate of tax on the top £24,860 of her income.*

She has been withdrawing £150,000 for several years now. With this much income, she also loses her Income Tax personal allowance every year. As a result, her total Income Tax bill for 2024/25 will be £43,963.

In 2025/26, Sam takes the same salary and dividend again, giving her the same Income Tax bill. Hence, over two years, her total tax bill will be £87,926.

Sam could instead consider withdrawing £200,000 in 2024/25 and £100,000 in 2025/26: the same total income but split differently. If she does this, her Income Tax bills will be £63,638 and £20,039 respectively: a total tax bill of £83,677.

Sam saves £4,249 by following this strategy. In 2024/25, she has to pay Income Tax at 39.35% on an extra £50,000 of dividend income: £19,675. However, in 2025/26, her taxable income falls by £50,000 to £100,000, so her Income Tax personal allowance is fully retained. She would have paid 56.25% tax on the first £25,140 of that income (see Chapter 18) and 39.35% on the final £24,860: a total of £23,924. The difference is £4,249 (£23,924 – £19,675).

Sam could repeat this strategy, withdrawing income of £100,000 every second year in order to protect her personal allowance. The bi-annual saving of £4,249 amounts to around 4% of Sam's annual after tax income, so it's well worthwhile and shows how company owners can use 'roller-coaster income' (see Chapter 8) to lower their tax bills.

If both Sam and the company meet the necessary conditions, even more might be saved by varying income over a longer cycle. If Sam withdraws income of £250,000 in tax year 1, and £100,000 in each of tax years 2 and 3, she would save £8,498 over the three years compared with taking income of £150,000 in each year.

Following this pattern for six years would produce total savings of £16,996 over that period, compared with £12,747 using a bi-annual strategy: so we can see the potential benefits of a longer cycle. All of this naturally assumes the current Income Tax rates continue to apply for the foreseeable future.

Salary versus Dividends

In Chapter 9 we saw the 'optimal' salary for most company directors this year is £12,570. Company owners who are additional rate taxpayers may be able to make a small saving by paying themselves a salary of £9,100 instead.

The saving only arises where the company has no spare National Insurance employment allowance available and is usually a rather pathetic £46: hardly worth mentioning.

A salary of £12,570 always remains preferable where the company has spare employment allowance available.

Couples

Couples with combined income of £250,280 or more (i.e. at least £125,140 each if split equally) can make annual savings of up to £3,858 following the method we examined at the end of Chapter 18.

Chapter 20

The Cost of Taking Larger Salaries

Some company owners may desire the convenience of a larger salary, even if this is not strictly speaking 'optimal'. Some may take a bigger salary for other reasons.

While these factors could sometimes outweigh tax considerations, it's worth understanding the additional tax cost arising. In some cases, it may be a lot more than the company owner realises.

For example, if the owner of a company making profits of £150,000 takes a salary of £30,000 instead of £9,100 and extracts the company's remaining profits as dividends, he or she will be £2,250 worse off.

If the owner of a company with profits of £250,000 takes a salary of £50,000 instead of £9,100, he or she will be £2,798 worse off.

These extra tax costs represent a significant additional burden. To make up for the extra tax suffered, the first director would need to make **seven thousand pounds** of extra pre-tax profit in their company. The second director would need to make an extra £6,280.

So, what's easier, changing the level of salary you take so you can pay £2,000 or £3,000 less tax, or finding a way to make an extra £6,000 or £7,000 profit?

Interestingly, despite all this, **very** large salaries actually become preferable to dividends in some cases. We'll look at this situation in Chapter 21. It will often require company profits of at least £280,000 before it begins to pay off, although it can be beneficial at lower profit levels in some circumstances.

Chapter 21

Big Earners

At really high income levels, things change and, in some cases, it becomes more beneficial for director/shareholders to take most of their income as salary.

Where the company's profits exceed around £280,000, the 'optimal' salary for a director to take (assuming there is only one director) is the salary that will reduce the company's profits to £50,000. (This is assuming the director intends to withdraw all, or at least most, of the company's profits.)

To calculate this salary, we need to take account of the employer's National Insurance arising, so it is not simply a case of deducting £50,000 from the company's profits. Let's look at an example to see how it can be done.

Example: Elon's company makes a profit of £500,000 before tax. He wishes to withdraw all his after-tax profits as a combination of salary and dividends. There is no spare employment allowance available, so he can only take a salary of £9,100 free from National Insurance, reducing the company's taxable profit to £490,900.

This exceeds our target profit level by £440,900 (£490,900 – £50,000). To work out Elon's 'optimal' salary, we first divide this figure by 1.138 (one plus the 13.8% rate of employer's National Insurance).

£440,900/1.138 = £387,434

We now add back the £9,100 that is free from National Insurance, to produce Elon's optimal salary: £396,534.

How can we make sure Elon gets exactly the right salary? Simple: take a look at the technique discussed at the end of Chapter 1.

Having derived the optimal salary, let's now compare the outcome of either taking this large salary, or a small salary of £9,100. In both cases, we will assume Elon takes the company's remaining after tax profits as dividends.

	Small Salary	**Large Salary**
Company's tax	£	£
Company profit	500,000	500,000
Less: Salary	9,100	396,534
Less: Employer's NI	0	53,466
Net Profit	490,900	50,000
Less: Corporation Tax*	122,725	9,500
After-tax profit/dividend	368,175	40,500
Director's tax		
Total income	377,275	437,034
Income Tax	133,005	180,383**
National Insurance	0	9,941
After-tax income	244,270	246,710

* 25% with the small salary; 19% with the large salary
** Higher for Scottish taxpayers

Taking the large salary leaves Elon with £2,440 more in after tax income (£246,710 – £244,270).

A saving of £2,440 might seem like peanuts to someone like Elon, but he would need to increase his company's profits by over £5,000 to get the same after-tax income following the small salary/large dividend method.

The reason we see a tax saving by paying very large salaries at this level is because of the difference in marginal tax rates at high income levels. Taking everything into account, including Corporation Tax and employer's National Insurance, at this level a dividend suffers an overall marginal tax rate of just over 54.5%, but salary suffers slightly less, at 53.4%.

(In fact, the part of the dividend falling into the 26.5% marginal Corporation Tax rate band suffers an overall rate of 55.4%.)

Hence, the more the company's profit increases above our £280,000 threshold, the greater the savings yielded by following the large salary method. In a similar situation, but where the company is making a profit of £600,000, the saving would increase to £3,525; at a profit of £750,000 it's £5,153.

Partial Extraction

So far in this chapter, we have only looked at director/shareholders who wish to extract all their company's after-tax profits by way of salary or dividend.

With profit levels of this magnitude, however, many company owners may not be extracting all their company's profits and will reinvest part of them to fund future growth.

Large salaries can still be beneficial under these circumstances: provided the director/shareholder wishes to extract a substantial sum. For example, let's say Elon wishes to limit his net, after-tax income to £200,000. Let's see how he might do this:

	Small Salary £	Large Salary £
Company's tax		
Company profit	500,000	500,000
Less: Salary	9,100	354,177
Less: Employer's NI	0	47,621
Net Profit	490,900	98,202
Less: Corporation Tax*	122,725	22,274
After-tax profit	368,175	75,928
Less: Dividend	295,182	500
Company cash	72,993	75,428
Director's tax		
Total income	304,282	354,677
Income Tax	104,282	145,583**
National Insurance	0	9,094
After-tax income	200,000	200,000

* 25% with the small salary; 19% on the first £50,000 and 26.5% on the remainder with the large salary
** Higher for Scottish taxpayers

This time, rather than Elon enjoying £2,440 in extra after-tax income, the company retains £2,435 (£75,428 – £72,993) extra cash, so it's more or less the same saving.

In fact, the large salary route can produce savings when the director/shareholder wishes to take total net, after-tax income of more than around £118,000, although sometimes it would need to be more than £196,000: it all depends on the company's profit level, although this needs to be at least £280,000.

Remember, all these figures are based on the assumption the company will still have profits of at least £50,000 after paying the large salary.

Is the Salary Justified?

An important point to bear in mind is that the large salaries discussed in this chapter are only worthwhile if the company obtains Corporation Tax relief for them (and at a marginal rate of at least 25%).

This means the remuneration paid to the director (their salary) must be justified by the work they do in the company's business.

While this issue is seldom challenged by HMRC, we have to consider whether, for example, the work done by someone like Elon warrants a salary of almost £400,000. And remember, it is the director's total remuneration package we need to consider, including any company pension contributions made on their behalf and other benefits provided.

I would, however, make two key points in this context:

- If the director is actively running the company, there is a strong argument that its high profits are entirely down to the director's efforts, and any salary covered by those profits must therefore be justified.
- In a case like Elon's, HMRC are collecting almost £200,000 in Income Tax and National Insurance: there is very little incentive for them to challenge the way a director in this situation has chosen to structure their pay.

Cashflow

Another key issue to bear in mind is cashflow. Using the large salary technique may sometimes accelerate tax liabilities.

Income Tax and National Insurance due on a salary is payable under PAYE by the 22nd of the month following payment. The Corporation Tax relief for these costs doesn't follow until nine months after the end of the company's accounting period (in most cases: see Chapter 2 regarding large companies making profits in excess of £1.5m).

By contrast, the tax due on a dividend under the self-assessment system will generally be payable in two instalments on 31st January during the tax year and the following 31st July (see Chapter 6).

If the salary is paid monthly, the cashflow impact is both complex and significant: it would generally mean the overall saving needs to be quite large to make the large salary method worthwhile.

However, the cashflow impact is both simpler and vastly improved if the salary (or most of it) is paid as a single lump sum bonus after the end of the accounting period (but within nine months) using the method we examined at the end of Chapter 1.

Let's say, for example, Elon's company has a June accounting date and his salary, or bonus, of £396,534 in respect of the year ending 30th June 2024 is paid in a single lump sum in March 2025 (after the 5th).

(Note: we're reverting to the first part of the example above for the purposes of this illustration.)

To be fair, let's also say all his dividends paid out of the company's profits for the year ending 30th June 2024, are paid during 2024/25. We will also assume, for the sake of illustration, that, whichever method he follows, the Income Tax due on his dividend income for 2024/25 would have been payable in two equal instalments on 31st January and 31st July 2025 (it won't usually be this simple, but it's a reasonable approximation in most cases: see Chapter 6).

Lastly, again in the spirit of fairness, we'll assume the salary of £9,100 payable under the small salary/large dividend method would also be paid in March 2025.

Let's now compare the tax cash inflows/(outflows) under the two methods:

	Small Salary	Large Salary	Cumulative Saving/(Cost)
31/1/2025 (1)	(£65,593)	(£7,870)	£57,723
1/4/2025 (2)	£2,275	£115,500	£170,948
22/4/2025 (3)	(£1,820)	(£228,051)	(£55,283)
31/7/2025 (4)	(£65,593)	(£7,870)	£2,440

1. First payment on account under self-assessment in respect of dividend income
2. Reduction in the amount of Corporation Tax paid due to tax relief for Elon's salary and related employer's National Insurance
3. Income Tax and National Insurance paid under PAYE
4. Second payment on account under self-assessment in respect of dividend income

As we can see, Elon and his company are £55,283 out of pocket for a little over three months, from 22nd April to 31st July. But they are at least £57,723 ahead for the slightly shorter period from 31st January to 22nd April. Hence, all in all, the cashflow impact is broadly neutral.

Similar results can be achieved for companies with other accounting dates although, in some cases, this will mean the large salary/bonus is paid, and taxable, in the next tax year. That's alright in principle as long as:

- The director is still getting taxable income of at least £100,000 in the current tax year,
- This includes a salary of at least £9,100, and
- The director does not have more income from outside the company next tax year than this tax year

If these conditions aren't met, it may be preferable to pay the large salary/bonus in the current tax year. This won't be as good from a cashflow perspective, but the overall saving achieved by the large salary technique will still be obtained.

As a slight aside (but a relevant one) it's worth pointing out that delaying *dividends* to next tax year would carry a significant risk that dividend tax rates could be increased.

Delaying a salary or bonus is far less risky as the new Labour Government has pledged not to increase the rates of Income Tax or National Insurance applied to salaries.

Alternative Profit Extraction Strategies

Although we have seen that, at high income levels, a salary could be better than dividends, it is still a very costly way for an additional rate taxpayer to take money out of a company, with an overall tax burden of 53.4%.

It is therefore only worth looking at these super-size salaries when other options have been considered and either exhausted or found to be unsuitable.

Additional Factors to Consider

There are several factors that could make the large salary technique more or less attractive or, in some cases, not viable at all. Unless stated to the contrary, all the amounts quoted below assume all remaining after-tax profits are taken as dividends.

The Employment Allowance: So far, we have assumed the employment allowance is not available in respect of the director's salary. This is generally a fair assumption for companies with profits at the levels we have been looking at. If the employment allowance is available, however (e.g. if all the employees are aged under 21), additional savings will arise under the large salary route, and it could be beneficial for owners of companies with profits of just £160,000 or more.

Older Directors: Directors over state pension age are exempt from employee's National Insurance. This makes the large salary route considerably more attractive, with savings available to owners of companies with profits between around £107,000 and £119,000, or from £150,000 upwards.

If the employment allowance is also available, the large salary method, as described above, could be beneficial whenever company profits exceed £62,570.

It is, however, better for these older directors to extract the maximum amount of salary covered by the employment allowance (see Chapters 4 and 11 for guidance) where this is greater.

Younger Directors: There is no employer's National Insurance payable on the first £50,270 of salary paid to directors under the age of 21. As a result, the large salary method may be beneficial when the company has profits of more than around £157,500.

If the employment allowance is also available, the large salary method could produce savings when the company's profit is between £106,000 and £112,500, or when it is £141,000 or more.

Scottish Directors: The large salary technique is not beneficial for directors under state pension age who are Scottish taxpayers, due to the higher Income Tax rates on salaries. For those over state pension age, savings are just about possible, but it would take profits of over £1,000,000 unless the employment allowance is also available.

In this latter case, where the salary is completely free from National Insurance, the technique may be beneficial where the company's profits exceed around £210,000.

Other Income: Where the director has income from other sources outside the company, this could mean the large salary route becomes preferable at lower profit levels. For example, if a director also has rental income of £30,000 in 2024/25, the large salary method becomes preferable where the company's profits exceed £200,000.

If someone like Elon had rental income of £30,000, the large salary route would save them £3,924, i.e. £1,484 more than we saw above.

Pension or self-employment income will have a similar effect. Employment income from another source may bring another beneficial factor into play, which we will look at in Chapter 26.

In some cases, where a director has interest income, the large salary method could lead to them losing out on the starting rate band (see Chapter 26). This could cost up to £1,000 in extra Income Tax, but there may still be savings overall.

Dividend income from another source will not generally make any difference to the savings available under the large salary method.

See Chapter 25 for some more examples of the impact of other income on whether the large salary method is beneficial.

Multiple Directors: Where there is more than one director, much higher company profit levels will usually be required before the large salary technique is beneficial.

In the simplest case, with no other complicating factors, where a company is co-owned by a couple and profits are shared equally, it would generally require company profits of at least £655,000 before the large salary method is worthwhile.

Nonetheless, couples may benefit from the large salary method at much lower profit levels in some cases. Such as:

- Where the directors are over state pension age: profits of £164,000 may be sufficient, or just £136,000 if they are each receiving the full state pension of £11,502 this year
- Where the employment allowance is available: profits of £480,000 may be sufficient
- Where the directors are over state pension age *and* the employment allowance is available: any profit over £75,140 may be sufficient (but the maximum salaries covered by the employment allowance will be better if these are greater)

And lower profit levels will also be sufficient where the directors have other income from outside the company. For example, two directors under state pension age running the company and sharing profits equally, who each have other income from outside the company of £40,000, could benefit from the large salary method where company profits exceed around £400,000, or just £250,000 if the employment allowance is available.

Note that, when using the large salary method for two directors, both salaries must be taken into account in working out what level of salary to pay.

For example, if the company is making profits of £400,000, using the large salary method would mean the directors' salaries plus related employer's National Insurance should total £350,000, or £175,000 each (to reduce the company's profits to £50,000). Assuming the employment allowance is not available, that means paying each director a salary of £154,882. This is calculated in a similar way to Elon's salary at the start of the chapter, as follows:

£175,000 – £9,100 = £165,900
£165,900/1.138 = £145,782
£145,782 + £9,100 = £154,882

As for a single director, these salaries can effectively be put in place retrospectively by declaring a bonus following the method described at the end of Chapter 1.

Finally, it is important to remember both directors must be doing sufficient work for the company to justify their large salaries. This may not always be the case for a couple who co-own a company. The solution may sometimes be to pay a large salary to one of them and just £9,100 or £12,570 to the other: but that's the kind of calculation that needs to be done on a case by case basis.

Associated Companies: All our analysis so far has been based on the assumption the company has no associated companies. Where there are associated companies, the 'optimal' large salary becomes the amount that reduces the company's profit to the point at which its Corporation Tax rate drops to 19%: that's £25,000 where there is one associated company, £16,667 where there are two... and so on.

On the other hand, the amount of Corporation Tax saved by paying a large salary will generally reduce. For example, if Elon's company had one associated company, his optimal salary would increase to £418,502, but it would only save him £1,800. A profit of at least £335,000 will generally be required before there is *any* saving under this scenario. And it gets worse if there are more associated companies.

As always, other factors may improve the situation, so savings are still possible, but it will need some detailed calculations to decide if that's the case.

In Summary

There are far too many potential combinations of different factors for us to examine every possibility here. However, with annual savings potential running into several thousand pounds, the large salary method is certainly worth looking into for high earners.

In the simplest case, where none of the complications we have looked at arise, savings are available this year where company profits exceed around £280,000.

Savings will be increased where:

- Some spare employment allowance is available,
- The director is over state pension age,
- The director is aged under 21, or
- The director has other income

Savings can arise at lower profit levels where these factors are present. But the savings will be reduced, or even eliminated, if:

- There is more than one director,
- The director is a Scottish taxpayer, or
- There are any associated companies

Apart from Scottish taxpayers under state pension age, some savings can still arise, even when these factors are present, but it will necessitate a higher level of company profit.

Chapter 22

Alternative Profit Extraction Strategies

Company owners faced with losing their personal allowance or paying additional rate tax on their salary or dividends may wish to consider alternative profit extraction strategies, including:

- Gifting shares in the business to family members, including family members who are higher rate taxpayers (see Part 5).
- Making personal or company pension contributions (see Chapters 33 and 34).
- Keeping cash inside the company until the business is sold or wound up (see Chapter 36). At this point, it may be possible to pay just 10% CGT on the extracted funds.

Pension Contributions

Company owners who pay themselves small salaries can only make small pension contributions *personally*: your pension contributions cannot generally exceed your earnings (dividends don't count as earnings).

For example, if you pay yourself a salary of £9,100, you can only make a pension contribution of £9,100 personally (£7,280 contributed by you, with a further £1,820 added to your pension by the taxman).

Company owners who wish to make bigger pension contributions can either pay themselves higher salaries or get their companies to make the contributions on their behalf.

A higher salary usually comes with a punitive National Insurance bill, so company pension contributions are often the preferred route.

Company pension contributions enjoy Corporation Tax relief, providing they are not excessive (see Chapter 34).

The Pension Taper

High income earners face another restriction: the annual allowance. This is the maximum amount that can be invested in a pension each year and, for high earners, it can be reduced from £60,000 to just £10,000.

Fortunately, following changes made in 2020 and 2023, this pension taper now only kicks in at much higher income levels than previously. As a result, many high earning company owners can benefit from much larger pension contributions than before.

The first thing you have to calculate is your 'threshold income'. If your threshold income is no more than £200,000, you are completely exempt from tapering and can make pension contributions just like anyone else.

Your threshold income is, broadly speaking, your total taxable income. This includes your salary, dividends, rental profits, interest income and any other taxable income you receive.

From this, you deduct any pension contributions you have made *personally* (you deduct the gross contributions). You can also deduct qualifying loan interest (see Chapter 31), relief for trading losses, most other forms of loss relief, and a few other, more obscure reliefs, as listed in Section 24 of the Income Tax Act 2007.

Employer pension contributions are ignored when calculating threshold income. But you must add back any salary sacrificed in exchange for employer pension contributions.

Example 1: *Dirk takes a salary of £9,100 and a dividend of £190,900 out of his company. He has no other income so his total taxable income is £200,000. His company makes a pension contribution on his behalf but we ignore that when calculating his threshold income. He doesn't make any pension contributions personally, so his threshold income is exactly £200,000. Dirk is unaffected by the tapered annual allowance. This means his annual allowance for the current tax year is £60,000.*

Example 2: *Beric is a company owner who pays himself salary and dividend income totalling £200,000. He also has taxable rental profits of £50,000, so his total taxable income is £250,000.*

His company makes a pension contribution of £50,000 on his behalf, but we ignore this when calculating his threshold income. He doesn't make any pension contributions personally.

Beric's threshold income is therefore £250,000. Because this exceeds £200,000, he is potentially affected by the tapered annual allowance.

If your threshold income exceeds £200,000, the next thing you have to calculate is your 'adjusted income'.

Broadly speaking, your adjusted income is your total taxable income *plus* any pension contributions made by your company (your employer).

You also add back any contributions to an occupational pension scheme under a net pay arrangement (where your contributions are deducted from your salary before calculating PAYE).

As with threshold income, you can again deduct qualifying loan interest, relief for trading losses, most other forms of loss relief, and other reliefs listed in Section 24 of the Income Tax Act 2007.

Your £60,000 pension annual allowance will only be reduced if your adjusted income exceeds £260,000.

Your annual allowance is reduced by £1 for every £2 your adjusted income exceeds £260,000. For example, an individual with adjusted income of £290,000 will have their annual allowance reduced by £15,000 (£30,000/2), giving them an annual allowance of £45,000.

The annual allowance cannot fall below £10,000: this is the minimum level of the allowance for those affected by the taper.

Pension contributions that exceed the tapered annual allowance face the annual allowance charge. The excess contributions will be added to your income and taxed. If the charge exceeds £2,000, it may be possible to have it paid out of your pension savings. This may only be possible if total contributions to the scheme in question exceed the £60,000 annual allowance.

Example 2 continued: As we saw earlier, Beric has total taxable income of £250,000 and his company makes a contribution of £50,000 on his behalf. His adjusted income is therefore £300,000 (£250,000 + £50,000).

His annual allowance is cut by (£300,000 – £260,000)/2 = £20,000

His annual allowance is therefore £60,000 – £20,000 = £40,000

He faces an annual allowance charge on £50,000 – £40,000 = £10,000

Beric can avoid the charge by getting his company to make a smaller pension contribution (no more than £43,333). Alternatively, he may be able to extract less income from his company (no more than £180,000) to ensure his total taxable income reduces to £230,000 and he is able to benefit from a tapered annual allowance of £50,000. Company owners may find it easier than others to control their taxable income to reduce their threshold income and adjusted income. However, if they do this, they may have to be wary of triggering a special anti-avoidance rule (see below).

Company owners will find it fairly easy to calculate their adjusted and threshold income when it comes to salaries and dividends.

Problems may arise when the company owner has other income that is less predictable, for example rental income from properties. Company owners who are also landlords may not know precisely how much taxable income they have earned (and thus their tapered annual allowance) until *after* the tax year has ended. By then it will be too late to make pension contributions.

Those who wish to benefit from pension contributions and think they may be affected by the tapered annual allowance may need to estimate their taxable income just *before* the end of the tax year.

The Tapered Annual Allowance and Carry Forward
All is not lost if your pension contributions exceed your tapered annual allowance for the year. Those affected by the tapered annual allowance can still carry forward any unused annual allowance from the three previous tax years. For example, if your annual allowance this year is reduced from £60,000 to £40,000 and you make a £25,000 pension contribution, you will have £15,000 left to carry forward to next year (£40,000 – £25,000).

Carry forward could act as a lifeline for those whose pension contributions accidentally exceed the tapered annual allowance in any given year. Beric in the above example will avoid the annual allowance charge if he has at least £10,000 of unused annual allowance from the three previous tax years.

Example: *Mario is a company owner with taxable income of £200,000. He gets his company to make an £80,000 pension contribution (utilising £20,000 of unused annual allowance carried forward from previous years). His adjusted income is £280,000 but his threshold income is £200,000, so his annual allowance for the current year is not reduced.*

If your threshold income does not exceed £200,000, you cannot be subject to the tapered annual allowance, even if your adjusted income is greater than £260,000.

Anti-Avoidance Rule
There is an anti-avoidance rule to prevent anyone entering into an arrangement that involves reducing their adjusted or threshold income and increasing their income in a different tax year.

The anti-avoidance provisions apply when it is reasonable to assume the main purpose, or one of the main purposes of the arrangement, is to reduce the impact of the tapered annual allowance. If the anti-avoidance provisions apply, then the relevant arrangement will be ignored for the purposes of calculating the tapered annual allowance.

It is unclear how this anti-avoidance rule could be applied to company owners who vary their income from year to year.

Enjoying over 55% Tax Relief
Thanks to the changes made in 2020 and 2023, many additional rate taxpayers are unaffected by the tapered annual allowance and can make fairly big pension contributions with full tax relief.

Any company owner with taxable income of no more than £200,000 can get their company to make a pension contribution of up to £60,000 every year. Other high earning company owners can make the following maximum pension contributions:

Taxable Income	Maximum Contribution*
£230,000	£50,000
£260,000	£40,000
£290,000	£30,000
£320,000	£20,000
£350,000+	£10,000

* Applies from 2023/24 onwards. Ignores potential carry forward from previous tax years.

Additional rate taxpayers currently face a combined marginal tax rate of up to 55.4% on their dividend income (Corporation Tax and Income Tax). After tax, a company owner could be left with just £446 from each £1,000 of pre-tax profit.

By contrast, with a pension contribution, the whole £1,000 can be paid into the director's pension fund. Income Tax will be payable when they eventually take the money out, but the effective tax rate could be between 15% and 30%, leaving them with between £700 and £850 after tax. (See Chapter 33 for an explanation of how these tax rates are calculated.)

Thus, the director can choose between £446 today and £700 to £850 in the future. It's easy to see why pensions are such powerful tax shelters!

Chapter 23

Using a Company versus Self-Employment

Most company owners probably realise that if they take all of their income as salary, they could end up paying significantly more tax than a self-employed person (sole trader or partner) with the same income. This is because of the additional employer's National Insurance payable on most salary income.

It's interesting to note that, even if a company owner structures their pay in the most tax efficient manner, taking most of their income as dividends, they could still end up paying significantly more tax than a self-employed person. This situation will typically arise when the company owner withdraws most or all of the company's profits and is a high income earner.

Table 6 compares the total after-tax income of a company owner with that of a self-employed business owner at different profit levels. It is assumed the business owner has no other taxable income in both cases.

For the company owner, it is assumed the 'optimal' salary is taken and all the remaining after-tax profits are extracted as dividends. At profit levels up to £120,000 (in this scenario), that 'optimal' salary is £12,570 (because the company owner's taxable income is less than £100,000); at higher profit levels, the 'optimal' salary is £9,100.

The 'Extra Income' column is the additional income enjoyed by the *self-employed* person. For example, when profits are £100,000, a self-employed person will enjoy £2,449 more after-tax income than a company owner.

TABLE 6
After-Tax Income Compared
Company Owner vs Self Employed

Profits	Company Owner	Self-Employed	Extra Income
£30,000	£25,143	£25,468	£325
£40,000	£32,534	£32,868	£334
£50,000	£39,925	£40,268	£343
£60,000	£47,234	£46,111	(£1,123)
£70,000	£52,255	£51,911	(£343)
£80,000	£57,124	£57,711	£587
£90,000	£61,994	£63,511	£1,518
£100,000	£66,863	£69,311	£2,449
£110,000	£71,732	£73,111	£1,379
£120,000	£76,602	£76,911	£310
£130,000	£80,806	£81,440	£634
£140,000	£84,316	£86,740	£2,424
£150,000	£87,532	£92,040	£4,509
£175,000	£97,201	£105,290	£8,090
£200,000	£108,345	£118,540	£10,195
£225,000	£119,490	£131,790	£12,301
£250,000	£130,634	£145,040	£14,406
£300,000	£153,295	£171,540	£18,245

Notes:
1. Company owner withdraws all the profits of the business
2. Company owner takes optimal salary of £9,100 or £12,570 (see above) and remaining income as dividends
3. No spare employment allowance available
4. No associated companies
5. Business owner is under state pension age but over 21 in both cases
6. Self-employed tax includes Income Tax and National Insurance
7. Self-employed tax bills are higher in Scotland (see Table 8 below)

At profit levels of around £52,500 to £73,500, the company owner enjoys a little extra income, but this 'sweet spot' is very much the exception that proves the rule: generally, the self-employed business owner is better off.

The best saving for company owners is around £1,140 and comes at a profit of £59,600. Whether even that is enough to make up for the extra costs and admin burden involved in running a company is perhaps questionable.

(There's another little sweet spot for profits around £125,000, but with a maximum saving of £240, it's hardly worth mentioning.)

It's also worth pointing out that an increase in dividend tax rates could wipe out even these small savings!

In short, the general conclusion is that, if you intend to extract all your profits every year, using a company will not usually save you any tax and, at higher profit levels, will lead to significant costs.

This picture changes over the years though: twenty years ago, using a company could lead to significant tax savings at many profit levels. That may happen again but, for the time being, we wouldn't suggest self-employed business owners form a company just to save tax if they need all their profits to live on every year.

But there are many other reasons to form a company, and the non-tax benefits, such as limited liability protection, could often outweigh the tax considerations.

Furthermore, none of this necessarily means all owners of companies with significant profits would be better off self-employed. If profits are kept inside the company to help it grow, the only tax payable will be Corporation Tax. Clearly, paying Corporation Tax at 25% or 26.5% is a lot better than the 47% tax paid by self-employed additional rate taxpayers (50% in Scotland).

It is in these circumstances, when profits are reinvested, that companies are most powerful as tax shelters. For example, where a company has profits of £500,000 and only half the after-tax profits are paid out as dividends, the total tax bill will be around £40,000 less than the tax paid by a self-employed person.

Would the Employment Allowance Help?
If at least £479 of the employment allowance is available, the 'optimal' salary becomes £12,570 at all the profit levels covered in Table 6. This leads to some small savings for company owners, with the company owner better off at all profit levels up to around £76,000. But the overall saving for the company owner is still modest, peaking at £1,418 for a profit of around £59,100.

Partnership versus Company

Table 6 above is based on a comparison between a sole trader and a single company director. If we compare a partnership to a company with more than one director, the company becomes even less favourable.

For example, a couple in partnership together who each have a profit share of £150,000 would each enjoy after tax income of £92,040, as shown in Table 6.

If they formed a company, however, and both extracted half the after-tax profits by way of salaries of £9,100, with the remainder taken as dividends, their after-tax income would be £86,816 each.

Hence, staying in partnership would mean they had £5,224 (£92,040 – £86,816) of extra income each, rather than the £4,509 shown in Table 6 for a sole trader with profits of £150,000.

Nonetheless, a company could again yield tax savings when the couple limit the amounts they withdraw each year. For example, if they each took a salary of £12,570 plus a quarter of the company's after-tax profits as dividends (£51,536 in this case), there would be an overall tax saving of over £31,000 compared with operating as a partnership. At the same time, the couple would have a healthy £112,363 of total after-tax income between them.

The employment allowance would again improve the position for the company owner couple, and it is more likely to be available where there are two directors. However, if we go back to our initial assumption that all profits are extracted, the difference the employment allowance makes is far too small to make a company worthwhile at any profit level.

Big Earners

As we saw in Chapter 21, large salaries can be preferable to dividends at high income levels. However, while this generates a saving compared with the usual small salary/large dividend route, that saving is not enough to alter what we saw in Table 6: namely that high income earners who wish to extract all their business profits each year would be better off operating as a self-employed trader (based purely on the tax position).

TABLE 7
After-Tax Income Compared
Company Owner vs Self Employed: High Income

Profits	Company Owner	Self- Employed	Extra Income
£300,000	£153,564	£171,540	£17,977
£350,000	£176,850	£198,040	£21,190
£400,000	£200,137	£224,540	£24,404
£500,000	£246,709	£277,540	£30,831
£600,000	£293,282	£330,540	£37,258
£700,000	£339,855	£383,540	£43,685
£800,000	£386,428	£436,540	£50,112
£1,000,000	£479,574	£542,540	£62,966

Notes:
1. Company owner withdraws all the profits of the business
2. Company owner takes optimal large salary plus dividends of £40,500
3. No spare employment allowance available
4. No associated companies
5. Business owner is under state pension age but over 21 in both cases
6. Personal tax includes Income Tax and National Insurance in both cases
7. Both sets of tax bills are higher in Scotland (this method of profit extraction is never optimal for Scottish taxpayers under state pension age)

This is illustrated by Table 7, which compares the total after-tax income of a company owner with that of a self-employed business owner at different profit levels.

For the company owner it's assumed the optimal salary is taken (i.e. the amount that reduces the company's profits before tax to £50,000, after accounting for employer's National Insurance) and the remaining £40,500 of after-tax profits is extracted as dividends.

The 'Extra Income' column is again the additional income enjoyed by the *self-employed* person. For example, when profits are £500,000, a self-employed person will enjoy £30,831 more after-tax income than a company owner.

Comparing the company owner's income of £153,564 when profits are £300,000 with the corresponding figure of £153,295 in Table 6, we can see the large salary method is slightly better at this profit level. However, the self-employed person is still £17,977 better off!

The table again reinforces the fact there is no tax benefit in running a highly profitable business through a company if you intend to extract all the profits each year.

However, at these profit levels, there are many other reasons to form a company. Furthermore, many company owners with this level of profit will not extract all the profits and will reinvest a significant proportion. As discussed above, this will yield significant savings.

For example, if a director whose company had profits of £800,000 restricted their own after-tax income to £250,000, the company would be left with around £218,000 of cash to reinvest after accounting for Corporation Tax and employer's National Insurance.

As a sole trader, the same person would have net, after-tax income of £436,540 but, after deducting the £250,000 they needed for personal reasons, there would only be £186,540 left to reinvest in the business.

Looked at another way, the total tax burden for the sole trader (Income Tax and National Insurance) would be £363,460, whereas the total tax burden for the company and its owner (Corporation Tax, Income Tax, and both types of National Insurance) would be £332,367: that's a saving of over £30,000 in this case.

So, there is no doubt companies can be tremendous tax shelters for successful businesses, when a reasonable proportion of profits are retained for reinvestment.

Scottish Business Owners
The higher Scottish Income Tax rates on self-employed business owners mean there is a very different picture in Scotland, as shown by Table 8. In fact, it's so different that, this time, the 'Extra Income' column means the extra after-tax income enjoyed by the *company owner*.

TABLE 8
After-Tax Income Compared
Company Owner vs Self Employed: Scottish Taxpayers

Profits	Company Owner	Self-Employed	Extra Income
£30,000	£25,143	£25,457	(£314)
£40,000	£32,534	£32,757	(£223)
£50,000	£39,925	£38,726	£1,199
£60,000	£47,234	£44,315	£2,919
£80,000	£57,124	£55,365	£1,759
£100,000	£66,863	£65,965	£898
£125,000	£79,036	£73,590	£5,446
£150,000	£87,555	£86,063	£1,492
£175,000	£97,224	£98,563	(£1,339)
£200,000	£108,368	£111,063	(£2,694)

Notes:
1. Company owner withdraws all the profits of the business
2. Company owner takes optimal salary of £9,100 or £12,570 (see above) and remaining income as dividends
3. No spare employment allowance available
4. No associated companies
5. Business owner is under state pension age but over 21 in both cases
6. Personal tax includes Income Tax and National Insurance in both cases

As we can see, at many profit levels, there are significant savings to be had by using a company for Scottish business owners. In fact, there is some saving at any profit level between around £44,600 and £158,000.

As with other taxpayers in the rest of the UK, the savings will be slightly greater if some spare employment allowance is available.

Scottish Partnership versus Company
The picture for Scottish couples in business together is again very different to their counterparts in the rest of the UK.

At modest profit levels, up to around £95,000, the couple would pay less tax operating as a partnership, or about the same if the employment allowance would be available if they operated as a company.

However, once profits exceed around £95,000, a company would generally produce savings for a Scottish couple in business together.

The savings persist until profits reach around £305,000, apart from a 'bad patch' between around £184,000 and £204,000, where the company could create a small additional cost (less than £700).

And, as ever, there are both other good reasons for forming a company, and far greater savings to be had if profits are retained and reinvested within the company.

A Word of Warning

Everything in this chapter is based on current tax rates. A change in rates will tip the balance and we fear the most likely change we may see is an increase in dividend tax rates, making companies less attractive, whatever their profit level (even if you're a Scottish taxpayer).

Property Businesses

This chapter has also focussed exclusively on trading businesses. Property letting or property investment businesses are quite different. For a thorough analysis of the position for these businesses, see the Taxcafe guide *Using a Property Company to Save Tax*.

Part 4

Company Owners with Income from Other Sources

Chapter 24

Keeping Income Below the Key Thresholds

In Chapter 8 we explained why company owners, when deciding how much income to withdraw from their companies, need to be aware of the following Income Tax thresholds and brackets:

- Over £50,270   Higher rate tax
- £60,000-£80,000   Child Benefit Charge
- £100,000-£125,140   Personal allowance withdrawal
- Over £125,140   Additional rate of tax

Basic rate taxpayers pay 8.75% Income Tax on their dividends. Once your income exceeds £50,270 you start paying 33.75% higher rate tax. However, dividend income that falls into the final three tax brackets is taxed at much higher rates:

- £60,000-£80,000   40.4% to 58.0%, or even more
- £100,000-£125,140   56.25% in many cases
- Over £125,140   39.35%

(Note: the £60,000-£80,000 bracket only applies to households in receipt of child benefit.)

When trying to avoid these extortionate tax rates, you must remember to include any other taxable income you receive. If you have taxable income from other sources it may force your company income, in particular your dividend income, into a higher tax bracket.

To avoid a potential tax sting, you may wish to reduce the amount of income you withdraw from your company or take other steps to reduce your tax bill.

The Order in which Income is Taxed

Income is taxed in the following order:

- Non-savings income:
  - Employment income
  - Self-employment income
  - Rental income
  - Pension income (including state pension income)
- Savings income (interest, etc)
- Dividend income

Most importantly for the purposes of this guide, dividends are always treated as the top slice of income.

Let's say you expect to earn £10,000 of rental income during the current tax year but, so far, have not withdrawn any income from your company. As things stand, all of your rental income will be tax free, being covered by your Income Tax personal allowance.

Let's say you now decide to withdraw a salary of £12,570 and a dividend of £37,700 from your company (the maximum amount you can withdraw tax free or taxed at just 8.75%, in the absence of any other income). The decision to take a salary means you now have £22,570 of non-savings income and your Income Tax bill will increase by £2,000:

£22,570 – £12,570 personal allowance = £10,000 x 20% = £2,000

And what about your dividends that are supposedly taxed at no more than 8.75%?

Thanks to your rental income, £10,000 of your dividend income will now be pushed into the higher rate tax bracket and taxed at 33.75% instead of 8.75%, resulting in additional tax of £2,500.

In summary, having £10,000 of rental income increases the company owner's tax bill by £4,500!

Income from Other Sources

With the exception of self-employment and pension income, it may be possible to extract all the other types of income listed above from *your own company*: employment income, rental income, interest income, and dividend income.

We've already talked extensively about salaries (employment income) and dividends. If your company uses a property that you own personally (for example, an office or shop) it can also pay you rent; and if your company borrows money from you it can pay you interest.

In Chapters 30 and 31 we take a look at whether it is tax efficient to get your company to pay you rent or interest and how much.

In this part of the guide the focus is on company owners who have income from *other sources*: i.e. income that does not come from their own company. More specifically, the focus is on company owners who have income from other sources that is subject to *Income Tax*.

Some income (e.g. most interest income and stock market dividends) can be sheltered from Income Tax inside an ISA or pension scheme.

It is also possible to shelter assets from Income Tax inside another company. Many property investors do this. Corporation Tax is still payable on any rental profits produced by the properties but the Income Tax position of the company owner will be unaffected, unless those profits are extracted.

Those company owners who do have a significant amount of taxable income from other sources, and cannot shelter it from Income Tax, may wish to reduce the amount of income they withdraw from their own companies, so as to avoid paying Income Tax at some of the extortionate rates listed at the beginning of this chapter.

Control
One of the benefits of being a company owner is you can control how much income you withdraw from your business. This allows you to control your Income Tax bill from year to year.

Income from other sources is often less easy to control. For example, it may not be possible to shift it from one tax year into another tax year. You may be able to control the dividends declared by your own company but if you own a few shares in BP you can't force their directors to increase or lower the company's dividend!

TABLE 9
Avoiding the Tax Thresholds
Maximum Dividend 2024/25

Other Income	Threshold £50,270	£60,000	£100,000
£9,100	£41,170	£50,900	£90,900
£12,570	£37,700	£47,430	£87,430
£15,000	£35,270	£45,000	£85,000
£20,000	£30,270	£40,000	£80,000
£25,000	£25,270	£35,000	£75,000
£30,000	£20,270	£30,000	£70,000
£35,000	£15,270	£25,000	£65,000
£40,000	£10,270	£20,000	£60,000

Company owners who want to keep their taxable income just below any of the key Income Tax thresholds may therefore have to increase or decrease their *company income*: it may not always be possible to alter the income you receive from other sources.

Table 9 shows the maximum dividend you can withdraw during 2024/25 if you have other taxable income (including your company salary) and want to avoid some of the key Income Tax thresholds.

For example, if you have other taxable income of £20,000, a dividend of no more than £30,270 will prevent your income going over £50,270, which means you will avoid paying 33.75% tax.

A dividend no higher than £40,000 will ensure you avoid the Child Benefit Charge, where relevant.

A dividend of up to £80,000 will ensure your income does not exceed £100,000. A significant amount will be taxed at 33.75% and you may end up paying the maximum Child Benefit Charge but you will not lose any of your personal allowance.

Note, Table 9 is equally relevant to Scottish taxpayers because it is the *UK* thresholds that apply to your dividend income.

For example, a Scottish taxpayer with £40,000 of salary and rental income can still receive a dividend of £10,270 without paying 33.75% tax because it is the UK higher rate threshold that applies to dividend income.

We haven't included the additional rate tax threshold of £125,140 here because, as explained in Chapter 19, there is no benefit in avoiding it.

Predictability

At the start of a new tax year you may not know how much taxable income you will receive from other sources during the year. This could be problematic if you wish to withdraw dividends from your company *at the beginning of the tax year.*

If you withdraw dividends from your company and your other income then turns out to be higher than anticipated, you may end up paying more Income Tax than you expected on your company dividends.

Some types of income are, however, more predictable than others. For example, interest income, stock market dividends and pension income are arguably more predictable than, say, the profits of a sole trader business (self-employment income).

Some types of income, if not completely predictable, are more likely to end up being *less than expected*, rather than higher than expected. A rental property that normally generates rental income of £1,000 per month may lie empty for three months, thereby producing an annual income of £9,000 rather than £12,000.

If your income from other sources turns out to be less than expected, you may be able to get your company to pay you additional dividend income before the end of the tax year.

If your income from other sources turns out to be *higher than expected* you generally cannot reverse any dividends you have already taken out of your company, although it may be possible to do some emergency year-end tax planning (see Chapter 26).

Company owners who have unpredictable income from other sources may therefore wish to postpone paying dividends until closer to the end of the tax year, if they are concerned that their dividend income may fall into a heavily taxed bracket.

Chapter 25

Should I Pay Myself a Different Salary?

So far, we have shown that if you have income from other sources (e.g. rental income) you may wish to reduce your company *dividends* to avoid various tax thresholds.

Another important question is, "Should I pay myself a different salary?"

The answer to this depends on a number of factors, including:

- What you are trying to achieve
- Whether the employment allowance is available
- How much other income you have
- What type or types of other income you have

Not Exceeding the Thresholds

If you have a substantial amount of other income from outside the company (generally more than £37,700, or more than £31,092 for a Scottish taxpayer), you may want to reduce your salary in order to avoid exceeding one of the key Income Tax thresholds: £50,270, £60,000, and £100,000.

Scottish taxpayers have two additional thresholds to be aware of: £43,662 and £75,000, but can ignore interest or dividend income for the purpose of these.

So, for example, if you have other income of £53,000 and several small children, you might choose to reduce the salary you take from your company to £7,000 in order to avoid the CBC. (Or perhaps £6,500 so you can still take a £500 tax-free dividend.)

Maximising After-Tax Income

You might also wish to reduce your salary in other cases where you are seeking to maximise your total after-tax income without exceeding one of the key Income Tax thresholds.

Let's say you have rental income totalling £30,000 and a company making profits of around £125,000. You want to limit your total taxable income to £100,000 so that you retain your personal allowance. What's the best level of salary to take? Let's look at three options:

Salary	£0	£9,100	£12,570
Income Tax @ 20%	£0	£1,820	£2,514
Net Salary	£0	£7,280	£10,056
Dividends	£70,000	£60,900	£57,430
Income Tax @ 8.75%	£1,730	£934	£630
Income Tax @ 33.75%	£16,784	£16,784	£16,784
Total Net Income*	£51,486	£50,462	£50,072

* This doesn't include the rental income or take account of the Income Tax on it. However, as long as total taxable income does not exceed £100,000, this is the same regardless of what salary is taken from the company.

So, in this scenario, the best after-tax income is produced by taking no salary at all. But this is far from the end of the story.

Firstly, taking no salary will mean you get no credit for state pension purposes. It may also create other problems. We'll look at these issues later in this chapter.

Secondly, we have only looked at the director's position and not the company's. A salary of £9,100 would have produced a Corporation Tax saving of £2,412 in this case: that's £1,388 more than the director's £1,024 Income Tax saving.

A salary of £12,570 may have been even better. Even if it gave rise to employer's National Insurance of £479 it would have produced a Corporation Tax saving of £3,458 and hence an overall net saving for the company of £2,979. That's another £567 saved for the company when the director's net income only falls by a further £390.

So, what's best for the director personally is not necessarily best overall. And that's why we need to look at the optimal position taking all these factors into account.

Optimal Salaries with Other Income

If you intend to pay yourself a salary of £12,570, as discussed in Chapter 9, and extract the rest of the company's profits as dividends, it may be possible to save a small amount of tax by reducing your company salary. The position depends on whether the company has any spare employment allowance and on how much other income from outside the company you have.

With Spare Employment Allowance

Where there is at least £479 of spare employment allowance available, a salary of £12,570 generally remains optimal for most directors, regardless of how much other income they have.

Although the salary may be subject to Income Tax, there will be no National Insurance payable by the director or the company.

No Spare Employment Allowance
Low Levels of Other Income

A salary of £9,100 may sometimes be slightly preferable where the company has no spare employment allowance available and you have at least £3,470 of other income from outside the company (excluding dividends and interest).

The savings are not significant, typically £143 for a basic rate taxpayer or £14 for a higher rate taxpayer (as we know, a salary of £9,100 is generally preferable for director/shareholders with total income over £100,000 in any case).

With less than £3,470 of other income (excluding dividends and interest) and no spare employment allowance available, the optimal salary for a basic or higher rate taxpayer is generally £12,570 less that other income. For example, with £2,000 of other income, the optimal salary will generally be £10,570. However, it's hardly worth worrying about this level of detail, as the savings are even less!

No Spare Employment Allowance
Significant Levels of Other Income

If the other income from sources outside the company is significant, a salary of £12,570 may remain optimal for some higher or additional rate taxpayers (including those with total taxable income of more than £100,000).

Generally speaking, the company will need to have profits of at least £63,049 before taking account of the director's salary (thus getting Corporation Tax relief at 26.5% on all the salary plus related employer's National Insurance): although there are some small savings to be had by less profitable companies under certain conditions.

How much other income it takes before a salary of £12,570 remains optimal (instead of £9,100) varies depending on the company's profit level: the higher the profit, the less other income it takes. Here are some examples:

Company Profit	Other Income Required
£63,049 to £77,000	£37,275
£80,000	£36,525
£90,000	£34,075
£100,000	£31,625
£110,000	£29,175
£120,000	£26,725
£128,500 to £200,000	£24,825

These figures assume:
1. Company owner withdraws all the profits of the business
2. No spare employment allowance available
3. No associated companies
4. Company owner is under state pension age but over 21

Alternatively, with high company profit levels, and significant amounts of other income from outside the company, it may be better to increase the salary even further: see below.

By Way of Explanation
The reason it's sometimes tax efficient to pay yourself a smaller salary when you have other income from outside the company is because that other income will effectively use up some or all of your personal allowance. Any salary that exceeds what's left of your personal allowance will give rise to an Income Tax liability.

If there is also any National Insurance payable, the total tax rate (Income Tax and National Insurance) will often exceed the combined tax rate on dividend income (Corporation Tax and Income Tax).

So, once you've exhausted both your personal allowance and your National Insurance free salary, dividends are generally better for those with low or modest amounts of other income (except for the big earners we looked at in Chapter 21).

However, with significant amounts of other income and a very profitable company, the Corporation Tax relief on that extra £3,470 of salary, combined with the fact it means you have less dividends taxed at 33.75% or 39.35%, outweighs the Income Tax and employer's National Insurance on the salary.

Reducing Your Salary: Other Factors to Consider

Aside from the issues discussed above, there are reasons why you may not wish to reduce your salary, or why it may not be practical to do so:

- To make pension contributions personally (see Chapter 34).
- Because your income from other sources may not be known at the beginning of the year, when you may wish to start making monthly salary payments.
- Because the taxman may question any reduction in your salary (see Chapter 42).

However, when we are only looking at whether to pay yourself £9,100 or £12,570, the second point is easily dealt with by paying yourself a monthly salary of £758.33 (£9,100/12) for most of the year. Then, if you decide the higher salary is going to be better, simply pay an extra £3,470 as a bonus in March.

And a mere reduction from £12,570 to £9,100 is highly unlikely to give rise to any problem under the third bullet point.

Recent changes mean the optimal salary for nearly all director/shareholders is now always *at least* £9,100. It is, however, worth mentioning it may be important to pay yourself a salary above the lower earnings limit (£6,396 in 2024/25) to protect your state pension entitlement (see Chapter 12): unless, of course, your other income already includes sufficient qualifying earnings from a different source (over £6,396 from a different employment, or over £6,725 in profits from self-employment), or you are getting a credit via the child benefit system (see Chapter 17).

Dividends and Interest

Where your income from outside your company includes, or comprises, dividends or interest, the impact of reducing your salary will be different. We'll look at these types of 'other income' in Chapter 26.

Increasing Your Salary
For those with a company making substantial profits *and* significant amounts of income from other sources, the existence of that other income makes it more likely you will benefit from following the large salary method we looked at in Chapter 21.

In effect, the other income brings down the level of company profit required before the large salary method becomes optimal. The more other income you have, the lower the profit level you need. Here are some examples:

Other Income	Profit Level Required
£10,000	£238,000
£20,000	£210,000
£30,000	£200,000
£40,000	£197,000
£50,000	£194,000
£75,000	£186,500
£100,000	£179,000
£108,000 or more	£176,500

These figures assume:
1. Company owner withdraws all the profits of the business
2. No spare employment allowance available
3. No associated companies
4. Company owner is under state pension age but over 21
5. Company owner is not a Scottish taxpayer

Other income excludes dividends for this purpose. Higher profit levels may be required where the other income includes interest income: but not if there is also at least £17,570 of other income that is not interest or dividends.

We'll look at some other, more specific cases where the large salary method may be beneficial in the next chapter.

Summary: Optimal Salaries with Other Income
A salary of £12,570 generally remains optimal when the company has at least £479 of employment allowance available, or the company owner has significant amounts of income from other sources outside the company.

Low or modest amounts of other income (but at least £3,470) will generally mean a salary of £9,100 becomes optimal. However, the potential savings are not significant.

Other income of less than £3,470 will mean a different salary is theoretically optimal, but the impact will be even less significant.

Other income will also reduce the profit level at which the large salary method (Chapter 21) becomes optimal. However, company profits of at least £176,500 will generally still be required, unless there are other factors making this route more attractive (e.g. company owner is over state pension age or under 21, or there is spare employment allowance available). This method is not suitable for Scottish taxpayers under state pension age.

Chapter 26

The Different Types of Income

In this chapter, we will take a closer look at the different types of income you may earn from sources outside your company and how they may affect the income you decide to withdraw from your company.

As a general point, it's worth remembering, as discussed in Chapter 25, that significant amounts of other income from outside the company could mean the large salary method described in Chapter 21 becomes optimal for director/shareholders with highly profitable companies. This is equally true for all types of other income except dividends.

Employment Income

It is possible to have more than one source of employment income, for example:

- Salary from a second job with a separate employer, or
- Salary from a second company you own

If you have recently started out in business, it's possible you will have a second job (possibly a part-time job) to help pay the bills.

If you start a second company for a separate business venture there is, of course, nothing to stop you paying yourself a second salary.

For Income Tax purposes you are only entitled to one personal allowance (£12,570 at present). This generally means you can only have one tax-free salary (unless, of course, the two salaries, added together, total no more than £12,570). Some or all of the second salary may be taxed at 20%.

National Insurance is calculated differently. Directors who have more than one salary of £12,570 this year may not have to pay any National Insurance personally. This is because the earnings from each job may be treated separately.

If the two businesses are 'in association' however, the salaries will be added together and National Insurance may be payable. Employers are considered to be in association if:

- The businesses serve a common purpose, and
- There is significant sharing of things like premises, personnel, equipment, or customers

A second salary will generally be more tax efficient than a dividend, providing there is no National Insurance payable.

If you wish to pay yourself two salaries, it may be necessary to obtain professional advice to satisfy yourself the companies will not be treated by HMRC as being in association, with resulting National Insurance liabilities.

Finally, there may be other tax and non-tax reasons why you wish to pay yourself a second salary or a bigger second salary.

Salary from Other Job At Least £50,270
Where a company owner earns a salary of at least £50,270 (the upper earnings limit) from a different employment, it may be possible to reduce the employee's National Insurance rate on the salary they receive from their own company.

In other words, instead of paying 8% National Insurance, it may be possible to pay just 2% on all of the second salary the director receives from their own company.

This is because there is a limit to the amount of salary income on which you have to pay the main rate of National Insurance each year. Applications to pay the reduced rate can be made using form CA72A, available from HMRC's website.

Note, employer's National Insurance will still be payable on any amount over £9,100, unless the company has spare employment allowance available.

Nonetheless, where you are eligible to pay just 2% National Insurance on the salary you take from your company, it will often be tax efficient to increase your company salary.

Where there is NO spare employment allowance available, a higher salary may be beneficial provided that, after paying the salary, the company will still have a marginal Corporation Tax rate of 25% or 26.5% (i.e. a salary that reduces the company's profit before tax to £50,000 but no more than this).

Where there IS spare employment allowance available, the optimal salary will be the *greater* of the amount covered by the employment allowance or the amount that reduces the company's profit before tax to £50,000.

As usual, this assumes all remaining after-tax profits are taken as dividends. The position may differ in other cases.

Scottish directors will not benefit from an increased salary in this scenario if their total taxable income exceeds £100,000.

Self-Employment Income
You may have self-employment income if you have another business that is not a company (i.e. you're a sole trader or belong to a partnership). When we refer to self-employment income, we are talking about the taxable profits of your sole trader business, or your share of the taxable profits of a partnership.

Many entrepreneurs have multiple businesses and it's possible a second or third business will not be a company.

Companies can be wonderful tax shelters but unincorporated businesses have advantages of their own, including lower accountancy fees, more generous treatment of certain expenses, and more generous capital allowances for cars used in the business.

Self-employment income may be difficult to predict, especially close to the beginning of a new tax year, making it difficult to decide how much income to withdraw from the other company business.

Fortunately, as far as your self-employment business is concerned, it may be possible to do some emergency year-end tax planning to reduce your tax bill (for example, by making pension contributions or incurring other tax-deductible expenditure).

Rental Income
When we use the term 'rental income' what we mean is taxable rental *profit*. You may receive rents of £10,000 per year but your

taxable rental profit may only be £5,000, after deducting all the expenses property investors can claim.

Unlike interest income and stock market dividends, most rental income cannot be sheltered from Income Tax in an ISA, pension scheme or other tax shelter. There are, however a couple of exceptions:

- Commercial property held in a pension scheme
- Residential or commercial property held in a company

Some business owners place their business premises inside a self-invested personal pension (SIPP) to avoid Income Tax and CGT (see Chapter 35).

Others put their properties in a separate company. Corporation Tax is payable on the rental income and capital gains, but the company owner's Income Tax bill will be unaffected, unless the property company's profits are extracted.

Apart from these two exceptions, most landlords own their properties *personally*, which means they are fully exposed to Income Tax on rental profits. These rental profits may then need to be factored into the mix when deciding how much income you withdraw from your other company business.

For example, if you take a salary of £12,570 and expect to have taxable rental profits of £20,000, you can take tax-free dividend income of £500 plus additional dividend income of £17,200 taxed at 8.75%. This takes you up to the £50,270 higher rate threshold. Any additional dividend income you receive will be taxed at a rate of at least 33.75%.

If you take a salary of £12,570 and expect to have taxable rental profits of £50,000 you will pay at least 33.75% tax on any dividend income you receive from your company (apart from the first £500 covered by the dividend allowance).

Mortgage Tax Relief Restrictions
Landlords who own residential property can no longer deduct their mortgage interest from their rental income when calculating their taxable rental profits. Instead what they receive is a 'tax reduction' equal to the 20% basic rate of Income Tax.

These rules do not apply to commercial properties nor, in the current 2024/25 tax year, furnished holiday lettings. They also do not apply to properties held inside companies.

The reduced tax relief means many landlords have bigger taxable rental profits.

This in turn has pushed more of the dividend income they receive from their other company business over the higher rate threshold where it is taxed at 33.75% instead of 8.75%.

Tax Planning for Landlords
If you are a company owner and separately own mortgaged rental properties personally you will have to be careful about the amount of dividend income you pay yourself if you want to avoid going over the various tax thresholds.

Example: Jessie owns a small engineering company and some rental property. Because she earns rental income, she decides to pay herself a salary of £9,100 in 2024/25 (Chapter 25 explains why this might be the optimal salary for someone with modest income from other sources).

Her rental property produces income of £20,000 net of all expenses except mortgage interest. Her mortgage interest is £7,500 so her true rental profit is £12,500.

However, her taxable rental profit is £20,000 and it is this number she must use when deciding how much dividend income to take.

With a salary of £9,100 and taxable rental profit of £20,000 Jessie can pay herself a dividend of up to £21,170 before she becomes a higher rate taxpayer and has to pay 33.75% tax (£50,270 – £9,100 – £20,000).

Example: Cillian owns a software company and a portfolio of rental properties. Because he earns significant rental income and has a very profitable company, he decides to pay himself a salary of £12,570 in 2024/25 (Chapter 25 explains why this may be the optimal salary in this case).

His rental property produces income of £50,000 (net of all expenses except interest). His mortgage interest is £15,000 so his true rental profit is £35,000. However, his taxable rental profit is £50,000.

With a salary of £12,570 and taxable rental profit of £50,000, Cillian is a higher rate taxpayer and will pay 33.75% tax on his dividend income (except the first £500, covered by the dividend allowance).

Cillian can pay himself a dividend of up to £37,430 before he reaches the £100,000 tax threshold where his personal allowance will be gradually withdrawn. He will then pay tax at an effective rate of 53.75% on the next £25,140 of dividend income he receives (see Chapter 18 for an explanation of how the withdrawal of the personal allowance works).

For the rest of this guide, when we refer to 'rental income' received by an individual, unless expressly stated to the contrary, this means their taxable rental profits, after deducting all allowable expenses EXCEPT interest and finance costs relating to residential rental property.

In the case of non-residential property or, for 2024/25, furnished holiday lets, 'rental income' simply means rental profits.

Rental Losses
If you have rental losses brought forward from previous years you may not have to pay any Income Tax on the rental profit you make during the current tax year (providing the loss brought forward is big enough to offset the current year's profit).

If the rental profit you make during the current tax year is not taxable it does not need to be factored into the mix when deciding how much income you withdraw from your company.

However, because of the restrictions on relief for interest and finance costs discussed above, most residential landlords with rental losses brought forward have seen these effectively eroded away over the last few years and turned into what is officially termed 'unused residential property finance costs', better known as 'unrelieved interest'.

Where you have unrelieved interest brought forward rather than old-style rental losses, it will attract tax relief at the 20% basic rate, the same as your current interest costs, but it will not reduce your taxable rental profit, which will therefore still have to be factored into your decision-making when considering how much income to withdraw from your company.

Pension Income

If you have any pension income, this will usually need to be taken into account when deciding how much income to withdraw from your company. Most pension income is taxable, including:

- Your UK state pension, where applicable
- Occupational pensions
- Private pensions
- Income withdrawn under a drawdown arrangement
- Foreign pensions (subject to the terms of any applicable Double Tax Treaty)

However, there is one key exemption to be aware of, namely the 25% tax-free lump sum available from most private pension schemes.

Where there is no spare employment allowance available, the optimal salary level for a company owner who has £3,470 or more of pension income is generally £9,100 this year, regardless of whether or not they are over state pension age.

For smaller amounts of pension income, the optimal salary will generally be the greater of:

- £9,100, or
- £12,570 LESS their total non-savings income for the year (pension income is classed as non-savings income)

For those under state pension age, the optimal salary where there IS spare employment allowance available will generally be £12,570.

This may also be the optimal salary where the director has significant amounts of income from outside the company (in total), and the company has profits of £63,000 or more (see Chapter 25).

Where there is spare employment allowance available, directors over state pension age will benefit from the National Insurance free salaries we looked at in Chapter 11 (£27,216 where the company is run by two directors with no other employees). In most cases, this will be the optimal salary for them to take from their company.

Whether the employment allowance is available or not, it will often be better for directors over state pension age with very profitable companies to use the large salary method we looked at in Chapter 21, where this produces a higher salary.

Alternatively, as with any other director, it may make sense to restrict the amount extracted from the company to avoid exceeding one of the key Income Tax thresholds: £50,270, £60,000 or £100,000. Remember, it is the director's total income from all sources that needs to be considered (including dividends and interest).

Dividends for Pension Recipients

Once a director in receipt of pension income has worked out their optimal salary, the next step is to decide how much dividend income they would like to take. As usual, any amount covered by the dividend allowance will be tax free. Beyond that, we are back into the usual tax planning territory.

Example: George and Gracie are the owner/directors and only employees of Like Old Times Ltd. In 2024/25, they each receive a state pension of £11,502 and each take a salary of £27,216 out of the company. They have no other income from outside the company.

If they each take dividends of £11,552 out of the company, £500 (each) will be tax free and the remaining £11,052 (each) will be taxed at 8.75%.

Any further dividends will be taxed at 33.75% and if they take any more than £61,282 each in total, they will start to lose their personal allowances, leading to further tax costs.

We've assumed in this example that George and Gracie each own 50% of the shares in their company.

Note that, at company profit levels over around £105,000, the large salary method covered in Chapter 21 will often be more beneficial in this scenario.

Example: Bob is below state pension age, but enters a drawdown arrangement and takes £50,000 out of his pension scheme during 2024/25. However, only £16,000 of this is taxable as the remaining £34,000 represents his 25% tax free lump sum.

Bob also takes a salary of £9,100 out of his company, but has no other sources of income.

It's still worth Bob taking a dividend of £500 as this is tax free. He can also take up to a further £24,670 in dividends this year that will only be taxed at 8.75% (£50,270 – £16,000 – £9,100 – £500 = £24,670).

If Bob had taken only his 25% tax free lump sum, it would have had no impact on his company income and he could then have taken an optimal salary of £12,570 plus dividends of up to £37,700 without suffering any tax at 33.75%.

Interest Income

Most personal interest income can be sheltered from tax inside an ISA or SIPP. Other tax-free investments include index-linked savings certificates (when they're available) and offset mortgages (instead of earning interest, your savings are used to reduce the interest on your mortgage). Paying off personal debts is also effectively a way to earn tax-free interest (you pay less interest on your debts and that reduction is not taxed: unless it counts as qualifying loan interest, which we will look at in Chapter 31).

Wealthier individuals, with large cash balances or holdings of corporate and government bonds may, however, have a significant amount of *taxable* interest income and there may also be times in life when less wealthy taxpayers have significant amounts of taxable interest income:

- You sell your home and have a large cash lump sum
- You lend money to a friend or family member
- You receive a big dividend and put the cash in the bank
- You lend money to your company (see Chapter 31)

This income may need to be factored into the equation when you decide how much income to withdraw from your company.

The £5,000 Starting Rate Band

When it comes to interest income, many company owners are in a fortunate position. They can receive up to £5,000 of interest *tax free* each year thanks to the 0% starting-rate band.

The starting rate is supposed to benefit those with low incomes. Hence the £5,000 starting rate band is reduced by any *non-savings* income you have in excess of the personal allowance, including:

- Employment income
- Self-employment income
- Pension income
- Rental income

Hence, if your non-savings income (for example your rental income) exceeds £17,570 in total (£12,570 + £5,000), none of your interest income will be covered by the starting rate band.

Of course, most regular salary earners and self-employed business owners will have more than £17,570 of non-savings income. Many *company owners* are in a different position, however. Note that the above list of non-savings income does NOT include dividends. Dividends are the top slice of income and do not use up the starting rate band.

Because company owners often pay themselves small salaries and take the rest of their income as dividends, they will often have little or no taxable non-savings income. As a result, many can earn at least £5,000 of tax-free interest.

Example: *Mandy is a company owner with a salary of £12,570, dividend income of £32,700, and interest income of £5,000. Her salary is tax free thanks to her personal allowance and she therefore has no taxable non-savings income that uses up her starting rate band (her dividend income does not count). Her interest income is fully covered by her £5,000 starting rate band and taxed at 0%.*

Many directors will thus pay 0% tax on their interest if they:

- Take a small salary from their company,
- Do not have another source of employment income,
- Do not have a sole trader or partnership business,
- Don't earn much, if any, rental income, and
- Do not receive much, if any, pension income.

It is important to point out that the 0% starting rate band is not given in addition to your basic rate band (currently £37,700). Instead it is part of your basic rate band.

If you qualify to use the starting rate band, your basic rate band will be reduced, possibly pushing some of your dividend income into a higher tax bracket.

The Personal Savings Allowance

The personal savings allowance exempts the first £1,000 of your interest income from tax if you're a basic rate taxpayer and the first £500 if you're a higher rate taxpayer. Additional rate taxpayers get nothing.

The personal savings allowance operates separately from, and in addition to, the starting rate band. This means some company owners can earn up to £6,000 of tax-free interest every year.

Income covered by the personal savings allowance uses up some of the band it falls into. For example, if you have £49,400 of salary and rental income, and £1,000 of interest income, you will have total income of £50,400.

As a higher rate taxpayer, you will therefore be entitled to a £500 personal savings allowance. Thus £500 of your interest income will be tax free and this will use up £500 of your basic rate band, leaving £370 taxed at 20%. The final £130 will be taxed at 40%.

The personal savings allowance is helpful to company owners who cannot use the starting rate band because they have too much non-savings income such as rental income. Most can enjoy £1,000 or £500 of tax-free interest. It may also be useful for extracting interest from your own company (see Chapter 31).

Interest Income Examples

The somewhat complex operation of the starting rate band and personal savings allowance is best explained with some examples. These examples are all based on the current, 2024/25 tax year.

Example: Samantha is a company owner with a salary of £12,570 and interest income of £5,000. She also has £10,000 of rental income.

Her salary is covered by her personal allowance but thanks to her rental income she has £10,000 of taxable non-savings income. Because her taxable non-savings income exceeds the £5,000 starting rate band, none of her interest income is covered by the 0% starting rate.

However, because she is a basic rate taxpayer (her total income is less than £50,270) she is entitled to a £1,000 personal savings allowance. So £1,000 of her interest income will be tax free, the remaining £4,000 will be taxed at 20%.

Example: Elaine is a company owner with a salary of £9,100, rental income of £7,500, interest of £1,500 and dividends of £20,000 (total income £38,100).

There is no Income Tax on her salary and the first £3,470 of her rental income is covered by her remaining personal allowance. The final £4,030 of her rental income is taxed at 20% and uses up £4,030 of her £5,000 starting rate band. Thus £970 of her interest income is covered by her remaining starting rate band and is tax free.

As a basic rate taxpayer, she is also entitled to a £1,000 personal savings allowance, so the final £530 of her interest is also tax free. The first £500 of her dividend income is covered by the dividend allowance; the remaining £19,500 is taxed at 8.75%.

Example: Ollie is a company owner with a salary of £12,570 and dividends of £37,700. He also has interest income of £5,500 (total income £55,770).

There is no Income Tax on his salary and £5,000 of his interest income is tax free thanks to the 0% starting rate band (dividends do not count as non-savings income and do not use up the starting rate band). Because his total income is £55,770, he is a higher rate taxpayer and is entitled to a £500 personal savings allowance, so the final £500 of his interest income will also be tax free.

Turning to his dividend income, Ollie has £32,200 of his basic rate band remaining (£50,270 – £12,570 – £5,500). Of this £500 will be tax free thanks to the dividend allowance and £31,700 will be taxed at 8.75%. The final £5,500 of his dividend income is taxed at 33.75%.

Although all of Ollie's interest is tax free it uses up some of his basic rate band, pushing £5,500 of his dividend income over the higher rate threshold where it is taxed at 33.75%.

Example: Mark is a company owner with salary and rental income totalling £50,000 (his non-savings income) and dividends of £20,000. He also has interest income of £5,000. Total income: £75,000. Because his taxable non-savings income exceeds the £5,000 starting rate band, none of his interest is covered by the 0% starting rate. However, as a higher rate taxpayer, he is entitled to a £500 personal savings allowance. The final £4,500 of his interest income is taxed at 40%. Turning to his dividend income, the first £500 will be tax free thanks to the dividend allowance and the final £19,500 is taxed at 33.75%.

Making the Most of Your Personal Allowance

In Chapter 4 we mentioned that the personal allowance can be allocated to any income the taxpayer receives. Those with interest income are more likely to save tax by allocating some of their personal allowance from their interest income to their dividend income. This is because their interest income will still be tax free thanks to the 0% starting rate.

__Example:__ In 2024/25, company owner Jameel has salary income of £9,100, interest income of £4,000 and dividend income of £50,000. If all his personal allowance is allocated to his salary and interest, his tax bill will be calculated as follows:

Salary		**Income Tax**
Personal allowance	£9,100	£0
Interest		
Personal allowance	£3,470	£0
Starting rate	£530	£0
Dividend		
Dividend allowance	£500	£0
Taxed at 8.75%	£36,670	£3,209
Taxed at 33.75%	£12,830	£4,330
Total tax		£7,539

This is not the optimal outcome. Jameel can reduce his tax bill by reallocating some of his personal allowance from his interest income to his dividend income. This is because his interest income will still be tax free thanks to the 0% starting rate.

Salary		**Income Tax**
Personal allowance	£9,100	£0
Interest		
Starting rate	£4,000	£0
Dividend		
Personal allowance	£3,470	£0
Dividend allowance	£500	£0
Taxed at 8.75%	£33,200	£2,905
Taxed at 33.75%	£12,830	£4,330
Total tax		£7,235

In this case, Jameel saves £304. This is because his salary does not fully use up his personal allowance, so £3,470 of his dividend income can be tax free instead of taxed at 8.75%. His interest income remains tax free thanks to the 0% starting rate.

Good tax software should perform this calculation automatically.

Scottish Company Owners with Interest Income
The Scottish Parliament can tax most types of income but not interest and dividends. So Scottish taxpayers will not pay more tax on their interest income than other taxpayers.

This year it's only when Scottish company owners have salary income and other income subject to Scottish tax of more than £28,867 that they will pay more tax than other UK taxpayers.

Thus, in all of the above examples the company owners will pay the same tax on their interest and dividend income if they live in Scotland. Samantha and Elaine will, however, pay less tax on their rental income if they live in Scotland, whereas Mark will pay more tax on his salary and rental income.

There is one quirk to watch out for though: a Scottish taxpayer with taxable income (excluding dividends and interest) of more than £43,662 becomes a higher rate taxpayer and sees their personal savings allowance halved from £1,000 to £500.

Stock Market Dividends
The big difference between dividends from your own company and stock market companies is that stock market dividends can be completely sheltered from Income Tax in an ISA or SIPP.

In practice, many investors end up with a mixture of shares held inside and outside the tax protection of ISAs and SIPPs (for example, those who want to invest more than the current £20,000 ISA allowance but do not want to put money in a pension).

These investors could consider:

- Holding high-income shares inside an ISA (to protect the dividends from Income Tax), and
- Holding growth shares that produce capital gains outside an ISA (because some capital gains will be tax free anyway thanks to the annual CGT exemption: see Chapter 44)

This simplistic strategy will not always produce the biggest tax savings, however. If you bought Apple shares back in 2003, before their 90,000% rise, you would be kicking yourself if you didn't stick them in an ISA!

Stock Market Dividends: How Big a Problem?
If you have significant dividends from stock market companies, and the shares are not sheltered inside an ISA or SIPP, you may want to reduce the dividends you extract from your own company to avoid going over one of the key Income Tax thresholds.

However, our gut feeling is that stock market dividends do not cause a significant tax problem for most small investors. Even if you own, say, £100,000 worth of shares outside an ISA or SIPP you will probably receive no more than £5,000 per year in dividends, producing an Income Tax bill of £1,688 for a higher rate taxpayer.

Remember, of course, that you only get one dividend allowance each tax year, so stock market dividends may use up some or all of this allowance: meaning you are able to take less tax-free dividends from your own company, or none at all.

Short-Term (Emergency) Tax Planning

If your total taxable income is higher than expected, there are some steps you can take to reduce it before the end of the tax year:

Pension Contributions
Everyone under age 75 can make a gross pension contribution of £3,600 per year. The taxpayer personally contributes £2,880 and the taxman tops up the pension plan with £720 of basic rate tax relief. To make bigger pension contributions you require earnings: generally salary income or self-employment profits.

If you have a salary of £9,100 you can make a gross pension contribution of £9,100 (£7,280 from you, £1,820 from the taxman). Your basic rate band will be increased by £9,100, so up to £9,100 of your dividends will escape higher rate tax.

If you have a modest amount of self-employment income, you can generally make an additional gross pension contribution equivalent to the taxable profits of the business, thereby eliminating any tax problem caused by this type of income. See Chapters 33 and 34 for more on pension contributions.

Tax Deductible Expenditure

Company owners who also have income from self employment can reduce their taxable income by incurring tax deductible expenditure before the end of that business's accounting period. Possibly the easiest way is to incur expenditure that qualifies for an immediate tax deduction thanks to the annual investment allowance.

Do beware, however, if you don't have a 31st March or 5th April accounting date for your sole trader or partnership business, the way your tax-deductible expenditure reduces your taxable profits will effectively be spread over more than one tax year. For full details see the Taxcafe guide *Small Business Tax Saving Tactics*.

Company owners who also have income from property can reduce their rental profits by spending money on property repairs before the end of the tax year: e.g. replacement kitchens and bathrooms.

Long-Term Tax Planning

Company owners with significant amounts of income from other sources may be able to take the following steps to shift income to another entity or person:

Self-Employment Income

Consider putting the business into a second company (Company 2) so that Corporation Tax is payable rather than Income Tax and National Insurance.

Dividends can then be extracted from Company 2, taking into account dividends withdrawn from Company 1. This will allow you to control your Income Tax bill from year to year.

Of course, it's not always advantageous to incorporate a second business. Sole traders and partnerships enjoy certain tax benefits, including more generous tax treatment of various expenses (including home office, travel, and car capital allowances).

Incorporation could also cost you a significant amount in professional fees and having a second company will generally lead to an increase in the Corporation Tax bill for your first company (unless it has profits of less than £25,000, or more than £250,000).

Another possibility for sole traders may be to transfer their sole trade business into their existing company. This may sometimes cost less overall in Corporation Tax than having two companies; there are also cases where it will make no difference or cost more.

Furthermore, while it is possible for a single company to operate two distinctly separate businesses, there are significant commercial implications to this strategy, which must be considered.

Rental Income
Tax can be saved by:

- Transferring properties to your spouse if he/she pays Income Tax at a lower rate.
- Holding commercial properties inside a pension scheme.
- Holding investment properties inside a company, so that Corporation Tax is payable instead of Income Tax and the extraction of rental profits (as dividends) can be controlled. See the Taxcafe guide *Using a Property Company to Save Tax*.
- Consider alternative investments (e.g. blue chip shares) that can be sheltered from tax in an ISA or pension scheme.

Interest Income
Some company owners can receive up to £6,000 of tax-free interest and most can receive at least £500 (except additional rate taxpayers). Where tax is payable on your interest income, or you fear it will push some of your dividend income into a higher tax bracket, the following strategies can be adopted:

- Transfer savings into an ISA or SIPP
- Use savings to pay off debt or take out an offset mortgage
- Transfer cash to family members who pay tax at a lower rate (but not minor children)
- Invest in assets that produce capital growth rather than interest

Large cash transfers to anyone other than your spouse may have Inheritance Tax implications, although these can be beneficial.

Stock Market Dividends
Tax can be saved by holding shares in an ISA or SIPP, or by transferring holdings to your spouse, or possibly other family members. However, transfers of shareholdings to anyone other than your spouse may have both CGT and Inheritance Tax implications.

Part 5

Splitting Income with Your Family

Chapter 27

Splitting Income with Your Spouse or Partner

In Chapter 14 we saw that couples can double up the tax-free salary and dividend and the amount of dividend income taxed at just 8.75%.

That's all very well if the couple own and run the company together. But what if your spouse/partner isn't involved in the business, for example if the company was started before you met or if they have a separate career and receive salary income from another employer?

In situations like these it may be possible to save Income Tax by gifting shares in the company to your spouse/partner. It may even be possible to save tax by paying them a salary as well.

The amount of tax that can be saved depends on individual circumstances, for example how much profit the company makes and how much taxable income each person has already.

Tax savings are typically achieved where one spouse/partner is a higher rate taxpayer (paying 33.75% tax on their dividend income) and the other spouse/partner has no income at all, has income less than the personal allowance, or is a basic rate taxpayer.

However, it's not just these couples who can save tax. It's possible to pay Income Tax at more than 33.75% on dividend income that falls into any of the following tax brackets:

- £60,000-£80,000   Child Benefit Charge
- £100,000-£125,140   Personal allowance withdrawal
- Over £125,140   Additional rate tax

If your income falls into one of these tax brackets, you may be able to save tax by transferring income to your spouse/partner, even if they are a higher rate taxpayer.

Before we look at some sample tax savings, it is important to point out there are also potential dangers when it comes to splitting dividend income with your spouse/partner. We will return to this important issue later in the chapter.

Capital Gains Tax (CGT)

If you wish to split your dividend income with your spouse/partner, you generally have to transfer shares in the company to them.

In the case of married couples, a gift of shares would be exempt from CGT. CGT will, however, be payable if the spouse who receives the gift later disposes of the shares. The original base cost of the spouse who made the transfer will be used to perform the CGT calculation.

Gifts between unmarried couples are normally subject to CGT. However, the couple may be able to jointly elect to claim holdover relief.

Holdover relief allows a chargeable gain to be deferred (held over) when gifts of qualifying business assets are made. The person who receives the shares may eventually have to pay CGT on the original owner's held over gain, as well as their own, when the shares are sold.

To qualify for holdover relief, the company must generally be a regular trading company.

Unmarried couples who want to split their income face a further potential danger (see below).

Giving the Business Away

To successfully split your dividend income with your spouse/partner, it is essential that genuine beneficial ownership of shares in the company is handed over. This means your spouse/partner must be able to do what they like with any dividends and any proceeds from a sale of the business.

As we shall see shortly, it is also safer to transfer ordinary shares rather than shares that have fewer voting rights or other rights.

It is probably wise to have any dividends received by your spouse/partner paid into a separate bank account in their name, to show HMRC you have not retained control of the money.

Dividends are generally payable in proportion to shareholdings. So, if you normally take a dividend of £100,000 and want to transfer £40,000 of this income to your spouse/partner, you will generally have to transfer 40% of the business to them or, to be more precise, 40% of your shares in the company.

Because this sort of tax planning, if done correctly, involves effectively giving away ownership and control of part of your business, it is only suitable where there is a significant amount of trust between the parties involved.

How Much of the Business Should Be Transferred?
For many company owners, a 50:50 ownership split with their spouse or partner will prove optimal, but a smaller stake can be transferred if the founder wants to retain more control over the business.

Example: Steve owns 100% of Steve's Spices Ltd, a small trading company. Steve currently pays himself a salary of £15,000 and dividends of £80,000.

His total income is £95,000, which means he is close to the £100,000 threshold. If his income rises above this threshold, he will start to lose his Income Tax personal allowance.

As things stand, he will pay Income Tax of £18,139 on his dividend income in 2024/25 (see Chapter 5 for how dividends are taxed).

Steve's wife, Lara, does not own any shares in the company, but she does receive rental income of £14,000 from a buy-to-let property. This means she can receive dividends of up to £36,270 this year before she becomes a higher rate taxpayer (£50,270 – £14,000). Of this, £500 will be tax-free and the rest will be taxed at just 8.75%.

Steve therefore transfers 45% of the ordinary shares in the business to Lara. The company continues to pay total dividends of £80,000 but now Steve's dividend is £44,000 and Lara's is £36,000.

Lara's total taxable income is now £50,000 and the tax bill on her dividend income is £3,106. Steve's total taxable income is now £59,000 and the tax bill on his dividend income is £5,989.

Overall, the total tax on the dividend income has been reduced by £9,044.

Furthermore, Steve's income is now well below the £100,000 threshold, which means he doesn't have to worry about losing his Income Tax personal allowance.

Additional tax savings may be achieved if the couple are currently receiving child benefit. As we know from Chapter 17, the Child Benefit Charge is payable if the highest earner in the household has income of more than £60,000.

Because Steve's income has fallen from £95,000 to £59,000, he will no longer be subject to the Child Benefit Charge, saving the couple an additional £2,212 if they have two qualifying children.

Potential Tax Savings

The potential tax savings from transferring dividend income to your spouse/partner will vary from case to case. The analysis set out below is based on the current 2024/25 tax year.

Spouse/Partner Has No Income

If you are a basic rate taxpayer (income under £50,270) and your spouse/partner is a 'house-spouse' with no taxable income, they can receive tax-free dividends of up to £13,070 this year (made up of the £12,570 personal allowance and £500 dividend allowance). The potential tax saving is £1,144 (£13,070 x 8.75%).

If you are a higher rate taxpayer and your spouse/partner has no taxable income, they can receive less heavily taxed dividends of up to £50,270 this year. The first £13,070 will be tax free and the remainder will be taxed at 8.75%.

By contrast, you as a higher rate taxpayer could be paying at least 33.75% tax on all of this income.

For example, let's say you gift enough shares in the company so that your spouse/partner receives dividend income of £40,000. Your spouse/partner will pay £2,356 tax (first £13,070 tax free, the remainder taxed at 8.75%).

If we assume you would have paid tax at 33.75% on all of this income, this would have amounted to £13,500, so the net tax saving in this example would be £11,144.

The tax saving may be even greater if you have income of more than £100,000 before you transfer shares. Reducing your income may allow you to claw back some or all of your personal allowance, which will produce an additional tax saving.

Spouse/Partner is Basic-Rate Taxpayer
Even if your spouse/partner works and has taxable income, it may be possible to save tax by gifting shares in the business to them. Again, the tax savings will vary from case to case.

Example: *Rupert is a company owner who expects to have a taxable income of £75,000 this year, made up of a £60,000 dividend and £15,000 of salary and other income. He will pay 33.75% tax on £24,730 of his dividend income (£75,000 – £50,270 higher rate threshold).*

His wife, Wendy, receives taxable income of £30,000 from another source. Thus, she has £20,270 of her basic rate band left and can receive £20,270 of dividends that will be less heavily taxed in her hands.

If Rupert gifts one third of the shares to Wendy and the company normally pays dividends of £60,000, she'll receive £20,000. The first £500 will be tax free thanks to the dividend allowance and tax of £1,706 will be payable on the remaining £19,500 (at 8.75%). Rupert would've paid £6,750 tax on this income so the tax saving is £5,044.

Spouse/Partner is Higher-Rate Taxpayer
If you and your spouse/partner are both higher rate taxpayers (income over £50,270) it may still be possible to save tax by gifting them shares in the company.

If your income exceeds £100,000 some or all of your personal allowance will have been withdrawn and it may be possible to save more tax by transferring dividend income to your spouse/partner.

Example: *Saul is a company owner who expects to have a taxable income of £130,000 this year, made up of £120,000 of dividend income and £10,000 of salary and other income. With this much income all of his personal allowance will be withdrawn.*

His wife Kylie has income of £60,000 from another source. If Saul transfers 25% of the company to Kylie she will receive dividend income of £30,000. The first £500 will be tax free but she will pay 33.75% tax on the rest (£9,956).

Saul's income will fall from £130,000 to £100,000 which means he will recover all of his personal allowance and his tax bill will fall from £35,803 to £20,039.

All in all, the couple will save £5,808 in tax by transferring the dividend income to Kylie, even though she is also a higher rate taxpayer.

Where you have income significantly over £125,140 and are an *additional rate* taxpayer, it may be possible to save tax by gifting shares to a higher rate taxpayer spouse/partner, but if your income is not reduced below £125,140, the tax savings are not huge: just £56 on every £1,000 of dividend income transferred.

It's also important to be careful that the dividend income transferred to your spouse/partner does not push *their* total taxable income over the £100,000 threshold, so that they begin to lose their personal allowance. In most cases, this would wipe out the saving and turn it into an overall additional tax cost!

Spouse/Partner is Additional-Rate Taxpayer
There is a situation where it may actually be beneficial to transfer dividend income to your spouse/partner, even if they are an additional rate taxpayer with income over £125,140. This arises where your income falls into the £100,000 to £125,140 bracket and you are suffering Income Tax at effective rates of up to 56.25% on some of your dividend income.

__Example Revisited:__ Let's go back to Saul and Kylie in our last example, but change just one thing: let's say Kylie's income from another source is £150,000 instead of £60,000.

Saul transfers 25% of the company to Kylie as before and she receives the same £30,000 of dividend income. The first £500 will be tax free and she will pay 39.35% tax on the rest: £11,608.

Saul will recover his personal allowance and his tax bill will fall from £35,803 to £20,039, as before. The couple now save £4,156. It's not quite as good as we saw before, but it's not bad considering Kylie is an additional rate taxpayer.

Will the Tax Savings Last?

There are many reasons why any tax savings that may be achieved in one tax year by splitting income with your spouse/partner may not be achievable in full in future tax years, including:

- Changes to tax rates and thresholds
- Changes to personal circumstances

For example, it's important to remember that the higher rate threshold is to remain frozen at £50,270 until 5th April 2028. As a result, more and more basic rate taxpayers are likely to become higher rate taxpayers. This may make it less attractive for some higher rate taxpayers to shift income to spouses/partners who are currently basic rate taxpayers. If your spouse/partner's income simply increases with inflation, they will have less of their basic rate band left to enjoy dividends taxed at just 8.75%.

Worthwhile Income Tax savings can usually only be achieved if your spouse/partner has a lower tax rate than you. It is possible that, over time, your tax rate will fall or your spouse/partner's tax rate will increase. This could eliminate or even reverse any initial Income Tax saving that is achieved.

Your tax rate could fall if the company's profits fall, resulting in lower dividends. Your spouse/partner's tax rate could rise if their income from other sources increases (for example, if another business they own produces bigger profits).

There are many different permutations. The key point is that couples should look further ahead than just one tax year when deciding what proportion of the company each should own.

HMRC Attacks on Income Shifting

Income splitting arrangements like those described in this chapter have come under attack in the past. The taxman has tried to prevent dividends being paid to non-working spouses/partners, or spouses/partners who do just a small amount of work for the company.

In particular, the taxman's target has been small 'personal service companies' (IT consultants and the like) where most of the work is carried out by one person.

It all came to a head in the notorious 'Arctic Systems' case. HMRC tried to use the so-called settlements legislation to prevent Geoff Jones, a computer consultant, from splitting his dividend income with his wife.

The settlements legislation is designed to prevent income being shifted from one individual to another via a 'settlement', for example by transferring an asset or making some other 'arrangement'.

In the Arctic Systems case Mr Jones did most of the work in the company. Mrs Jones did a few hours admin each week. Because Mr Jones only paid himself a small salary despite all the work he did, more money was left to pay out as dividends to Mrs Jones. HMRC therefore decided a settlement had taken place and tried to have Mrs Jones' dividend income taxed in her husband's hands.

HMRC originally won the case but the decision was overturned by the House of Lords. The judges agreed with HMRC that a settlement had taken place **but** decided that the settlement provisions could not be applied because in this case the couple were protected by the exemption for gifts between spouses. This exemption applies where:

- There is an outright gift of property to a spouse, and
- The property is not wholly or mainly a right to income

On the first point, the judges ruled that, although Mrs Jones had subscribed for her share when the company was set up (i.e. it was not strictly speaking gifted to her by her husband), her share was essentially a gift because it contained an 'element of bounty': the share provided a benefit that Mr Jones would not have given to a complete stranger.

On the second point, the judges also ruled that a gift of *ordinary* shares is not wholly or mainly a right to income because ordinary shares have other rights: voting rights and the right to capital gains if the company is sold or wound up.

Thanks to the courage of Mr and Mrs Jones, who were prepared to fight HMRC all the way to the House of Lords, this exemption should safeguard most types of income splitting arrangements between married couples where ordinary shares are involved.

For this reason, some tax advisers are of the opinion that married couples should make hay while the sun shines, i.e. they should split their dividend income with their spouses while they can.

Preference Shares

The outcome of the Arctic Systems case may have been different if another type of share other than ordinary shares had been involved. In another tax case (*Young v Pearce*), wives were issued with preference shares that paid income but had very few other rights. The shares did not have voting rights and did not entitle the spouses to receive any payout in the event of the company being sold (other than the original £25 payment for the shares).

All the preference shares provided was a right to receive 30% of the company's profits as a dividend. The court therefore decided the preference shares provided wholly or mainly a right to income.

Thus, the exemption for gifts between spouses was not available and the settlement rules applied. The wives' dividends were therefore taxed in the hands of their husbands.

Unmarried Couples & Other Family Members

Although HMRC was defeated in the Arctic Systems case, the judges did agree that a settlement had taken place. The taxpayers only won the case thanks to the exemption for gifts between *spouses*.

There is still uncertainty as to where this leaves income-splitting arrangements between other groups of individuals, in particular, *unmarried* couples.

HMRC may take the view that the settlements legislation applies to unmarried couples and other family members, especially where small personal service companies are involved.

However, to date the taxman has not pursued these individuals aggressively so, again, it may be a case of making hay while the sun shines.

To protect against any potential attack the best defence is probably to have both individuals equally involved in the business (a bit of admin or bookkeeping will not suffice, as Mr and Mrs Jones discovered).

HMRC's main concern seems to be personal service companies (IT consultants and other businesses where the profits are generated from one person's services). Larger businesses that have other employees, premises, equipment, etc, may be safer because the profits come from various sources, not just one person's work.

Future Danger?
In 2007, draft income shifting legislation was published but fortunately never made it onto the statute books after being widely condemned for being completely unworkable.

That draft legislation essentially sought to prevent business owners from receiving dividends unless they effectively earned them! This would have undermined the whole basis of shareholder capitalism: dividends are supposed to be a reward for being an entrepreneur and setting up or investing in a business.

Although income shifting legislation is on the back burner for now, it could be introduced in the future and could upset some income splitting arrangements. This danger was highlighted by a recent announcement of some new reporting requirements to apply from 2025/26:

- Director/shareholders are to report dividends from their own companies separately to stock market dividends
- Director/shareholders must also report their percentage shareholdings in their own companies

An additional proposed requirement to report employees' hours worked under PAYE has been pushed back to at least April 2026 and there is some hope it may be shelved altogether.

Maybe we're being paranoid, but we fear these proposals could be HMRC beginning to gather the data they need to enable them to have another go at income-shifting legislation later this decade. So, like we said, make hay while the sun shines!

Dividend Waivers
Dividend waivers are used by company owners who wish to relinquish their rights to dividends. They can be commercially justifiable, for example if a shareholder waives their dividend to protect the company's cash.

To be effective it is necessary to draw up a formal deed that is executed before the dividend is declared or paid.

Company owners have tried using dividend waivers to avoid tax by diverting income to their spouse/partner: a higher rate taxpayer may try to divert a disproportionate share of the company's profit to their spouse/partner who is a basic rate taxpayer.

HMRC may use the settlements legislation to attack arrangements where shareholders end up with excessive dividends, i.e. more of the company's distributable profit than their shareholding would normally entitle them to. Because dividend waivers involve simply a transfer of income, not assets, they are not protected by the exemption for outright gifts to spouses (see above).

Example: *Mrs M owns 80 ordinary shares in M Limited and also has significant taxable income from other sources. Mr M owns 20 shares and has no other income. The company has retained profits of £50,000. Mrs M waives her right to a dividend and the company then declares a dividend of £2,000 per share. Mr M thus receives a dividend of £40,000, most of which he hopes will be taxed at no more than 8.75%.*

HMRC could apply the settlements legislation in this situation. Clearly a dividend of £2,000 per share could not have been paid on all 100 shares, so the waiver enhanced Mr M's dividend.

This would therefore be seen as a 'bounteous arrangement': it is unlikely Mrs M would have agreed to do the same thing with a third party. £32,000 of the dividend paid to Mr M would therefore be taxed in Mrs M's hands.

Some of the factors HMRC will look for when deciding whether to apply the settlements legislation to dividend waivers include:

- Insufficient retained profits to pay the same rate of dividend on all issued share capital.
- Even if there is sufficient profit to pay the same rate of dividend per share for the year in question, there has been a succession of waivers over several years and, in the absence of the waivers, the total dividends payable exceed the company's retained profits.
- Waiving shareholders wish to benefit non-waiving shareholders.
- Non-waiving shareholders pay tax at a lower rate.

In summary, company owners should be careful of entering into arrangements to waive dividends where there is no commercial reason for the waivers and no evidence the waivers are for non-tax reasons.

Salaries for Spouses/Partners

If your spouse/partner also works for your company they can be paid a salary. Please note, you cannot pay them a salary if they do no work for the company. And you cannot pay them more than is justified for the duties they perform. If you do, the company may be denied tax relief for the expense.

If your spouse/partner is a director then the accompanying legal responsibilities will also justify some remuneration being paid. This factor alone is generally given a lot of weight and will almost always justify a salary up to the level of the personal allowance. However, it remains important for your spouse/partner to be actively carrying out their duties as a director (attending board meetings, reviewing company accounts and other important documents, etc).

If your spouse/partner has no taxable income from other sources, a small salary will be more tax efficient than simply paying them dividends.

Why? Unlike dividends, which are paid out of the company's after-tax profits, salaries are a tax-deductible expense for the company. In other words, in addition to any *Income Tax* savings enjoyed by the couple, a salary will also save the company *Corporation Tax*.

For example, a salary of £12,570 will save a company at least £2,000 in tax, taking into account the small amount of National Insurance that is usually payable. The savings will be greater for companies with a Corporation Tax rate of more than 19%.

To minimise National Insurance, salary payments should generally be made monthly instead of as a lump sum. If, however, your spouse/partner is a director, the payment can be made as a lump sum because company directors pay National Insurance on an annual basis.

Second Jobs

What if your spouse or partner already has income from other sources, e.g. a salary from another job? Is it still tax efficient to get your company to pay them a small salary?

Firstly, it's important to point out that if they work for another employer the employment contract may prevent them working for you as well.

If there is no such restriction, paying your spouse or partner a small National Insurance free salary could lead to an overall saving of several hundred pounds in some cases. Why? Because for basic rate taxpayers the combined tax rate (Corporation Tax and Income Tax) for dividend income is at least 26.1%, compared with 20% for salaries.

Thus, paying your spouse/partner a salary of, say, £9,100 could lead to an overall saving of around £555 (£9,100 x 6.1%), providing there is no National Insurance payable.

Where the company has a marginal Corporation Tax rate of more than 19% (see Chapter 1), paying your spouse or partner a salary will be even more attractive because that salary will enjoy more Corporation Tax relief (up to 26.5%).

Chapter 28

Splitting Income with Your Children

It is possible to gift shares in your company to your children. Because they will have their own Income Tax personal allowance and dividend allowance it may be possible for them to receive tax-free dividends of up to £13,070 each in 2024/25, plus an additional £37,200 taxed at just 8.75%.

However, it is important to point out this type of tax planning generally only works when *adult* children are involved (i.e. children 18 or older).

Transfers of income to minor children are generally ineffective as the income would be taxed in the parent's hands. This section therefore deals exclusively with adult children.

If you gift shares in the company to your adult children there will potentially be CGT payable, as if you had sold the shares to them for their full market value. However, it may be possible for both the parent and child to jointly elect to hold over the capital gain.

To qualify for holdover relief the company must, generally speaking, be a trading company.

The safest route is probably to use ordinary shares, which means your children will obtain full ownership and voting rights in respect of their share of the business, not just a right to receive dividends.

There is a potential tax trap for family members who are gifted shares and are also employees of the company. In certain cases, where shares are obtained because of an individual's employment, a gift of shares can be subject to Income Tax charges.

However, there is an exemption where shares are given in the 'normal course of domestic, family, or personal relationships'.

So, in most family companies, where shares are transferred to a spouse/partner or adult children, the transfer should not give rise to any employment tax charges.

There is nevertheless a danger that, in certain circumstances, HMRC may argue the individuals received shares by virtue of their employment, not because they are family members.

For example, if the individual only receives a small salary from the company (i.e. below market rate) HMRC may have more grounds to argue that the gift was made to increase the individual's remuneration from the company.

If shares are transferred to a family member who is an employee and to other employees who are not family members, this could indicate the gift was made because of the family member's employment.

On the other hand, if shares are gifted to several family members (some of whom are not employees) this may indicate the gift was made solely because of the family relationship.

It may be wise in such circumstances to document the reasons for the gift and (as always) obtain professional advice.

Salaries for Children
It's often worth getting your company to employ your children (including your minor children) at certain points in time. The salary payments will be a tax-deductible expense for the business, providing the payments can be justified by the duties performed. (In one tax case a son's wages were disallowed because there were no time records or other evidence to justify the payments.)

The income will generally be tax free in the hands of the children, if they're at school, college, or university and have no other taxable income.

A tax deduction coupled with a tax-free receipt is the best possible outcome when it comes to extracting money from your company!

Children under 21 can be paid up to £12,570 with no Income Tax or National Insurance consequences for either them or the company (assuming they have no other taxable income).

For those who are 16 and over, employee's National Insurance will be payable on any salary in excess of £12,570 at 8%. To avoid employee's National Insurance on salaries paid to non-directors, it is important to make regular weekly or monthly payments of no more than £242 or £1,048 respectively.

There is no employer's National Insurance on salaries of up to £50,270 paid to employees under 21 and apprentices under 25. The exemption is not lost if the employee earns more than £50,270: employer's National Insurance is only payable on the excess.

It's important to note the restrictions on the hours and work children can do because this affects how much you can pay them.

Restrictions on Work and Hours
Children are of compulsory school age up to the last Friday in June in the academic year of their 16th birthday. After this, they are at the 'mandatory school leaving age' and can apply for a National Insurance number and work full time.

Until that time there are restrictions on the hours and types of work that can be carried out. For starters, it is generally illegal to employ children under 13 in any capacity (unless they're involved in acting or modelling).

Other children under school leaving age must not work:

- Without an employment permit if local byelaws require it
- In factories or on industrial sites
- During school hours
- Before 7.00 am or after 7.00 pm
- For more than one hour before school (local byelaws permitting)
- For more than four hours without taking a one-hour break
- In occupations prohibited by byelaws/legislation (e.g. pubs)
- If the work will harm their health, wellbeing, or education
- Without having a two week break during the school holidays in each calendar year

More Restrictions on Hours Worked

During term time children under school leaving age can work for no more than 12 hours per week including a maximum of:

- Two hours on school days and Sundays
- Five hours on Saturdays for 13 to 14 year olds; eight hours for 15 to 16 year olds

During school holidays, 13 to 14 year olds may work a maximum of 25 hours per week. This includes a maximum of:

- Five hours on weekdays and Saturdays
- Two hours on Sunday

During school holidays, 15 to 16 year olds under school leaving age may work a maximum of 35 hours per week. This includes a maximum of:

- Eight hours on weekdays and Saturdays
- Two hours on Sunday

National Minimum Wage & Living Wage

If your children are below the compulsory school leaving age, the national minimum wage does not apply. From 1st April 2024, the hourly rates for older children are as follows:

- £11.44   Living wage, 21 and over
- £8.60   for those aged 18-20
- £6.40   for those aged 16-17
- £6.40   for apprentices under 19 or in their first year

Part 6

Other Profit Extraction Strategies

Chapter 29

Loans to Directors

It used to be illegal for companies to make loans to directors. This is no longer the case and loans of any size are now permitted.

With the exception of loans under £10,000 they generally have to be approved by the company's shareholders. For most small companies this is obviously not a problem because the shareholders and directors are the same people!

You cannot take a loan from your company for an indefinite period without any tax consequences. If that was possible most company owners would never pay themselves taxable dividends.

The attractiveness of taking a loan from your company is limited by two potential tax charges:

- a 33.75% tax paid by the *company* (the Section 455 charge)
- a benefit-in-kind charge paid by the *director*

Fortunately, it is possible to avoid or mitigate the damage caused by these taxes, if you understand the rules.

The Section 455 Charge
Most small family companies are 'close companies'. A close company is one controlled by five or fewer 'participators', or by any number of participators who are also directors. Broadly, a participator is a shareholder.

If a close company lends money to a participator *the company* will have to pay a 33.75% tax charge on the loan. This is known as the Section 455 charge. Failure to pay this charge will result in penalties and interest.

However, there are two reasons why this charge is not as bad as it first appears:

1. Short-Term Loans Escape the Section 455 Charge

The 33.75% tax does not apply if the loan is repaid within nine months of the end of the company's accounting period. This is the normal due date for the company's Corporation Tax. This means short-term loans to directors do not attract a company tax charge.

Example: Bill Ltd's accounting period ends on 31st December 2024. The company made a £10,000 loan to Bill, the sole shareholder and director, in July 2024.

Bill repays the loan before the end of September 2025. The company will not have to pay the 33.75% tax charge because the loan was repaid within nine months of the end of the accounting period in which it was made.

Example: The facts are the same as before except only £7,000 is repaid before the end of September 2025. The remaining £3,000 is repaid in October 2026. The company will pay a Section 455 tax charge of £1,013 (£3,000 x 33.75%).

2. The Section 455 Charge is Refundable

Even if the 33.75% tax does end up being paid because the loan is not repaid early enough, the tax will be refunded when the loan is repaid.

That's the good news. The bad news is the company will only be repaid nine months after the end of the accounting period in which the loan is repaid. In Bill Ltd's case this means the £1,013 tax will not be repaid until 1st October 2027.

Exemption for Minority Shareholders

This exemption isn't much use to most small company owners. Nevertheless, it is worth mentioning that there is no 33.75% company tax charge if you own 5% or less of the company's ordinary shares.

There are some qualifying criteria: total loans to the individual cannot exceed £15,000 and the individual must work full time in the company's business. When it comes to the 5% limit you must include shares owned by you, your spouse and other 'associates' (e.g. close relatives).

Although there is no company tax charge on small loans to minority shareholders, there will still be a potential benefit-in-kind charge for the individual.

The Benefit-in-Kind Charge
If no interest is payable on the loan, or if the interest paid to the company is less than the 'official rate', the director will have to pay Income Tax on the benefit in kind.

The official rate of interest is 2.25% for the current 2024/25 tax year, which, considering what has happened to actual interest rates in the real world, represents quite a bargain.

If the interest charged on a loan to a director is less than 2.25%, a benefit-in-kind charge is payable.

Employer's National Insurance is also payable, although there is no employee's National Insurance payable by the director.

As far as Income Tax is concerned, most articles on benefits in kind state that basic rate taxpayers pay 20% tax and higher rate taxpayers pay 40% tax.

It's not as simple as that if you're a company owner taking a small tax-free salary and the rest of your income as dividends. The amount of Income Tax payable on the benefit depends on the level of salary and whether the director has income from other sources such as rental income.

Directors who are higher rate taxpayers will effectively suffer between 33.75% and 45% tax on the benefit. The lower 33.75% tax rate is payable to the extent that the taxable benefit is covered by the director's personal allowance. The 45% rate then comes into force and is a combination of the 20% tax suffered on the benefit in kind itself and the 25% increase (from 8.75% to 33.75%) in the tax suffered on an equivalent amount of dividend income.

For example, if the loan is for £20,000 and no interest is charged, the director will potentially face the following benefit-in-kind charge as a higher rate taxpayer:

£20,000 loan x 2.25% interest x 45% tax = £203

The company will also have to pay Class 1A National Insurance:

£20,000 loan x 2.25% interest x 13.8% = £62

The benefit in kind is reduced if interest is paid to the company. For example, if you pay 1.5% interest, the benefit in kind will be calculated using an interest rate of 0.75% (2.25% less 1.5%). If you pay 2.25% interest there will be no benefit in kind charge.

Note that the benefit in kind is only reduced if there is a formal obligation to pay interest to the company. For this reason, it is probably advisable to have a properly drawn up loan agreement.

If you do pay interest on the loan, the good news is you will be paying the money to your own company, not a bank. However, the company will pay Corporation Tax on the interest it receives.

It must also be remembered that money inside a company is generally less valuable than money outside a company. If you wish to withdraw the interest back out as a dividend, there is likely to be an Income Tax charge.

Should Directors Pay Interest?
Let's compare the outcome under two scenarios: an interest-free loan, or paying interest at the official rate.

We will assume the loan is for £30,000, the official interest rate is 2.25%, and the director suffers Income Tax at an effective rate of 45% on any benefit in kind. We will also assume, for now, that the company has a marginal Corporation Tax rate of 26.5%.

With an interest-free loan, the benefit-in-kind charge paid by the director will be:

£30,000 x 2.25% x 45% = £304

The National Insurance paid by the company will be:

$$£30,000 \times 2.25\% \times 13.8\% = £93$$

The employer's National Insurance is a tax-deductible expense, so the net cost would be £68 (£93 less 26.5% Corporation Tax relief).

$$\text{Total cost of loan: } £304 + £68 = £372$$

Note too that your accountant will probably also charge a fee to complete a P11D form to report the benefit of an interest-free loan to HMRC. If the director already has other benefits to report, however, reporting one more may not cost very much.

Let's now look what would happen if the director pays interest at the official rate. On a £30,000 loan, the director will currently pay £675 interest to the company (£30,000 x 2.25%). The company will pay 26.5% Corporation Tax on this interest so the cost will be:

$$£675 \times 26.5\% \text{ Corporation Tax} = £179$$

Even if the after-tax interest is paid out as a dividend, producing an Income Tax charge of £167 for a higher rate taxpayer (£496 x 33.75%), the total tax cost will be £346.

This is a little less than the cost of an interest-free loan. However, the difference is small, so it may be other factors (such as accountancy fees or simplicity) that determine which route is best.

In the above example we assumed the company has a marginal Corporation Tax rate of 26.5%. Paying interest at the official rate becomes more attractive when the company has a lower marginal Corporation Tax rate. For example, taking all the same facts as above, but with the lowest Corporation Tax rate of 19%, the total cost of an interest-free loan would be £379, the cost of paying interest at the official rate would be £313, and the saving generated would increase to £66. Still not much, but better.

The Official Rate of Interest
Back in 2009, the official rate of interest was 6.25%. Despite the recent phenomenal rise in real interest rates, the official rate was only increased from 2% to 2.25%.

Whether this beneficial state of affairs will last is a mystery. One wonders if the official rate has simple been overlooked. If the official rate was, say 6%, the tax cost of directors' loans would almost triple. It remains to be seen whether loans to directors will become more expensive in future, despite the Bank of England's recent small interest rate cut.

Exemptions from the Benefit in Kind Charge

There are two important exemptions from benefit in kind charges: loans to invest in another company, and loans for no more than £10,000.

Neither exemption makes any difference to the requirement to pay the Section 455 company tax charge. Remember, however, that the company tax charge does not apply to short-term loans (up to 21 months in some cases) and is repayable.

Loans to Invest in Another Company

There is generally no benefit in kind charge on certain *qualifying* loans. A qualifying loan is one where the interest (if interest was charged) would be a tax-deductible expense for the director.

An example of a qualifying loan would be one given to an individual so they can acquire an interest in another close company carrying on qualifying activities: namely either trading or letting property to unconnected third parties.

The person borrowing the money must generally hold more than 5% of the ordinary shares in the company in which the money is being invested.

Whether this is the most tax-efficient way to finance a new business venture is, of course, another question altogether, although we will return to this issue later.

Remember, the Section 455 company tax charge still applies, unless the loan is repaid within nine months of the end of the accounting period in which it is made.

Loans not Exceeding £10,000

There is no benefit-in-kind charge if all loans to the director/shareholder total £10,000 or less throughout the tax year.

It is important to understand that any sum due from the director to the company is counted as a 'loan', including goods or services that have been provided to the director but not paid for.

The Section 455 Corporation Tax charge still applies if the loan is not repaid on time. Nevertheless, this exemption allows a director/shareholder to take a loan of up to £10,000 for up to 21 months with no adverse tax consequences.

Larger Short-Term Loans

By taking a loan for no more than £10,000 and repaying it on time, both the 33.75% Section 455 tax charge and the benefit-in-kind charge can be avoided. What if you want to borrow more than the tax-free limit for a short period: how does this compare with paying yourself additional taxable dividends?

Example: Penelope owns Pitstop Hotels Ltd, which has a 31st December accounting date. Penelope normally withdraws a salary of £12,570 and enough dividend income to use up her basic rate band. It's the beginning of January 2025 and Penelope would like to withdraw some additional money from Pitstop Hotels, over and above her usual salary and dividend income. She needs £13,500 for some home improvements.

If she takes the money as a dividend, she will need to withdraw £20,377. There will be an Income Tax charge of £6,877 payable by 31st January 2026, leaving her with the required £13,500.

Instead she decides to take an interest-free loan of £13,500 from her company on 6th January 2025. Because it's an interest-free loan and the loan is for more than £10,000, she will be subject to a benefit-in-kind charge (paying interest to her company at the official rate would be more tax efficient, but she decides an interest-free loan will be simpler).

The loan will also be subject to the 33.75% Section 455 tax charge unless it is repaid by the end of September 2026 (nine months after the end of the company's accounting period on 31st December 2025).

She repays the loan on 5th September 2026, after 20 months. The loan falls into the 2024/25 tax year (3 months), the 2025/26 tax year (12 months) and the 2026/27 tax year (5 months). We'll assume the official rate of interest in 2025/26 and 2026/27 is 4% (although we have no idea what the actual official rate will be in future tax years).

Penny will face the following Income Tax charges:

2024/25: £13,500 x 2.25% x 3/12 x 45%   *£34*
2025/26: £13,500 x 4% x 12/12 x 45%   *£243*
2026/27: £13,500 x 4% x 5/12 x 45%   *£101*
Total   *£378*

The National Insurance paid by the company will be:

2024/25: £13,500 x 2.25% x 3/12 x 13.8%   *£10*
2025/26: £13,500 x 4% x 12/12 x 13.8%   *£75*
2026/27: £13,500 x 4% x 5/12 x 13.8%   *£31*
Total   *£116*

This is a tax-deductible expense, so the total net cost to the company may be just £85 (at a marginal Corporation Tax rate of 26.5%: which is likely if Penelope is extracting income of £50,270 from the company each year). The total cost of the loan is therefore likely to be £463 (£378 + £85).

To repay the £13,500 loan, Penelope withdraws additional dividend income, over and above what she normally takes, of £20,377 during the 2026/27 tax year. The Income Tax on this additional dividend is £6,877, payable by 31st January 2028.

By taking a loan in 2025 instead of a taxable dividend, Penelope has managed to defer paying Income Tax of £6,877 for two years.

The likely cost is £463 in this scenario, although it could be significantly lower if the official rate of interest remains at 2.25%.

Additional points to note:

- If Penelope thinks her marginal Income Tax rate in 2026/27 may be higher than in 2024/25, she may be better off paying herself a dividend in January 2025 instead of taking a loan. In particular she may have to watch out for the £100,000 personal allowance withdrawal threshold.

- If Penelope can repay the loan out of her regular dividend income taxed at just 8.75% (i.e. without having to withdraw an additional dividend taxed at 33.75%) she may be able to *save* £6,877 Income Tax, not just defer paying it.

Longer-Term Loans

Arguably, one could say it's worth every higher rate taxpayer director borrowing £10,000 from their company. There would be no benefit in kind charge but, as we know, a Section 455 charge at 33.75% will arise if the loan is not repaid within nine months of the end of the accounting period in which it is made.

So, if the loan is left outstanding for a longer period, the director has extracted £10,000 from the company at a cost of £3,375.

BUT that's still cheaper than the cost to a higher rate taxpayer of getting a net sum of £10,000 by way of a dividend. To get £10,000 net of tax at 33.75% means taking a dividend of £15,094 and paying £5,094 in Income Tax: £1,719 more than the Section 455 charge.

For an additional rate taxpayer to get a net sum of £10,000 by way of a dividend would mean taking a dividend of £16,488 and paying £6,488 in Income Tax at 39.35%: £3,113 more than the Section 455 charge (the company charge is still at 33.75%, even if the director is an additional rate taxpayer).

Having borrowed £10,000 though, the director needs to be very careful. Even just £1 more borrowed for just one day would lead to a benefit in kind charge for the whole tax year. If the official rate rose to, say, 6%, this could cost a total of up to £337 in combined Income Tax and National Insurance (net of Corporation Tax relief).

And remember, borrowing will include any goods or services provided to the director but not *immediately* paid for.

Hence, perhaps, if following this strategy, it may be best to leave a little leeway and only borrow, say £9,000.

Greater borrowings (potentially without limit) will enjoy similar benefits if used to invest in a qualifying close company. As we said above, this may not be the best way to finance, or structure, such an investment, but it could well beat taking a dividend.

Example: Dick owns Muttley Ltd, a successful trading company with over £200,000 in surplus cash sitting in its bank account. Together with three friends, Dick is planning to set up Pigeon Properties Ltd, a property investment company. Dick and his friends are each going to invest

£100,000 in Pigeon Properties Ltd (made up of 25 £1 shares and a loan to the company of £99,975, but it will all qualify).

Dick has no other resources available, so he will have to obtain the cash he needs from Muttley Ltd. So far this tax year, he has already taken a salary of £12,570 and dividends of £80,000, giving him taxable income of £92,570. He needs that income (£75,039 net of tax) to fund regular living expenses.

To get a further net sum of £100,000 in 2024/25, he will need to take additional dividend income of £171,200, which will suffer Income Tax of £71,200, leaving him with the required sum of £100,000.

On the other hand, if Dick borrows £100,000 from Muttley Ltd, the Section 455 charge will amount to just £33,750, saving £37,450 compared with taking a dividend.

Not only can this strategy lead to a massive, immediate saving, it's worth remembering that tax paid under the Section 455 charge is ultimately repayable, tax paid on dividend income is not.

In fact, so great is this saving it may sometimes be worth contemplating this type of strategy even when the loan does not qualify for the benefit in kind exemption.

Let's say Dick was not going to invest in a qualifying company, but needed the £100,000 for some other type of investment (perhaps residential rental property owned personally). Let's also say his loan is interest free. For future years, let's assume the official rate rises to 4%, Muttley Ltd is paying Corporation Tax at 25%, and Dick takes a salary of £12,570 plus dividends of £80,000 to give him the same total taxable income of £92,570 as at present.

The annual benefit in kind on the loan will therefore be £4,000 (£100,000 @ 4%), leading to the following costs:

Income Tax	
Benefit in kind £4,000 x 20%	£800
Dividend pushed into higher rate £4,000 x 25%	£1,000
Employer's National Insurance £4,000 x 13.8%	£552
Corporation Tax relief thereon £552 x 25%	(£138)
Total annual cost	£2,214

In this example, it will take seventeen years before the cumulative annual cost of the loan exceeds the initial saving of £37,450.

Furthermore, assuming Dick eventually repays the loan and hence Muttley Ltd recoups the £33,750 Section 455 charge, it will take 32 years before the cumulative annual cost exceeds the tax he would have suffered if he had taken a dividend.

As we have seen, for higher rate taxpayers, taking loans from your company can be a cheaper option than taking dividends. Where money is borrowed to make investments outside the company, and thus can reasonably be expected to ultimately be repaid, such a strategy may make sense.

However, borrowing long term from your own company simply to fund regular living expenses is not generally a good idea, due to the ultimate costs that could arise if the loan eventually has to be written off (see further below). Furthermore, if the company runs into financial difficulty, its creditors will be able to force you to sell personal assets in order to repay your loan.

Large loan balances also carry a risk of legal challenge, as it is questionable whether the director is fulfilling their duty to act in the best interests of the company: unless a market rate of interest is being paid and the company could not have obtained a better return by investing the funds elsewhere.

Loans to Family
You cannot necessarily avoid the Section 455 tax charge and benefit-in-kind charge by making loans to family members. For example, both the Section 455 charge and the benefit-in-kind charge apply to loans to spouses and children of the director/shareholder and other close relatives.

The Section 455 charge also applies to loans to business partners. The charges do not apply to loans to friends and some more distant relatives BUT you will incur the taxman's wrath if the benefit of the loan passes back to you or a close relative.

Loans Written Off
If the loan is formally released or written off by the company, the amount is likely to be treated as a deemed dividend for Income Tax purposes. In most instances, the amount released will also be subject to employer's National Insurance, like a benefit in kind.

This treatment was confirmed in the case of Stewart Fraser Ltd, which involved a write off of loans by a close company to an employee shareholder. The loan write offs were treated as distributions taxable on the employee and HMRC successfully argued that National Insurance was also payable by the company.

Because of this National Insurance cost, you may wish to consider declaring a dividend to settle the debt, providing the company has sufficient distributable reserves. One drawback of this is a dividend would have to be paid to all shareholders pro rata.

A loan written off in these circumstances will not be deductible for Corporation Tax purposes. Any Section 455 tax charge paid is, however, refunded to the company if the loan is released or written off. The safest course of action may be to ensure that any loan is always repaid, wherever possible, rather than written off.

Paperwork
Although it's simple in small companies to obtain shareholder approval for loans, it's important to get the paperwork right. There should be a proper loan agreement with written documentation outlining the nature of the loan, the company's liability and the amount and purpose of the loan.

The shareholders should then grant their approval at a meeting or by written resolution, again with all the appropriate documentation. Shareholder approval is not required for loans of up to £10,000, although it is good practice to continue to produce the same paperwork, where possible, as this may provide more certainty as to the tax treatment of the borrowed money.

Financial Reporting Standard 102 (FRS 102)
A recent financial reporting standard (FRS 102) may affect the accounting treatment of directors' loans in certain circumstances.

Where interest is not charged at a market rate, the loan may have to be discounted in the company's accounts. For example, if the market interest rate is 5%, and an interest-free loan of £100,000 is made to a director and is repayable after three years, the present value of the loan is £86,384:

$$£100,000/(1.05 \times 1.05 \times 1.05) = £86,384$$

The initial shortfall of £13,616 would be treated as a 'distribution' for accounts purposes.

The tax treatment does not, however, follow the accounting treatment. The Section 455 charge is still based on the total amount of the loan and the director's taxable benefit will be calculated in the way described earlier in this chapter.

To avoid the complexities of FRS 102, tax commentators suggest it should be specifically recorded that directors' loan accounts are repayable on demand, or to charge a market rate of interest. Of course, it's only an accounting adjustment, and there's no tax cost involved, but it is a nuisance. And one indirect consequence is that the deemed distribution (e.g. £13,616 in our example) reduces the company's distributable profits available for paying dividends.

Loan Recycling
To prevent directors simply repaying loans before the Section 455 charge is payable, and then taking a new loan out straight away (known as 'bed and breakfasting'), there are some additional rules:

The 30 Day Rule
Relief from the Section 455 charge is denied if:

- A shareholder makes repayments totalling £5,000 or more to the company and within 30 days...
- new loans totalling £5,000 or more are made to the same person or their associates

For this rule to apply, the original loan and repayment can take place in the same or different accounting periods. The new loan must be in a subsequent accounting period to the original loan.

It's important to point out that the 30-day rule does not apply where the loan is repaid using amounts that give rise to an Income Tax charge, for example where a taxable dividend is declared and credited to the director's loan account.

Example 1: During accounting period 1 there is a loan outstanding of £6,000. Two days before the end of the accounting period £6,000 is repaid. Three days into accounting period 2 a new £6,000 loan is taken. The repayment will be matched with the new loan, not the old loan. The loan from accounting period 1 is treated as still outstanding and will be subject to the Section 455 tax charge if not repaid.

Example 2: *C Ltd is a close company in which Jim is a shareholder. C Ltd's accounting period ends on 31st March 2025. On 25th March 2025, Jim borrows £15,000 from C Ltd. If the loan is not repaid within nine months of the end of the accounting period, C Ltd must pay a 33.75% Section 455 tax charge (£5,063).*

On 1st December 2025, a dividend of £9,000, which is chargeable to Income Tax, is declared by C Ltd and credited to Jim's loan account. On the same day, Jim repays the remaining £6,000 of his loan. On 10th December 2025, Jim borrows £3,500 from the company. On 15th December 2025, Jim borrows a further £2,000.

The Section 455 tax charge is calculated as follows:

- £9,000 was repaid by applying a chargeable dividend towards the loan. This is ignored when it comes to applying the 30-day rule. The remaining £6,000 that Jim repays exceeds the £5,000 minimum repayment under the 30-day rule.

- Nine and fourteen days later respectively (i.e. within 30 days) Jim withdraws a further £5,500 (£3,500 + £2,000), which is also in excess of the £5,000 limit for new loans.

- The new loans (£5,500) are less than the repayments (£6,000). Relief from the Section 455 tax charge is denied on the lesser amount of £5,500, resulting in a tax charge of £1,856. Only the net repayment of £500 is recognised.

The Arrangements Rule
This rule applies even if the new borrowing takes place after 30 days. Relief from the Section 455 charge will be denied if:

- Prior to repaying the loan, the total amount owed by the shareholder to the company is £15,000 or more, and
- At the time of the repayment, arrangements had been made for new loans of £5,000 or more to replace the amounts repaid.

The relief denied is the lower of the amount repaid and the new loan. 'Arrangements' are not defined and HMRC will give the term a wide meaning.

Once again, the arrangements rule does not apply if the loan is repaid with a taxable dividend or bonus. In other words, if a loan account is credited with a taxable dividend this will be treated as a valid loan repayment.

Example: *Brigitte owes her company £25,000, which she borrowed on 1st June 2024 during the accounting period ended 30th June 2024.*

After the end of the accounting period, Brigitte takes a 45-day loan from the bank for £25,000 and uses it to repay the loan to her company. 40 days after repaying her company, Brigitte takes a new loan of £30,000 from her company and uses it to repay the bank.

There is a significant risk HMRC will argue that, at the time she repaid her company, Brigitte had made arrangements to withdraw a new amount from her company (to repay the bank), so the original loan will be treated as not repaid. Thus, the Section 455 charge will be payable on the initial £25,000 loan, unless a further repayment is made.

What is a Valid Income Tax Charge?
As mentioned above, the anti-avoidance rules do not apply if the amount repaid gives rise to an Income Tax charge in the hands of the director-shareholder. This will be the case if a loan is repaid by means of a dividend credited to the director's loan account that is included as income on the director's tax return (or where a bonus is paid subject to PAYE before being credited to the director's loan account).

According to HMRC, if a dividend is first paid out in cash and the money is then paid back into the company and credited to the director's loan account, the exemption does not apply.

HMRC also contends that, if the director owns the business premises and the company pays them rent, the exemption does not apply to rent credited to the director's loan account.

Chapter 30

Rental Income: Better than Dividends

Many company owners own their business premises *personally* and the company pays them rent.

Paying yourself rent is often more tax efficient than paying yourself a higher salary. Like salaries, rental payments are a tax-deductible expense (providing the rent does not exceed a market rent). But, unlike salaries, there is no National Insurance cost.

Following increases in dividend tax rates in recent times, rental income is also more tax efficient than dividend income and has become even more attractive for those whose companies face higher Corporation Tax rates (Chapter 1).

Of course, there are also non-tax reasons why you may wish to pay yourself rental income instead of withdrawing dividends from your company. For starters, to pay dividends the company must have sufficient distributable profits. There is no such requirement when it comes to paying rent.

Secondly, with rental income it is relatively straightforward to pay yourself a fixed monthly amount throughout the year, for example by setting up a standing order from your company bank account to your personal bank account. This could be helpful if you have to personally pay various costs associated with the property, especially mortgage interest.

With rental income there is no requirement to continually do all the paperwork that often accompanies dividends, for example holding directors' board meetings and shareholder meetings.

How much better off could you be by paying yourself rental income instead of dividends? It all depends on your personal circumstances, for example how much taxable income you have and the amount of tax-deductible mortgage interest you have.

Example 1: Basic Rate Taxpayer

Warren is a company owner and a basic rate taxpayer. He personally owns the property out of which the company operates but the company currently doesn't pay him any rent. He does not have any tax-deductible mortgage interest to offset.

During the current 2024/25 tax year he decides to pay himself a small salary of £9,100 (see Chapter 25). He also has other taxable income that uses up the balance of his £12,570 Income Tax personal allowance. He withdraws the rest of the company's profits as dividends.

Let's say he gets the company to pay him rental income of £10,000 per year. After paying Income Tax at 20% he will be left with £8,000.

If the company had not paid him rent it would have had an extra £8,100 at most to pay dividends (£10,000 profit less at least 19% Corporation Tax). Warren would have been left with £7,391 at most after paying 8.75% Income Tax.

By getting the company to pay him rent Warren is better off by at least £609. This is because, for basic rate taxpayers, the combined tax rate on dividends is around 26.1% (at least), compared with 20% for rental income.

Example 2: Higher Rate Taxpayer

The facts are exactly the same except Warren is a higher rate taxpayer. If he gets the company to pay him rental income of £10,000, after paying Income Tax at 20% he will be left with £8,000.

However, his rental income will use up £10,000 of his basic rate band, which means £10,000 of his dividend income will be taxed at 33.75% instead of 8.75%, resulting in additional tax of £2,500. Overall Warren will be left with £5,500 (£8,000 – £2,500).

Since Warren is a higher rate taxpayer, it is likely that his company will have annual profits in excess of £50,000, so we will now assume it has a marginal Corporation Tax rate of 26.5%. If the company had not paid him any rental income, it would have been left with an extra £7,350 to pay out as dividends and Warren would have been left with £4,869 after paying Income Tax at 33.75%.

Rental income is again more tax efficient than dividends for a higher rate taxpayer, with a saving of up to £631 on £10,000 of rental income. If the company has a lower marginal Corporation

Tax rate, however, the saving will be less: £531 at a Corporation Tax rate of 25%, or just £134 if the Corporation Tax rate is 19%.

Example 3: Higher Rate Taxpayer

This time we'll assume Warren's premises are more substantial and he gets the company to pay him rental income of £37,700. Along with his salary and other non-dividend income this will take him up to the £50,270 higher rate threshold. After paying 20% tax on his rental income he will be left with £30,160 of this income.

His rental income will use up his entire £37,700 basic rate band, which means £37,200 of his dividend income will be taxed at 33.75% instead of 8.75%, resulting in additional tax of £9,300 (it's £37,200 and not £37,700 because of the dividend allowance).

Overall Warren will be left with £20,860 (£30,160 – £9,300) from his rental income of £37,700.

If the company had not paid him £37,700 of rental income, it would have been left with an extra £27,710 of after-tax profit to pay out as dividends (again assuming a marginal Corporation Tax rate of 26.5%). Warren would then have been left with £18,358 after paying Income Tax at 33.75%.

In this example, Warren is £2,502 better off by paying himself rental income. If the company's Corporation Tax rate were 25%, he would be £2,128 better off and, even at the lowest possible Corporation Tax rate of 19% (which is unlikely), he would still be £629 better off.

Mortgage Interest and Other Property Expenses

Many company owners who personally own their business premises will also have a mortgage over those premises on which they personally pay the interest. These interest payments can be offset against your rental income, effectively making some or all of it 'tax free'.

Note that, although tax relief on mortgage interest for residential property has been reduced (see Chapter 26), mortgages used to buy commercial properties are unaffected.

Most company owners will instinctively realise it would be foolish not to receive rental income if they also have mortgage interest to set off (or other tax-deductible property expenses). Tax-free rental income has to be better than a taxable dividend!

Example 4: Higher Rate Taxpayer

Warren has a salary and other income of £12,570, is a higher rate taxpayer and has tax deductible mortgage interest of £5,000. If he gets the company to pay him rental income of £10,000, he'll have a taxable rental profit of £5,000. After paying Income Tax at 20% he will be left with £4,000 (£10,000 – £5,000 interest – £1,000 tax).

His taxable rental income will use up £5,000 of his basic rate band, which means £5,000 of his dividend income will be taxed at 33.75% instead of 8.75%, resulting in additional tax of £1,250. Overall Warren will be left with £2,750 (£4,000 – £1,250).

If the company had not paid him any rental income, it would have been left with an extra £7,350 to pay out as dividends (again assuming a marginal Corporation Tax rate of 26.5%) and Warren would have been left with £4,869 after paying Income Tax at 33.75%. After paying his interest costs Warren would be £131 out of pocket.

Overall, Warren is £2,881 better off paying himself rental income.

At lower Corporation Tax rates, Warren might not be quite as badly off under the dividend route, but taking £10,000 of rental income from the company will always leave him at least £2,384 better off.

Summary

The above examples illustrate it is often more tax efficient to get your company to pay you rent instead of dividends. Rental income is most tax efficient to the extent you have tax deductible costs to offset, such as mortgage interest. The savings vary from case to case, so it is essential to do your own number crunching.

Business Asset Disposal Relief (BADR)

Although you may save Income Tax by paying yourself as much rental income as possible, there is one reason why you may prefer to get your company to pay you a below-market rent. If you sell your company, you may be able to claim BADR, which means you could pay CGT at just 10%.

Trading premises can also qualify for BADR, even if you own them personally. But you cannot claim the relief if your company has paid you a full market rent (although rent paid for periods before 6th April 2008 is ignored). If your company pays you a rent that is lower than the market rent, or if you owned the property before April 2008, a partial claim can usually be made.

If BADR is not available when you dispose of your premises, you will be subject to CGT at the normal rates for commercial property. Higher rate taxpayers pay 20% CGT and 10% tax is payable to the extent your basic rate band is not used up by your income.

So, it's possible that, even without BADR, company owners will be able to benefit from a 10% tax rate on at least some of their capital gains by making sure they don't have much taxable income in the year they sell their trading premises.

Furthermore, since the lifetime maximum cumulative claim for BADR by any individual has been reduced to just £1m, many company owners will exhaust their potential relief on the sale of the company itself, so that there is none remaining for the gain on their business premises: in which case, there is no disadvantage in paying yourself a full market rent.

Capital Allowances

Company owners who also own the company's business premises personally may be entitled to claim capital allowances on part of the cost of the property. However, where less than full market rent is charged, the company owner can only claim a suitable proportion of the available capital allowances. For example, if the rent charged equates to 75% of a full market rent, 75% of the available allowances may be claimed.

This means the Income Tax advantages of paying yourself full market rent may be even greater than we have seen so far: and this may be enough to outweigh any potential loss of business asset disposal relief.

For further details of the capital allowances available on business property, see the Taxcafe guide *How to Save Property Tax*.

Chapter 31

Pay Yourself Tax-Free Interest Income

If your company owes you money you can make it pay you interest. In some cases, the interest will be both a tax-deductible expense for the company and tax free in your hands: the best case scenario when it comes to extracting money from your company.

In this situation, extracting interest income may be more tax efficient than other types of income, including dividends.

How can interest income be tax free? For starters, interest is not subject to National Insurance. As for Income Tax, there is the 0% starting rate band for up to £5,000 of savings income.

There's also the personal savings allowance which shelters up to £1,000 of interest income from tax if you're a basic rate taxpayer and £500 if you're a higher rate taxpayer (additional rate taxpayers do not benefit).

In Chapter 26, we looked at company owners with income from *other sources*, including interest from investments. In this chapter, we're looking at a different type of interest income: interest that comes out of your own company.

The £5,000 Starting Rate Band
Not everyone can benefit from the 0% starting rate. It's designed to benefit those with very low income. Hence the £5,000 starting rate band is reduced if you have any *taxable non-savings income*.

Non-savings income includes income from employment, self-employment, pensions, and rental properties. Crucially, it does not include dividend income.

Furthermore, thanks to the personal allowance, the first £12,570 of non-savings income you receive is effectively not taxable and thus cannot reduce the £5,000 starting rate band (unless your total income exceeds £100,000).

For example, if you have a salary of £12,570 this year and no other income apart from dividends, you won't have any taxable non-savings income and can receive £5,000 of tax-free interest.

You may also be able to receive up to £1,000 of additional tax-free interest thanks to the personal savings allowance.

But if you have a salary of £12,570 and rental income of more than £5,000, your rental income will eat up your entire starting rate band, so none of your interest income will be tax-free under the 0% starting rate.

You may, however, be able to receive up to £1,000 of tax-free interest thanks to the personal savings allowance.

The £5,000 starting rate band is not given in addition to the basic rate band: it is part of the basic rate band. In other words, if you have £5,000 of interest income your basic rate band will be reduced by £5,000.

This means some of your dividend income may be pushed into the higher rate tax bracket.

This may reduce the attractiveness of extracting interest income from your company, but will not usually eliminate the benefit altogether.

The Personal Savings Allowance
The personal savings allowance operates separately from, and in addition to, the starting rate band. This means some company owners will be able to pay themselves up to £6,000 of tax-free interest per year.

The personal savings allowance is especially useful to company owners who cannot use the starting rate band because they have too much non-savings income, e.g. rental income.

They can typically extract £1,000 (basic rate taxpayers) or £500 (higher rate taxpayers) of tax-free interest from their companies.

Lending to Your Company
There are lots of circumstances in which company owners may lend money to their companies. For example, it may be a new

company that needs some cash to get started or a well-established company that needs money to buy some new equipment.

In some cases, company owners lend money to their companies indirectly, for example when a dividend is declared but the cash is not withdrawn immediately, perhaps because the company owner wants to reinvest it to help the business grow.

The Mechanics of Extracting Interest Income

There is no requirement for a director to charge interest on a loan account with their own company but, if they do, it must not exceed a reasonable commercial rate.

If the company pays more than a commercial rate, the excess payment could be treated as salary income and subject to Income Tax and National Insurance.

Interest paid to a director on their loan account will usually be an allowable expense for the company, providing the money is used for business purposes. The interest will therefore provide Corporation Tax relief.

Although your interest income may ultimately be tax free, the company will have to deduct Income Tax at 20% and pay this to HMRC quarterly, using form CT61 (which can be requested online). If this results in a tax overpayment, you can reclaim the excess through your self-assessment tax return. The company should also issue you an annual interest certificate.

While interest can be a very tax efficient way to extract money from your company, the additional reporting duties and payments may put some company owners off. However, both the negative cashflow impact and admin burden can be mitigated by paying interest annually, during the quarter to 31st March.

Another way to improve cashflow is to have the company pay you interest up to twelve months in arrears, after the end of its accounting period.

For example, let's say your company owes you £5,000 in interest for the accounting period ending 31st March 2025. Provided the company pays this interest by 31st March 2026, it will still be able to claim tax relief, saving it between £950 and £1,325 in Corporation Tax on 1st January 2026.

Let's say the company pays you during the quarter ending 31st March 2026. The £1,000 (20%) tax charge it needs to deduct and pay over to HMRC is only due by 14th April 2026 and you will only need to pay any further Income Tax due by 31st January 2027. That's good, generally positive, cashflow!

While this is good for cashflow purposes, however, one thing to watch is that this income now falls into a later tax year for Income Tax purposes, so you will need to factor this into your planning: especially if you're looking to maximise the benefit of your starting rate band and/or personal savings allowance.

How Much Tax Can You Save?
This will depend on *how much* and what *type* of income you earn.

Example 1
Basic-Rate Taxpayer, No Taxable Non-Savings Income
Gillian is a company director with salary and other non-savings income (e.g. rental income) of £12,570. She has £15,000 of dividend income. She charges her company £5,000 interest for a substantial loan she made to help it buy new equipment. Interest is at a commercial rate.

The interest will be a tax-deductible business expense, saving the company at least £950 Corporation Tax (£5,000 x 19%). Gillian has no taxable non-savings income, so all of her interest income will be tax free, being covered by the £5,000 starting rate band (although the company will initially have to withhold 20% tax and pay this to HMRC).

If instead Gillian decided to NOT pay herself interest, the company would have an extra £5,000 of taxable profit. After paying at least £950 Corporation Tax there would be an extra £4,050 at most that could be paid out as dividends taxed at 8.75%, leaving Gillian with £3,696.

The potential tax saving is at least £1,304.

Example 2
Higher-Rate Taxpayer, No Taxable Non-Savings Income
As before Gillian has £12,570 of salary and other non-savings income and £5,000 of interest from her company. However, this time she has dividend income of £50,000, which means she pays 33.75% tax.

Gillian can enjoy £5,000 of tax-free interest income but because the starting rate band is part of the basic rate band an additional £5,000 of her dividends will be taxed at 33.75% instead of 8.75%, resulting in additional tax of £1,250. So, effectively Gillian receives £3,750 after tax.

If she did not pay herself interest, the company would have an extra £5,000 profit. As the company is already paying dividends of £50,000, it is reasonable to assume it will have a marginal Corporation Tax rate of 26.5%. Hence, after Corporation Tax, there will only be £3,675 of the extra profit remaining to pay out as further dividends. This would leave Gillian with just £2,435 after tax.

Hence, for a higher rate taxpayer with no taxable non-savings income the maximum potential saving is £1,315 (£3,750 – £2,435).

The saving will be less where the company has a lower marginal Corporation Tax rate. However, even at the lowest possible Corporation Tax rate of 19%, there would be a saving of £1,067 in this scenario.

Example 3
Basic-Rate Taxpayer, No Starting Rate Band Available
This time Gillian has £17,570 of salary and rental income, £5,000 of interest income and £15,000 of dividend income.

Because she has £5,000 of taxable non-savings income (£17,570 – £12,570 personal allowance) she will have no starting rate band available. However, thanks to the personal savings allowance, £1,000 of her interest income will be tax free and the rest will be taxed at 20%, leaving her with £4,200.

If Gillian did not pay herself interest, the company would have an extra £5,000 of taxable profit. After paying at least £950 Corporation Tax there would be an extra £4,050 at most that could be paid out as dividends taxed at 8.75%, leaving her with £3,696.

So, in this case, Gillian is at least £504 better off paying herself interest. Not only is £1,000 of her interest Income Tax free, the remaining £4,000 is taxed at just 20% (remember the total combined tax rate on dividend income is at least 26.1% for a basic rate taxpayer).

Example 4
Higher-Rate Taxpayer, No Starting Rate Band Available
This time Gillian has £17,570 of salary and rental income, £5,000 of interest income and £50,000 of dividend income. Once again, she will have no starting rate band available. However, thanks to the personal savings allowance, £500 of her interest income will be tax free and the rest will be taxed at 20%, leaving her with £4,100.

An additional £5,000 of her dividend income will be taxed at 33.75% instead of 8.75%, resulting in an additional Income Tax charge of £1,250. So effectively Gillian ends up with £2,850 after tax.

If instead she had decided to not pay herself interest, the company would have an extra £5,000 of taxable profit. As the company is already paying dividends of £50,000, it is reasonable to assume it will have a marginal Corporation Tax rate of 26.5%. Hence, after Corporation Tax, there will only be £3,675 of the extra profit remaining to pay out as further dividends. This would leave Gillian with just £2,435 after tax.

So, in this case Gillian is £415 better off paying herself interest.

The tax saving will be less if the company has a lower marginal Corporation Tax rate, but it would still be £366 if the company is paying tax at 25% and, in the unlikely event that the company's Corporation Tax rate is only 19%, there remains a saving of £167.

Making the Most of Your Personal Allowance
If you pay yourself a salary of £9,100 and do not have any other non-savings income, you will have spare personal allowance of £3,470 (£12,570 – £9,100) to set against your interest or dividends.

In Chapter 26, we saw how you can save tax by allocating your spare personal allowance to your dividend income rather than your interest income (if your interest is tax free anyway).

In that chapter, we were focusing on interest income from investments but the same principle applies when you extract interest income from your own company.

Example 5
Higher-Rate Taxpayer, Spare Personal Allowance

Roisin's company pays her a salary of £9,100 and she extracts the remaining profits as dividends totalling £50,000. She has no other income and therefore has spare personal allowance of £3,470 to use against her dividends. She ends up with after-tax income of £52,865.

Let's now assume Roisin receives £5,000 of interest from her company. This also reduces the amount of profit that can be distributed as dividends. At a marginal Corporation Tax rate of 26.5%, this reduces her dividends by £3,675, but the reduction will be more where the company has a lower marginal Corporation Tax rate.

*If her spare personal allowance of £3,470 is set against her **interest income**, she will end up with after-tax income of £53,876, or £1,011 more than before.*

*But if her spare personal allowance is set against her **dividends**, she will end up with £54,180, an additional £304.*

Overall, Roisin ends up £1,315 better off by extracting £5,000 of interest from her company but the maximum saving is only achieved if she allocates her personal allowance correctly. If the company has a lower marginal Corporation Tax rate, the overall saving will be less, but it will always be at least £1,067, of which £304 comes from allocating the personal allowance correctly.

Tax-Free Loan Repayments

Apart from the beneficial tax treatment of interest income, it's worth pointing out that some or all of the outstanding balance on a director's loan account can be paid out tax free at any time.

Having such an amount 'banked' inside your company that can be withdrawn tax free at any time could prove useful, for example if the director unexpectedly requires additional money that would be taxed heavily as a salary or dividend.

The only potential cost of making loan repayments is where the director is claiming qualifying loan interest on amounts borrowed to invest in the company. Let's say, for example, a director borrowed £100,000 and then loaned that sum to their own company. Provided the company was carrying on a qualifying business (trading or letting property to unconnected third parties will qualify), the director can claim the interest paid on their personal borrowing for Income Tax purposes (it can be set against any personal income, not just against interest income).

As long as the company continues to owe the director at least £100,000, they may continue to claim full Income Tax relief for their personal interest cost. However, if the company repays part of the director's loan so that the balance falls below £100,000, the director's qualifying loan interest claim must be restricted accordingly.

Having said that, losing some of the tax relief for the director's personal interest costs will almost certainly be a lot cheaper than the Income Tax suffered on additional dividends taken out of the company instead of a loan repayment.

Note that qualifying loan interest is subject to an annual cap, which is generally the greater of £50,000 or 25% of the director's total income for the year. That's usually enough for most people though. For further details, see the Taxcafe guide *Using a Property Company to Save Tax*.

Summary

Some company owners may be able to save over £1,000 by getting their companies to pay them interest.

The potential tax saving is a lot smaller if there is no starting rate band available, for example if the taxpayer has a significant amount of salary income or rental income.

For many taxpayers the additional tax paperwork will nullify the tax savings: although this burden can be significantly reduced by making a single, annual interest payment.

Finally, it's important to remember the interest you charge your company must be at no more than a commercial rate. However, in most cases, your loan to the company will be unsecured and for no fixed term. Hence, it will be more akin to an overdraft than a mortgage or personal loan and the question of what constitutes a commercial rate can be judged in that context.

Chapter 32

Charitable Donations:
You or the Company?

Who should donate to charity: you or your company?

In this chapter we'll focus on the tax benefits and drawbacks of both types of donation, although *non-tax* factors may be more important.

For example, charitable donations by your company could enhance its reputation and good standing in the community, which in turn could help its business.

Donations by Your Company

Charitable donations are a tax-deductible expense for Corporation Tax purposes. So, if your company donates £1,000, its taxable profits will be reduced by £1,000, saving between £190 and £265 in Corporation Tax.

The company can also enjoy tax relief when it gives money to community amateur sports clubs, a list of which can be obtained by entering 'community amateur sports clubs registered with HMRC' into a search engine like Google.

No gift aid declaration is necessary for company donations (see below for more on gift aid declarations).

Nevertheless, you should still obtain documentation from the charity to support the donation, just as you would for any other business expense.

Charitable donations cannot create or increase a trading loss. If the donation exceeds the company's taxable profit, the excess will not enjoy any Corporation Tax relief and cannot be carried forward to the next year.

Donations do not enjoy automatic Corporation Tax relief if there are strings attached, for example a condition that the charity will buy goods from the company (or anyone connected with the company). However, where the donation was clearly intended to benefit the company's business, the cost may still be allowable as a regular business expense, like advertising.

For more information on charitable donations by companies, as well as other tax-deductible donations, such as to community amateur sports clubs, or in aid of grassroots sports, see the Taxcafe guide *Putting it Through the Company*.

Donations by You Personally

If you make a charitable donation of, say, £80 the charity can claim £20 gift aid. Essentially what the charity is doing is reclaiming from HMRC the 20% basic rate tax you will typically have paid on £80 of after-tax income.

The charity will require you to make a gift aid declaration. This entails stating you have paid sufficient tax to cover the basic rate tax the charity reclaims.

It is important that you are actually liable for the tax the charity reclaims. The tax can be either Income Tax or CGT (but not National Insurance).

For example, a company owner with a salary of £12,570 and dividend of £20,000 will face an Income Tax bill of £1,706 in 2024/25.

If that company owner makes an £8,000 charitable donation, the gift aid rules require that the donor has paid tax of £2,000. The company owner will therefore have to make up the shortfall of £294.

Higher Rate Taxpayers

Higher rate taxpayers who make charitable donations can claim higher rate tax relief when they submit their tax returns.

Example: Melinda, a company owner who takes most of her income as dividends, donates £80 to a charity. The gift aid on the donation is £20, resulting in a gross donation of £100.

Melinda's basic rate band is extended by £100, which means she will pay 8.75% tax instead of 33.75% tax on an additional £100 of dividend income. This will save her £25 Income Tax.

In summary, Melinda has effectively made a £100 donation with a net cost to her of £55. The basic rate tax relief goes to the charity, the higher rate tax relief goes to the person making the donation.

Protecting Child Benefit & Personal Allowance
Your family's child benefit is gradually taken away when the highest earner in the household has adjusted net income of more than £60,000. All the child benefit will be withdrawn when that person's income exceeds £80,000.

Your personal allowance is also gradually taken away when your adjusted net income exceeds £100,000. All of your personal allowance is withdrawn when your income exceeds £125,140.

Like pension contributions, gift aid donations reduce your adjusted net income and can therefore be used to increase your personal allowance or protect your family's child benefit payments, in addition to enjoying higher rate tax relief.

Example: Hassan is a company owner with salary and dividend income of £110,000. He donates £4,000 to his favourite charity. The gift aid on the donation is £1,000, resulting in a gross donation of £5,000. As a result, his adjusted net income is reduced by £5,000 from £110,000 to £105,000. This in turn increases his personal allowance by £2,500.

If Hassan has taken a salary of £9,100 and the rest of his income as dividends, his £4,000 donation will save him £2,266 in Income Tax, meaning the net cost to him is only £1,734. If he has taken a salary of £12,570, his Income Tax saving will be £2,375 and the net cost of his donation will be just £1,625: that's more than £3 for the charity for every £1 it costs Hassan.

Carrying Back Donations to the Previous Tax Year
You can claim tax relief on donations a year early if you like. For example, you can claim tax relief for donations you have made during the current 2024/25 tax year when you submit your tax return for 2023/24.

Understandably, you can only claim tax relief for donations made between 6th April 2024 and the date you file your 2023/24 tax return, and the return must be filed on time (i.e. by 31st January 2025 if filed online).

This option to carry back donations is attractive if you want the tax relief sooner, or if you were a higher rate taxpayer during the previous tax year but you are not certain whether you will be a higher rate taxpayer this year.

When you come to submit your 2023/24 tax return, you will know for certain your taxable income for that year and thus how much tax relief you will obtain.

Similarly, carrying back donations may be attractive if your income in the previous 2023/24 tax year was in the £100,000 to £125,140 bracket (personal allowance withdrawal).

You may enjoy extra tax relief on your charitable donations if you do not expect your income to fall into this tax bracket this year.

Only specific donations may be carried back and not an arbitrary sum: for example, if you made a single net donation of £800 (£1,000 gross), you can either carry it back or not, you cannot carry back, say, £400.

By contrast, if you had made four separate donations of £200 each (even if to the same charity) you could carry back any combination of those donations totalling £200, £400, £600, or £800, thus giving you far greater flexibility.

For this reason, regular, small donations will offer more opportunities to optimise your tax position. Alternatively, if you want to make a large donation, break it up. For example, let's say you want to donate £8,000. Instead of a single, large donation, you could make payments of £4,000, £2,000, £1,000, £500, and two of £250. You could then carry back any combination of these donations totalling between £250 and £8,000.

Company versus Personal Donations

Let's now compare the tax relief enjoyed by companies on charitable donations with the tax relief enjoyed by individuals.

Example: Basic Rate Taxpayer
Beric's company has £1,000 in its bank account, which he would like to give to charity. If the company makes the donation, it will enjoy

Corporation Tax relief, so the whole £1,000 can be paid directly to the charity with no further tax consequences.

If instead Beric decides to make the donation personally, the company will pay at least 19% Corporation Tax, leaving £810 at most to pay out as additional dividend income.

Let's say Beric holds onto £10 and gives £800 to the charity. The taxman will add £200 of gift aid, leaving the charity with the same amount: £1,000. But that's not the end of the matter: Beric will still have to pay 8.75% tax on his £810 dividend: £71. Beric is worse off by £61 (£71 less the £10 of dividend income he held onto).

Thus, if you're a basic rate taxpayer, for every £1,000 that ends up with the charity you will have to pay at least 6.1% in additional tax, and it will be more if your company's Corporation Tax rate is more than 19%.

In this case, a company donation is clearly more tax efficient than a donation made personally by the company owner.

Example: Higher Rate Taxpayer
This time we'll assume Beric is a higher rate taxpayer. If the company makes the donation, it can pay £1,000 directly to the charity. Alternatively, Beric can pay himself additional dividend income. However, since he is a higher rate taxpayer, his company may have a marginal Corporation Tax rate of up to 26.5%, meaning his additional dividend could be as little as £735.

Beric may therefore have to add up to £65 out of his own pocket so he can give £800 to the charity. The taxman will add £200 of gift aid, resulting in the same donation of £1,000.

Again, that's not the end of the matter. Beric still has to pay Income Tax on the additional dividend. With a gross donation of £1,000, his basic rate band will be increased by £1,000. This means the £735 dividend will be taxed at just 8.75%, not 33.75%, so the tax will be £64. Furthermore, an additional £265 of his other dividend income will also be taxed at 8.75% instead of 33.75%, saving him an extra £66.

All in all, a £1,000 donation made by the company owner is up to £63 more expensive than a donation made by the company (£65 + £64 − £66). That extra cost could be as little as £13 in some cases (depending on the company's Corporation Tax rate), but the company donation will always be better overall.

Example: Additional Rate Taxpayer

Sophie is a company owner with a salary of £9,100 and dividend income of £150,000. If she makes a net charitable donation of £4,000, this will reduce her Income Tax bill by £1,530, and the charity will receive a total of £5,000 under gift aid.

Alternatively, if Sophie's company makes a gross contribution of £5,000, it will enjoy Corporation Tax relief on this sum, leaving between £3,675 and £4,050 less available to pay out as a dividend. After accounting for Income Tax at 39.35%, Sophie's after-tax income will reduce by between £2,229 and £2,456. But, since she is no longer paying £4,000 to the charity, she is somewhere between £1,544 and £1,771 better off overall.

It's pretty clear that additional rate taxpayers should get their company to make charitable donations wherever possible.

UK Charities Only

Note that only donations to UK-registered charities now enjoy relief under gift aid, or automatic relief for Corporation Tax purposes if paid by a company.

Chapter 33

Pension Contributions: Better than Dividends

Following the increase in dividend tax rates and the subsequent increase in Corporation Tax, some company owners may be thinking about paying themselves smaller dividends and getting their companies to make bigger pension contributions instead.

The Corporation Tax increase means many companies will enjoy more tax relief on pension contributions they make for their directors and employees, whereas profits used to pay dividends will have been more heavily taxed.

There are several reasons why pension contributions are an attractive alternative to dividends:

- Like salaries, company pension contributions enjoy Corporation Tax relief. In other words, they're a tax-deductible expense.
- Unlike salaries, there is no National Insurance on the income you eventually withdraw from your pension.
- When you eventually withdraw money from your pension up to 25% can be taken tax free.
- Pension income is taxed at the 'regular' Income Tax rates, typically 20% or 40%. By contrast, the combined tax rate on dividends (Income Tax and Corporation Tax) is now at least 26.1% for basic rate taxpayers and between 46.3% and 51.3% for higher rate taxpayers.
- When you start withdrawing income from your pension, you could find yourself in a lower tax bracket than you are now (many retirees are basic rate taxpayers). This means you could end up paying Income Tax at just 20%.

Putting all this together, it's possible you could ultimately pay Income Tax on your pension withdrawals at an overall effective rate of just 15%.

By contrast, you may face a combined tax rate that is possibly two, three, or even more, times higher if the same money is paid out as dividend income.

There is, of course, a major drawback with pensions: your money is locked away until you are 55 (rising to 57 in 2028). Nevertheless, when you do reach the minimum retirement age you can make unlimited withdrawals.

Another drawback with pensions is you are potentially exposed to any future increase in Income Tax rates. Essentially your savings are at the mercy of future governments.

Having said this, we do believe pension contributions are still worth making in many cases.

Example: Higher Rate Taxpayer
Lesleyanne is a company owner and a higher rate taxpayer (i.e. her taxable income is more than £50,270).

Let's say she is trying to choose between taking an additional £1,000 of the company's profit as a dividend and getting the company to invest £1,000 in her self-invested personal pension (SIPP).

Let's also say (as will often be the case) her company has a marginal Corporation Tax rate of 26.5%. Hence, with a dividend the company will first pay Corporation Tax of £265, leaving £735 to distribute. Lesleyanne will then pay Income Tax at 33.75%: £248. The total combined tax rate on the dividend is 51.3%.

By contrast, a company pension contribution will enjoy Corporation Tax relief, so the whole £1,000 will go straight into Lesleyanne's SIPP. Ignoring investment growth (it doesn't affect the outcome), when she eventually withdraws the money from her pension, the first £250 will be tax free and the remaining £750 will be subject to Income Tax.

If Lesleyanne is a basic rate taxpayer when she retires in the future, she will pay 20% Income Tax (£150), leaving her with £850 overall. Thus, her effective overall tax rate will be 15%.

If Lesleyanne is a higher rate taxpayer when she retires (for example, if she ends up with a significant amount of rental income from buy-to-let properties) she will effectively pay 40% tax on her taxable pension income (£300), leaving her with £700 overall. Thus, the effective tax rate on her pension withdrawals will be 30%.

In summary, Lesleyanne's choice is between paying tax at 51.3% on her additional dividend income and paying tax at 15% or possibly 30% on her pension withdrawals.

What this example shows is that, for company owners who have not yet built up significant pension savings, a company pension contribution is an extremely attractive alternative to additional dividend income.

Of course, we must never lose sight of the fact your pension savings are placed in a locked box until you are at least 55 (soon to be 57). So, a company pension contribution is only an attractive alternative to a dividend if you have already withdrawn enough money from your company to cover your living costs.

Example: Basic Rate Taxpayer
Poppy is a company owner and a basic rate taxpayer. She too is trying to choose between taking £1,000 of the company's profit as a dividend and a £1,000 company pension contribution. As she is a basic rate taxpayer, we will assume her company pays Corporation Tax at 19%.

With a dividend the company will pay £190 Corporation Tax, leaving £810 to distribute. Poppy will pay Income Tax at 8.75%: £71. The total combined tax rate on the dividend is 26.1%. (Note, if the company has profits over £50,000 the combined tax rate could be 32.9%.)

With a company pension contribution, the whole £1,000 will go straight into Poppy's SIPP. As with Lesleyanne, the effective tax rate on her pension withdrawals will be either 15% if she is a basic rate taxpayer when she retires or 30% if she is a higher rate taxpayer.

In summary, Poppy's choice is between paying tax at between 26.1% and 32.9% on her additional dividend income and paying tax at 15% or possibly 30% on her pension withdrawals.

A company pension contribution is a reasonably attractive alternative to dividend income. However, pension contributions may not be very attractive if Poppy is a higher rate taxpayer when she retires (for example, if she accumulates a significant amount of assets and the income takes her over the higher rate threshold before she starts withdrawing money from her pension).

Chapter 34

Pension Contributions: You or the Company?

In the previous chapter we showed that company pension contributions can be an attractive alternative to dividends. However, company directors can also make pension contributions *personally*, so a key question is: *"Who should make the contributions: the director or the company?"*

When you make pension contributions *personally* (as opposed to getting your company to make them) the taxman will top up your savings by paying cash directly into your pension. For every £80 you invest, the taxman will put in an extra £20.

Why £20? Your contributions are treated as having been paid out of income that has already been taxed at 20%, the basic rate of Income Tax.

The company that manages your pension plan, usually an insurance company or SIPP provider, will claim this money for you from the taxman and credit it to your account.

So, whatever contribution you make personally, divide it by 0.80 and you'll get the total amount that is invested in your pension pot (your gross pension contribution).

Example: *Peter is a company owner who takes most of his income as dividends. He invests £800 in a self-invested personal pension (SIPP). The taxman will top up his pension with £200 of basic rate tax relief, which means he'll have £1,000 in his pension pot: £800/0.80 = £1,000.*

If Peter is a higher rate taxpayer, he can also claim higher rate tax relief when he completes his tax return. This is given by increasing his basic rate band by the amount of his gross pension contribution.

Example continued: *Peter's gross pension contribution is £1,000 so his basic rate band will be increased by £1,000. This means £1,000 of his dividend income will be taxed at 8.75% instead of 33.75%, i.e. a 25% saving. Thus, Peter's higher rate tax relief is: £1,000 x 25% = £250.*

In total Peter will enjoy £450 of tax relief (£200 basic rate relief plus £250 higher rate tax relief). Peter's total tax relief is 45% of his £1,000 gross pension contribution and the overall cost of his £800 net contribution is just £550.

Directors with Small Salaries

To obtain tax relief on your pension contributions they have to stay within certain limits:

- **Earnings:** Contributions made by you *personally* must generally not exceed your 'relevant UK earnings'. Earnings include your salary, bonus and taxable benefits in kind but do NOT include your dividends.

- **The Annual Allowance:** Total pension contributions by you and your company must not exceed £60,000 per year, although it is possible to carry forward any unused annual allowance from the three previous tax years. The annual allowance may be reduced if your 'adjusted income' exceeds £260,000 (see Chapter 22).

For a company director taking a salary of £12,570 (see Chapter 9), the maximum personal pension contribution that can be made with tax relief is therefore £12,570.

This is the maximum *gross* contribution. The director would personally invest £10,056 (£12,570 x 80%) and the taxman will top this up with £2,514 of basic rate tax relief for a total gross contribution of £12,570.

Directors who want to make bigger pension contributions personally have to pay themselves bigger salaries. However, this may not be an attractive option because a bigger salary may be subject to employer's National Insurance (at 13.8%) or employee's National Insurance (at 8%), or both.

Company Pension Contributions

As a company owner, you can also get your company (your employer) to make pension contributions on your behalf. Company pension contributions are always paid *gross* (there is no top up from the taxman), but the company will normally enjoy Corporation Tax relief on the payment. For example, a company with a marginal Corporation Tax rate of 26.5% can make a pension contribution of £10,000 and enjoy £2,650 of tax relief.

You do not need a dedicated company pension scheme to make company pension contributions. Most firms that offer SIPPs allow your company to pay directly into your pension (these plans may not be qualifying schemes for auto-enrolment purposes).

How much can your company contribute? Unlike the contributions you make personally, the company's contributions are NOT restricted by the size of your salary.

In other words, the company can make a pension contribution that is bigger than your salary. However, there are other restrictions on company contributions:

* Total pension contributions by you and your company must not exceed the annual allowance (typically £60,000 this year) although you can carry forward any unused allowance from the previous three tax years.

* The company may be denied Corporation Tax relief on any pension contributions made on behalf of directors, if the taxman views them as 'excessive' (see below).

Corporation Tax Relief on Pension Contributions

Unlike the pension contributions that you make personally, tax relief for company pension contributions is not automatic.

Company contributions will only be a tax-deductible expense for Corporation Tax purposes if they are incurred wholly and exclusively for the purposes of the business.

There is a danger HMRC could deny Corporation Tax relief for 'excessive' pension contributions although, in practice, this is relatively rare.

When determining whether company pension contributions qualify for Corporation Tax relief, HMRC will look at the director's total remuneration package. The total package (including salary, pension contributions, and other benefits in kind) must not be excessive relative to the work the individual carries out and his or her responsibilities.

Relevant factors may include:

- The number of hours you work, your experience, and your level of responsibility in the company.
- The pay of unconnected employees in your company and other companies who perform duties of similar value.
- The pay required to recruit someone to take over your duties.
- The company's financial performance.

Extra care may be necessary in the event of a large one-off company pension contribution.

It may be sensible to document the commercial justification (for example, strong recent financial performance of the company) in the minutes of a directors' board meeting and hold a shareholders' meeting to approve the contribution.

In some cases, when a company is making pension contributions on behalf of all employees, including directors, of more than £500,000 in total, it may be necessary to spread tax relief for the excess over a number of years. These spreading rules will obviously not affect most small companies.

Although the risk that your company will be denied Corporation Tax relief may be small, it is important to stress that, when it comes to company pension contributions, unlike contributions made by individuals, there is no cast-iron guarantee the company will enjoy tax relief. That's why we would recommend speaking to a tax adviser before your company starts making significant contributions.

Pension Contributions: You or the Company?

Using some case studies, we will now compare company pension contributions with pension contributions made personally by company owners to see which is most tax efficient.

Case Study 1: Basic Rate Taxpayer
Eva owns Cassidy Ltd. She is a basic rate taxpayer and pays herself a salary of £12,570 this year (2024/25). She takes the rest of her income as dividends.

She also decides to use £1,000 of the company's pre-tax profit to fund a pension contribution. If Cassidy Ltd makes the contribution it can pay £1,000 directly into Eva's SIPP and the amount will be a tax-deductible expense.

Alternatively, Eva can pay herself a dividend to fund a pension contribution she makes personally. We'll assume the company pays 19% Corporation Tax on the £1,000 profit, leaving Eva with £810 to take as dividend income.

Eva holds onto £10 and invests £800 in her SIPP. The taxman will add £200 of basic rate tax relief, leaving her with the same amount in her pension: £1,000.

But that's not the end of the matter: Eva will still have to pay 8.75% tax on her £810 dividend, £71.

Eva is worse off by £61: £71 less the £10 of dividend income she held onto. And she would be even worse off if her company pays Corporation Tax at more than 19%.

Thus, if you're a basic rate taxpayer, for every £1,000 that ends up in your pension, you will have to pay at least 6.1% in additional tax. In this case, a company pension contribution is clearly more tax efficient than a contribution made personally by the director.

Other Important Points
If Eva wants more than £12,570 invested in her pension, making the contribution personally will be even more expensive.

She would have to pay herself a bigger salary and this could result in a significant amount of National Insurance becoming payable.

This is because, to enjoy tax relief, any pension contribution you make personally cannot exceed your earnings (i.e. salary).

The additional salary would typically attract 8% employee's National Insurance, plus 13.8% employer's National Insurance (unless the company has spare employment allowance).

Case Study 2: Higher Rate Taxpayer
This time we'll assume Eva is a *higher rate taxpayer* and again wants to make a £1,000 pension contribution.

If Cassidy Ltd makes the contribution, it can pay £1,000 directly into Eva's SIPP. Alternatively, Eva can pay herself an extra dividend. We'll assume the company pays 26.5% Corporation Tax on the £1,000 profit, leaving Eva with £735 to take as dividend income.

Thus, Eva may have to contribute up to £65 out of her own pocket to invest £800 in her SIPP. The taxman will add £200 of basic rate tax relief, resulting in the same gross pension contribution of £1,000.

Again, that's not the end of the matter. Eva still has to pay Income Tax on the additional dividend.

With a gross pension contribution of £1,000, Eva's basic rate band will be increased by £1,000. This means the extra dividend of £735 will be taxed at just 8.75%, not 33.75%, so the tax is £64.

Furthermore, an additional £265 of her other dividend income will also be taxed at 8.75% instead of 33.75%, saving her a further £66.

All in all, a £1,000 pension contribution made by the director is £63 more expensive than a contribution made by the company:

£64 Income Tax + £65 (cash added) – £66 extra relief = £63

A company pension contribution is again more tax efficient than a contribution made personally by the director, producing an overall saving of 6.3%. If the company has a lower marginal Corporation Tax rate, the saving will be smaller: e.g. just 1.3% if the company has a marginal Corporation Tax rate of 19% (i.e. profits less than £50,000).

Other Important Points

If Eva wants to enjoy full higher rate tax relief on a gross pension contribution of £12,570 (i.e. equal to her salary), she must have at least £12,570 of dividend income above the higher rate threshold (total income of at least £62,840 in 2024/25).

If Eva wants to make a pension contribution bigger than £12,570 personally, she will have to take a bigger salary and this may result in a significant amount of National Insurance becoming payable.

Case Study 3: Personal Allowance Withdrawal

Katie owns Melua Ltd, which has a marginal Corporation Tax rate of 26.5%. She takes a salary of £9,100 plus dividends of £100,900 to give her total income of £110,000.

Katie wants to make a £9,000 pension contribution. If Melua Ltd makes the contribution, it can pay £9,000 directly into Katie's SIPP. Alternatively, Katie can pay herself an extra dividend. However, with a marginal Corporation Tax rate of 26.5%, that £9,000 will only fund a dividend of £6,615.

Katie will have to contribute £585 out of her own pocket to be able to invest £7,200 in her SIPP. The taxman will add £1,800 of basic rate tax relief, resulting in the same gross pension contribution of £9,000.

As usual, that's not the end of the matter. Katie will pay 56.25% Income Tax on the £6,615 dividend: £3,721 (see Chapter 18 which explains why the tax rate is 56.25%).

However, Katie's pension contribution will increase her basic rate band by £9,000, meaning £9,000 more of her dividends are taxed at 8.75% instead of 33.75%, producing a saving of £2,250 (£9,000 x 25%). Furthermore, it also means she regains £4,500 of her personal allowance, saving a further £2,025 (£4,500 of her salary becomes tax free instead of taxed at 20% and £4,500 more dividend is taxed at 8.75% instead of 33.75%). Total tax relief: £4,275.

All in all, Katie's Income Tax bill is reduced by £554 if she makes the contribution personally. However, she had to pay £585 from her own pocket to top up her pension contribution so, in the end, the company contribution would leave her £31 better off overall.

So, our final conclusion in this scenario is basically that it doesn't matter whether pension contributions are made by the company or by the director personally.

However, it's worth remembering that:

- If the company had a lower marginal Corporation Tax rate, the personal pension contribution would become more attractive. Nonetheless, the position remains pretty marginal. At a Corporation Tax rate of 25%, the personal contribution saves £28; at the lowest possible Corporation Tax rate of 19%, it would save £264.

- If Katie wanted to put more than £9,100 into her pension, she would either have to increase her salary, at a considerable cost in Income Tax and National Insurance, or, more likely, get the company to make the contribution.

As an aside, it's worth noting that, for a director/shareholder like Katie, the effective rate of Income Tax relief on gross pension contributions made personally is 47.5%. That means, for each £800 of cash contribution, £475 is saved in tax, reducing the net outlay to just £325 to get £1,000 into the director's pension pot. This highly beneficial outcome does need the right conditions though. Once enough of the personal allowance has been restored to make sure the director's salary is tax free, the rate at which tax is saved begins to drop.

Case Study 4: Additional Rate Taxpayer
Let's take the same facts as Case Study 3 above, except that Katie takes dividends of £130,000 out of her company, giving her total income of £139,100 and making her an additional rate taxpayer.

A further dividend of £6,615 (as before) would now lead to additional Income Tax of £2,603 (£6,615 x 39.35%). However, Katie's gross pension contribution of £9,000 would mean £9,000 more dividends were taxed at 8.75% instead of 39.35%. The saving, at an effective rate of 30.6%, would be £2,754.

Overall, Katie's Income Tax bill is reduced by £151. However, as before, she will have had to pay £585 from her own pocket to top up her pension contribution so, in the end, the *company* contribution would leave her £434 better off.

So, the clear conclusion here is that additional rate taxpayers will be better off getting their company to make pension contributions on their behalf.

As usual, the saving reduces if the company has a lower marginal Corporation Tax rate. For example, at a Corporation Tax rate of 25%, the saving in this scenario is £352. However, even at the lowest possible Corporation Tax rate of 19%, there is still a small saving for additional rate taxpayers (£25 in Katie's case).

Lifetime ISAs

Those aged 18 to 39 can open a Lifetime ISA, which can be used to save for a first home or for retirement.

Up to £4,000 per year can be invested and receives a 25% Government bonus. So, if you put in £4,000, the Government will add £1,000. This is the same as the basic rate tax relief enjoyed on pension contributions.

It is possible to continue making contributions up to age 50. This means you can invest a total of up to £128,000 between age 18 and 50 with a Government bonus of up to £32,000.

Unlike a pension, your savings are not locked up inside a Lifetime ISA. However, if you withdraw money before reaching age 60, for any reason other than to buy your first home, there will be a 25% early withdrawal charge. This will claw back all the Government bonus, plus an additional 6.25% of the amount you invested.

Lifetime ISA versus Company Pension Contribution
The Lifetime ISA is an attractive alternative to saving in a pension if you are a basic rate taxpayer. Like pensions, they attract a top up from the Government but, unlike pensions, ALL the money you take out will be tax free.

Let's say a company owner who is a basic rate taxpayer is trying to decide between a £1,000 company pension contribution and using a dividend to fund a Lifetime ISA contribution.

A £1,000 pension contribution will attract Corporation Tax relief so the whole £1,000 will go directly into the company owner's pension.

If the same money is used to pay a dividend to fund a Lifetime ISA contribution, and assuming the company pays 19% Corporation Tax, £810 will be left to pay out. After paying 8.75% Income Tax, the company owner will be left with £739 to invest in a Lifetime ISA. Adding the Government bonus, the company owner will end up with £924 in the Lifetime ISA.

When the company owner reaches age 60, all withdrawals from the Lifetime ISA will be tax free, whereas only 25% of the money withdrawn from the pension will be tax free (although they can get it slightly earlier). The rest will possibly be taxed at just 20% if they are a basic rate taxpayer.

If we ignore investment growth to keep the example simple (it doesn't affect the outcome), with a Lifetime ISA the company owner will end up with £924; with a pension they will end up with just £850 after tax.

Thus, if you're a basic rate taxpayer, your retirement income could be up to 9% higher with a Lifetime ISA

And, if you're a higher rate taxpayer when you retire, you might enjoy up to 32% more income with a Lifetime ISA!

On the other hand, if your company is paying Corporation Tax at more than 19%, the advantage of a Lifetime ISA will be reduced, or could even be eliminated.

For example, at the highest marginal Corporation Tax rate of 26.5%, £1,000 of pre-tax profit will only fund a dividend of £735. After Income Tax at 8.75%, a basic rate taxpayer will be left with £671. If they put that in a Lifetime ISA, the Government will add £167 for a total investment of £838. In the end, if they're a basic rate taxpayer when they retire, a company pension contribution could have left them with £850, i.e. £12 more.

The difference is only marginal, however, and it's important to remember, if you're a higher rate taxpayer when you draw your pension, you might end up with only £700 after tax.

So, basic rate taxpayers who own a company making profits between £50,000 and £250,000 face a choice between a certain £838, or a possible £850 that might, in fact, only be £700.

We think you'd need to be pretty certain you were going to be a basic rate taxpayer in retirement before you went for the pension contribution, but it's up to you!

Higher Rate Taxpayers

What about higher rate taxpayers? Once again, a £1,000 pension contribution will attract Corporation Tax relief, so the whole £1,000 will go directly into the company owner's pension.

If the same money is used to pay a dividend to fund a Lifetime ISA contribution, the amount received by the director will vary depending on the company's marginal Corporation Tax rate. If we assume it's 26.5%, the amount left to pay a dividend will be £735. After paying 33.75% Income Tax, the company owner will be left with £487 to invest in their Lifetime ISA. Adding the Government bonus, the company owner will end up with £609 in their Lifetime ISA.

When the company owner reaches age 60, all withdrawals from the Lifetime ISA will be tax free, whereas only 25% of the money withdrawn from the pension will be tax free. The rest could be taxed at just 20% if they are a basic rate taxpayer at that point.

Ignoring investment growth again, with a Lifetime ISA the company owner will end up with £609, with a pension they will end up with £850 after tax.

Thus, your retirement income could be up to 40% higher with a pension.

If the company owner is a higher rate taxpayer when they retire (e.g. if they have a lot of income from other sources, such as rental property) they will end up with £700 from a pension, compared with £609 from a Lifetime ISA. So, again, a company pension contribution will generally be better.

Finally, it's also important to remember you can only invest £4,000 per year in a Lifetime ISA (with an additional £1,000 bonus from the Government), compared with the maximum gross pension contribution of £60,000 per year. Furthermore, you can only open a Lifetime ISA if you're under 40, and it's only possible to make contributions up to age 50.

Summary

Company pension contributions are generally more tax efficient than contributions made personally by directors.

There are a few exceptions and some cases where the position is fairly marginal.

Frankly though, if you go on the basis that company pension contributions are always best, you will usually be right and, even if you're not, you will rarely lose out by much.

Furthermore, making large pension contributions personally may mean taking a bigger salary, often leading to significant National Insurance costs.

Tax relief for company pension contributions is not automatic, however, and could be denied if the contributions are viewed as excessive, although this is rare in practice.

A Lifetime ISA may be an attractive alternative to a company pension contribution for basic rate taxpayers. Company pension contributions generally remain better for higher rate taxpayers, however.

Chapter 35

Putting Property into a Pension

In Chapter 30, we explained that company owners who own their business premises personally can get the company to pay them rent and this may be an attractive alternative to dividends.

Some company owners also use a SIPP or other pension plan to hold their business premises and, in this chapter, we'll take a look at the benefits and drawbacks of this alternative. Note that, while you can put *commercial property* into a pension, you cannot do this with residential property.

Holding business property in a pension has a number of benefits:

- **Tax-free rent:** There's no Income Tax payable by you on the rent your company pays into your pension. The rent is also a tax-deductible expense for the business.

- **No Capital Gains Tax:** When a property held inside a pension is sold there is no CGT payable.

- **Inheritance Tax exemption:** Assets held in a pension generally fall outside your estate for Inheritance Tax purposes.

Although the ability to roll up rental income tax free inside a pension is enticing, you must never lose sight of the fact that all the money you eventually withdraw from your pension, over and above your 25% tax-free lump sum, will be subject to Income Tax.

If you are a higher rate taxpayer at present, but expect to be a basic rate taxpayer when you retire, it's possible the rental income will ultimately be much less heavily taxed by going the pension route.

Similarly, although property held inside a pension can be sold without incurring CGT, when you eventually withdraw the capital gain most of it (typically 75%) will be subject to Income Tax.

If you are a basic rate taxpayer when you retire you will pay 20% tax and if you are a higher rate taxpayer you will pay 40% tax.

By contrast, if you sell commercial property you own personally, you will be subject to CGT. Commercial property benefits from the lower 20% CGT rate and it's possible some of the gain will be taxed at 10% if your basic rate band isn't used up by your other income. Some of the gain may also be covered by your annual exemption, although this is a measly £3,000 now.

In some cases, a sale of business premises owned personally will qualify for business asset disposal relief. If so, a tax rate of 10% may apply to the whole gain, although the relief will be restricted if your company has paid you rent at any time since 6th April 2008.

Business premises held inside your pension do not have to be sold when you retire. If your own company ceases to occupy the property, it can remain in your pension and be rented out to someone else and the rent will roll up tax free in your pension.

Although property held inside your pension may fall outside your estate for Inheritance Tax purposes, in most cases the family members that inherit your pension pot will have to pay Income Tax on any money they subsequently withdraw.

By contrast, if you own your company's business premises personally, the property may qualify for 50% business property relief, reducing the effective rate of Inheritance Tax on the property to just 20% in many cases.

Finally, when it comes to tucking away money inside a pension, we must never lose sight of the fact you will not be able to get your hands on any of the money until you are at least 55 (rising to 57 in 2028).

Clearly there are benefits to holding business property inside a pension, but it is by no means a 'no brainer'. There are benefits, but also drawbacks, and each case needs to be decided on its own merits with help from a professional.

Funding the Property Purchase

The purchase of a business property by a pension can be funded in several ways. Typically, you will use your existing pension savings, topped up with fresh contributions (including company pension contributions).

It is also possible for your pension fund to borrow money, but only up to 50% of its net assets. For example, if you have pension savings of £100,000 an additional £50,000 can be borrowed.

Some pension providers allow a part share in a property to be acquired by the pension plan, with the balance owned outside the pension.

Several individuals can also pool their pension savings to collectively buy a property.

Transferring Existing Property

If you already own the property, you can sell it to your SIPP, and this may allow you to release a sizeable amount of cash from your pension savings.

Transferring an existing property into a pension is likely to result in CGT becoming payable if the property has risen in value since you bought it.

Commercial property benefits from the lower 20% CGT rate and some of the gain may be taxed at just 10%. It is unlikely business asset disposal relief would be available in such cases.

A sizeable CGT bill may put off many existing property owners going down the pension route, but others may still be tempted by the prospect of receiving a large cash payment out of their pension savings.

The transfer may also result in a Stamp Duty Land Tax bill and VAT may be payable in certain circumstances, although it may be possible to claim a VAT refund.

In Specie Contributions

Properties have in the past been transferred into pensions as *in specie* pension contributions, with the member claiming Income Tax relief. In specie contributions are no longer permitted following a clamp down by HMRC because of perceived abuse.

Costs and Other Formalities

Not all pension providers deal with property purchases, so you may need to transfer your existing pension to a specialist provider.

When your property is held inside a pension, your business will have to be treated just like any other tenant, with no special favours, which means rent will have to be paid at a full market rate come hell or high water.

If rent is not paid, this will be treated as an unauthorised payment by your pension and HMRC may levy a charge of 40% on you personally and a charge of up to 40% on the pension itself.

Property SIPPs are also much more expensive to run than those that only allow you to invest in traditional 'stocks and shares'. Initial set up costs include legal fees, survey fees, lenders fees, and fees to the pension company managing your SIPP. Fees will also have to be paid for regular rent revaluations and a third party property manager may have to be appointed to collect the rent from your company.

Chapter 36

Sell Your Business and Pay 10% Tax!

One of the most tax-efficient ways to grow your wealth is to build up a successful company and then sell it. This allows you to convert heavily taxed income into a less heavily taxed capital gain.

Many company owners who receive dividends have a marginal Income Tax rate of 33.75%. Those with income over £125,140 have a marginal rate of 39.35%, and those with income between £100,000 and £125,140 often face a marginal tax rate of 56.25%.

But when you sell a company and receive a cash lump sum, which replaces all of this heavily taxed income, you could end up paying just 10% tax thanks to business asset disposal relief (previously known as entrepreneurs' relief, which was a much better name).

The lifetime limit used to be £10 million of capital gains per person. But in 2020 this was slashed to just £1 million. It could have been a lot worse: there were fears the relief would be abolished altogether. And, because it applies on a per person basis, couples can still enjoy £2 million of capital gains taxed at 10%.

Business asset disposal relief is, however, no longer very attractive to serial entrepreneurs, who build up and sell many businesses during their careers. Many will have already exhausted their £1 million allowance.

However, if you are denied the relief, all is not lost. You could end up paying CGT at 20% instead of 10%, but that's still a lot more attractive than the top tax rates for dividends.

It remains to be seen whether the new Labour Government will reduce the relief further or abolish it altogether. Such a move would not surprise many tax commentators.

Qualifying for Business Asset Disposal Relief

Company owners are entitled to business asset disposal relief when they sell their shares or wind up the company. The main qualifying criteria are:

- The company must be your 'personal company' which, generally speaking, means you must own at least 5% of it (but matters can get more complicated: see below)
- You must be an officer or employee of the company
- The company must be a 'trading' company

Each of these rules must be satisfied for at least **two years** before the company is sold or wound up.

Where the company has ceased trading, each of the rules must be satisfied for at least two years before it ceases trading. The disposal of the company must then take place within three years after trading has stopped.

Selling a Recently Incorporated Business

If you have only recently transferred an unincorporated business (a sole trade or partnership) into your company wholly or partly in exchange for shares, you don't have to own the shares of the newly formed company for two years. The period you owned the unincorporated business is added to the period you own the company shares in this situation.

Transferring Shares to Your Spouse/Partner Etc

You do, however, have to be wary of transferring shares to your spouse within the two years before selling the company. Transfers to spouses are exempt from CGT and your spouse can then claim business asset disposal relief when the business is sold, but they personally must satisfy the necessary conditions outlined above in their own right. This generally means the transfer must have taken place at least two years before selling the company for the spouse to qualify for business asset disposal relief.

Spouse transfers weren't always necessary when the lifetime limit for the relief was £10 million, but are probably more important now it is just £1 million. As we saw in Chapter 27, many company owners also transfer shares to their spouse to reduce the Income Tax payable on dividends.

Similar principles apply to transfers to an unmarried partner or other adult family member; although a holdover relief claim will be necessary (see Chapter 27).

What is a Personal Company?

As stated above, to qualify for business asset disposal relief the company must be your personal company. This means you must own at least 5% of the ordinary share capital and have at least 5% of the voting rights.

HMRC was concerned that ordinary shares encompass a very broad range of share arrangements, including those where the shareholders have restricted rights to dividends and company assets.

As a result, you must now also meet at least one of the following two conditions to qualify for business asset disposal relief:

- You must be entitled to at least 5% of the profits available for distribution and at least 5% of the assets available for distribution if the company is wound up, or
- In the event of a disposal of all the ordinary share capital of the company, you would be entitled to at least 5% of the disposal proceeds

Initially the Government introduced just one additional condition (the first bullet point above). However, several expert tax commentators pointed out this would have prevented owners of alphabet shares (common in many small family companies) from claiming the relief.

For example, where a company has A and B shares and a different rate of dividend can be declared on each type, it could be argued that neither type of shareholder is entitled to at least 5% of the profits available for distribution: because there is no dividend entitlement until the dividends are declared.

As a result, the second condition was tagged on. This allows the company owner to instead enjoy business asset disposal relief if they are entitled to at least 5% of the proceeds when the company is sold.

What is an Officer?
Company officers include non-executive directors and company secretaries, so you don't have to work full-time at the company to qualify for business asset disposal relief.

What is a Trading Company?
To qualify for business asset disposal relief, the company must be a trading company. HMRC regards the following as non-trading activities:

- Holding investment property, including property for letting
- Holding shares or securities
- Holding surplus cash

If there is substantial non-trading activity, you could be denied business asset disposal relief. HMRC generally regards non-trading activities to be substantial where either non-trading income or non-trading assets exceed 20% of the totals for the company as a whole. However, this test is only a rule of thumb and does not have any statutory basis. It must be remembered that, in cases of dispute, it is for the courts to decide the matter, not HMRC. For further analysis of this issue and the current legal position established in court, see Chapter 1.

Nonetheless, it remains the fact that if just 20% of the assets or income of the company are not trading assets or income, you may be denied business asset disposal relief when you sell your shares.

In this context, it is worth pointing out that business goodwill is a trading asset and should be taken into account, even if its value is not reflected on the company's balance sheet.

If your company doesn't own investment property or invest in other companies, the most serious danger is holding too much cash. In the early days of what was then entrepreneurs' relief, many people were concerned that excessive amounts of cash could result in the company losing its trading status and hence the relief (now business asset disposal relief) could be taken away.

However, more recent case law has placed far less emphasis on surplus holdings of cash than HMRC seemed to think was appropriate. After all, the legislation only talks about substantial non-trading *activity:* and there is not much activity involved in simply holding cash!

Remember, case law now tells us non-trading activities will only be regarded as substantial if they are of material or real importance in the context of the company's activities as a whole (see Chapter 1).

So, if, for example, a company has a trading business, whose total net assets are worth £700,000, plus surplus cash of £300,000, which is simply being held in a bank account and not actively invested then, while that cash amounts to 30% of the company's assets, it is clearly not a substantial activity and the company remains a trading company.

Nevertheless, while the 20% used as a benchmark by HMRC has no legal substance, and were it to relate purely to a holding of cash, they would be laughed out of court, there *would* still come a point when the cash held by a company came to be so significant that it threatened the company's trading status.

So, this brings us to the question of when is cash surplus? Let's say a company has £500,000 in its bank account. That's a lot of cash. But if that company buys £1 million of trading stock every month, the cash is only covering two weeks' supplies. It is therefore simply working capital, it is not surplus cash, and is part of the assets of the trade.

But larger holdings of cash proportionate to the size of the company's trading activities will eventually become surplus to the requirements of the company's business. Eventually, a large enough cash holding will begin to pose a risk.

However, even such large holdings should not be a problem if you can prove the cash was required for business purposes, for example as part of a well-documented expansion plan.

Like many aspects of tax law, this issue is something of a grey area and, in cases of doubt, professional advice is recommended. (And, despite all we have said, any holding that represents more than 20% of the company's assets will always cast a degree of doubt.)

If the company really does have a substantial amount of surplus cash that cannot be justified for business reasons, it may be necessary to extract it at least two years in advance to prevent the company's trading status being challenged on a sale of the company's shares.

You then have to weigh up the potential costs and benefits: the benefit being a CGT rate of 10% instead of 20% on a gain of up to £1 million (per person); the cost being the Income Tax on any additional dividends.

Associated Disposals of Business Premises

Many business owners purchase business premises *personally* and rent them to their company. The good news is business asset disposal relief is available when 'associated' assets like these are sold. The bad news is many company owners will not qualify!

The asset will only qualify for business asset disposal relief if you also make a 'material disposal' of shares in your company. The stake being disposed of must generally be at least 5%.

It is possible to claim business asset disposal relief on an associated disposal even if the stake in the business is sold or gifted to a family member, for example an adult child.

However, there must also be no 'share purchase arrangements' in place at the time of disposal. This rule is designed to prevent you from taking back your stake in the business after the property has been sold and business asset disposal relief has been claimed.

To qualify for business asset disposal relief the 'associated' asset must have been in use in the business for at least two years. The asset must also have been held for at least three years to qualify.

The relief is also restricted if you've received any payment for the use of the property since 5th April 2008 (e.g. if your company has paid you rent).

Where the property was acquired after 5th April 2008 and a full market rent was received throughout the period of its use in the company's trade, no business asset disposal relief is available.

Where the property was acquired at an earlier date, or rent was charged at a lower rate, there will be a partial restriction in the relief.

As we saw in Chapter 30, getting your company to pay you rent is an attractive alternative to dividends, especially when the company owner (who owns the property) has expenses such as mortgage interest that can be deducted for tax purposes.

Another advantage of charging your company rent is so that capital allowances can be claimed on the qualifying fixtures in the property. If a market rent is not charged, the property owner will not be treated as having a proper 'property business', which is necessary for them to make a full capital allowances claim (although a partial claim is possible where a lower level of rent is charged).

For newer properties, or those that have recently undergone conversions or improvements, the owner may also be able to claim the structures and buildings allowance (see the Taxcafe guide *How to Save Property Tax* for details). Again, the claim is restricted if the owner charges less than a full market rent.

In summary, company owners who own their business premises personally have to weigh the benefits of business asset disposal relief against the benefits of paying themselves rental income. The reduction in the relief's lifetime limit from £10 million to £1 million has made paying rent considerably more attractive.

Winding Up Your Company

It is not always possible to sell your company shares to a third party. Buyers are often fearful of acquiring companies outright for fear of taking on any unknown liabilities. Instead they often prefer to buy the assets (e.g. premises, goodwill, stock, and customer lists).

The disadvantage of an asset sale such as this is the double tax charge: the company will pay Corporation Tax on the sale, and you will pay Income Tax or CGT when you extract the after-tax proceeds.

Providing you meet the qualifying criteria, business asset disposal relief is still available if you wind up your company following an asset sale and extract the cash as a capital distribution.

There are generally two ways to wind up a company:

- Dissolution under the Companies Act
- Voluntary liquidation under the Insolvency Act

With a *dissolution*, CGT treatment is only possible if the total distributions are no more than £25,000. Where the total distributions exceed £25,000, they are taxed as dividends, possibly at 33.75% or 39.35%.

A *voluntary liquidation* ensures payments to shareholders are treated as capital distributions for CGT purposes. However, voluntary liquidation requires the appointment of a licensed insolvency practitioner with fees running to many thousands of pounds in some cases (the fees may be less if the company's affairs are simple and its main asset is cash).

To qualify for business asset disposal relief, the capital distribution must be made within three years of the cessation of trading.

The following criteria must be met for the two years before cessation of trading:

- The company must be your 'personal company' (see above)
- You must be an officer or employee of the company
- The company must be a 'trading' company (see above)

As discussed above, in some cases a large surplus cash balance (a non-trading asset) already held in the company before the sale, or cessation, of the business, may throw into doubt the ability to claim business asset disposal relief.

It goes without saying that in all cases where a winding up of the company is to be carried out, professional advice should be obtained to ensure the desired tax treatment of the distributions.

The Anti-Phoenixing Rule

The anti-phoenixing rule means a distribution made when winding up a company will sometimes be taxed as a dividend. This is to prevent company owners continually winding up companies and starting new ones to enjoy the lower CGT rates.

The rule applies where **all** of the following conditions are met:

- **Condition A & B:** The individual holds at least 5% of the ordinary share capital and voting rights immediately before the winding up and the company is a close company at some point in the two years before the winding up

- **Condition C:** Within two years after the distribution, the company owner carries on the same or a similar trade or activity to the company being wound up

- **Condition D:** It is reasonable to assume the main purpose or one of the main purposes of the winding up is to avoid Income Tax

With regards to Condition C, it makes no difference whether you operate as a sole trader, or through a partnership, a new company in which you have at least a 5% interest, or a connected person (e.g. your spouse or another close relative).

The test is clearly very subjective and it is feared it could catch many innocent situations, for example where a company owner retires, winds up their company, and a year later decides to take on a few clients or do some work for a family member involved in the same trade.

It is also feared Condition D could be applied broadly. For example, HMRC could argue that if a company owner decides not to pay surplus funds out as dividends prior to the winding up, there is as an 'arrangement' to reduce Income Tax.

HMRC has provided the following examples, which are intended to allay these fears and explain when the rules apply:

Example 1: Mr A has been the sole shareholder of a company which carries on the trade of landscape gardening for 10 years. Mr A decides to wind up the business and retire. Because he no longer needs a company, he liquidates the company and receives a distribution in a winding up. To subsidise his pension, Mr A continues to do a small amount of gardening in his local village.

Conditions A to C are met, because gardening is a similar trade or activity to landscape gardening. However, when viewed as a whole, these arrangements do not appear to have tax as a main purpose. It is natural for Mr A to have wound up his company because it is no longer needed once the trade has ceased.

Although Mr A continues to do some gardening, there is no reason why he would need a company for this, and it does not seem that he set the company up, wound it up, and then continued a trade, all with a view to receive the profits as capital rather than income.

In these circumstances, Mr A's distribution in the winding up will continue to be treated as capital.

Example 2: *Mrs B is an IT contractor. Whenever she receives a new contract, she sets up a limited company to carry out that contract. When the work is completed and the client has paid, Mrs B winds up the company and receives the profits as capital.*

Again, conditions A to C are met because Mrs B has a new company which carries on the same or a similar trade to the previously wound up company. Here, though, it looks like there is a main purpose of obtaining a tax advantage. All the contracts could have been operated through the same company, and apart from the tax savings, it would seem that would have been the most sensible option for Mrs B.

Where the distribution from the winding up is made in these circumstances, the distribution will be treated as a dividend subject to Income Tax.

Example 3: *Mrs C is an accountant who has operated through a limited company for three years. She now feels the risk involved in running her own business is not worth the effort, and so decides to accept a job at her brother's accountancy firm as an employee. Her brother's firm has been operating for eight years. Mrs C winds up her company and begins life as an employee.*

Conditions A to C are met because Mrs C is continuing a similar activity to the trade that was carried on by the company. She is continuing it as an employee of a connected party, triggering Condition C.

But looking at the arrangements as a whole, it is not reasonable to assume they have tax advantage as a main purpose, so Condition D will not be met. Mrs C's company was incorporated and wound up for commercial, not tax, reasons; although she works for a connected party, it is clear that other business was not set up to facilitate a tax advantage because it has been operating for some time.

In these circumstances, the distribution from the winding up will continue to be treated as capital, absent any other considerations.

Transaction in Securities

HMRC can also use the so-called 'transaction in securities' rules to attack distributions when a company is wound up if it thinks the main reason for the liquidation is to save Income Tax.

The transaction in securities rules are contained in vague legislation that can be used to convert capital gains into income subject to the dividend tax rates if HMRC takes the view that income has been incorrectly extracted as a capital gain.

This introduces a second obstacle for business owners who wish to liquidate their companies. Hence, given the wide-ranging nature of the transaction in securities legislation, most tax advisers recommend obtaining pre-transaction clearance from HMRC. While the liquidation of a long-standing company after it has ceased trading, or sold its business assets to a third party, will seldom be challenged, it is better to be safe than sorry.

The transaction in securities rules cannot apply if there is a simple, straightforward, genuine third-party sale of company shares, even if one of the main reasons for the sale is to save tax.

Overdrawn Directors Loan Accounts

When a director owes their company money, the overdrawn loan account is an *asset* of the company. When there is a members' voluntary liquidation, it is common practice to distribute this asset to the shareholders *in specie* (i.e. not as a cash payment).

In other words, instead of the director repaying the company and receiving the cash back as a liquidation distribution in their capacity as a shareholder, the distribution is handled as a paper transaction.

In the past, the distribution of the director's loan account during a liquidation was treated as a capital distribution and taxed at just 10% if the company owner was entitled to business asset disposal relief.

Apparently, however, HMRC is now taking the approach that such distributions are subject to Income Tax at the dividend tax rates (i.e. at up to 39.35%).

For this reason, several expert tax commentators recommend that directors with overdrawn loan accounts should pay back their loans to the company before the company enters liquidation.

Conclusion

There is some uncertainty amongst tax professionals as to how the various anti-avoidance measures will be applied in practice when a company is liquidated.

Where capital gains treatment is in doubt, it may make sense to pay actual dividends over several tax years, rather than making a single large distribution when you wind up the company.

Adopting a phased approach to the withdrawal of profits from your company may allow you to enjoy the 8.75% tax rate that applies to basic rate taxpayers, rather than the 33.75% or 39.35% tax rates that apply to higher and additional rate taxpayers.

Adopting this strategy over several tax years could allow a significant amount of cash to be extracted from the company, especially when the amounts taxed at 8.75% can be doubled up in the case of a company owned by a couple.

A Final Note on Business Asset Disposal Relief

Business asset disposal relief is complicated and constantly changing. This chapter is by no means a definitive guide.

There are various quirks in the legislation that we have deliberately ignored for simplicity's sake, but which could see the relief denied in certain circumstances. For this reason, anyone who wants to benefit from business asset disposal relief should seek advice from a tax professional with experience in this area.

And finally, please note that, although business asset disposal relief is currently available, we would not be surprised to see the relief reduced or scrapped altogether. In other words, it may be unwise to make plans under the assumption that the relief will still be available when you sell or wind up your company in the future.

Chapter 37

Employee Ownership Trusts

In the previous chapter, we saw how, thanks to business asset disposal relief, company owners may be able to pay just 10% CGT when they sell their businesses.

Many company owners have heard about business asset disposal relief, but did you know you can also sell your company TAX FREE to something called an employee ownership trust?

With an employee ownership trust the company ends up being owned by a trust for the benefit of employees generally (shares are not earmarked for individual employees).

Note, employee ownership trusts are not to be confused with the much discredited use of employee benefit trusts to give employees interest-free loans that were supposedly tax free.

The CGT relief for the sale of company shares to employee ownership trusts was introduced in the 2014 Finance Act and therefore has the Government's blessing.

A typical business sale would take place as follows:

- An employee ownership trust is established.
- Shares in the company are sold to the trustees of the employee ownership trust. An independent valuation will be required so the correct market value is used.
- The trust does not need to have any money to buy the company. The purchase consideration will typically take the form of a debt owed to the original shareholders.
- The company will then gift its earnings to the employee ownership trust to pay off the original owners over a number of years. These gifts of earnings are not an allowable expense for Corporation Tax purposes, so money will need to be retained by the company to settle its Corporation Tax bills.
- Payments from the employee ownership trust to the original owners will be exempt from CGT, providing various conditions are met (see below).

- The employees will only be indirect owners of the company and will therefore not receive dividends. Instead, the trustees of the employee ownership trust can arrange for bonuses to be paid by the company. Annual cash bonuses of up to £3,600 per employee are allowed free from Income Tax (but not National Insurance).

Qualifying Requirements

There are, of course, a number of conditions that have to be satisfied to qualify for the tax benefits:

- The company must be a trading company or the holding company of a trading group
- The trustees of the employee ownership trust must provide benefits to all eligible employees on the same terms. It is, however, possible to distinguish between employees based on their levels of pay, length of service, and hours worked.
- The trustees of the employee ownership trust must acquire at least 51% of the company and thus have a controlling interest. Up to 49% of the shares can, however, remain in direct ownership.
- The directors can remain at the company following the sale. However, the number of continuing shareholders (and any other 5% participators) who are directors or employees (or persons connected to them, such as close relatives) must not exceed 40% of the total number of employees. So, if a company has five employees only two of them can be the original shareholders. This is to show there has been a genuine change of ownership in the business. This condition must also be met for one year before the sale of the business.

It is possible for the CGT relief to be clawed back if a disqualifying event occurs in the same tax year that the employee ownership trust acquires shares in the company or in the following tax year.

The original owners will then be subject to CGT under the normal rules, as laid out in the previous chapter.

If any of the conditions for CGT relief are breached in a later tax year it is the trustees who will be liable for CGT. The CGT bill will be calculated using the original owners' base cost in the shares.

Employee ownership trusts are supposed to be long-term ownership vehicles but it is possible that the 51% controlling interest requirement could be breached if, for example, the trustees decide to sell shares in the business to a third party on the basis that the offer is in the interest of the beneficiaries of the employee ownership trust.

The sale of the business to the employee ownership trust must not be for tax avoidance purposes and could fall foul of the so-called 'transactions in securities' rules if one of the main purposes is to obtain a tax benefit.

For this reason, several tax commentators recommend obtaining advance clearance from HMRC to ensure the payments from the trustees to the original owners will not be treated as disguised dividends.

Of course, selling to an employee ownership trust will not appeal to all business owners. In particular, many will be put off by the potentially long delay receiving payment for their sale of the business. If the company starts making losses the employee ownership trust may be unable to pay the original owners.

Apart from the tax benefits, selling to an employee ownership trust is also seen as a useful way to solve succession issues, where there are no family members willing to carry on with the business and the owners are unwilling to sell to a competitor or third party with all the hassle this may involve.

Changes Ahead
There are proposals to change the employee ownership trust regime which may make them less flexible (for example preventing the previous owners of the company retaining control of the company via the employee ownership trust). The outcome of the consultation has not been published yet. If you are considering using an employee ownership trust, your professional adviser (don't do this without one) should be able to advise whether you are affected.

Part 7

Salary & Dividends: Practical Issues & Dangers

Chapter 38

How to Avoid the Minimum Wage Rules

If you take a small salary from your company (for example, £9,100 or £12,570) there may be a danger of falling foul of the national living wage.

Where wages are too low, HMRC will force the company to make up the shortfall. Bigger wage payments may result in bigger National Insurance bills for both the company and the director.

There is also a penalty equivalent to 200% of the unpaid wages with a maximum penalty of £20,000 per worker. Those found guilty will also be considered for disqualification from being a company director for up to 15 years.

However, the key point to note about the national living wage is that it only applies to directors if they have a contract of employment.

Due to the informal set up in many small companies, there may be some uncertainty as to whether an employment contract exists between the director and the company (employment contracts do not need to be in writing).

However, it is generally accepted among the tax profession that if you do not issue yourself with an explicit contract of employment, the minimum wage regulations do not apply.

This means you should be able to continue paying yourself a small salary, even if it is less than the national living wage.

However, risk averse company owners (those worried about potential penalties) might consider paying themselves enough salary to satisfy the minimum wage regulations.

National Living Wage Rates

The national living wage now applies to those aged 21 and over. From April 2024 the rate is £11.44 per hour.

If you spend, say, 35 hours per week actively managing your business, the total salary due for 2024/25 will be: 35 x 52 weeks x £11.44 = £20,821.

Such a salary could result in unwelcome National Insurance charges.

The National Insurance payable on this salary by the director would be £660 and £1,617 would be payable by the company (unless it has spare employment allowance available).

Of course, every case is different and some directors will be able to argue they spend fewer hours actively managing the business.

Although it may seem the best strategy is to simply not have a contract of employment, there may be other reasons why having such a contract is important.

Note that directors are exempt from the national living wage with respect to hours spent performing their duties as directors: as distinct from hours spent managing the business. In a small company, this can often be a difficult distinction to draw. But if, for example, the company owner appointed their spouse/partner as a director, but that spouse/partner did no other work for the company apart from fulfilling their duties as director, then the national living wage would not apply in their case.

Family Members Who Aren't Directors

It is possible some family members will be employees of the company but not directors. These individuals are subject to the national minimum wage or living wage for all hours spent working in the business. The exemption for members of your own household does not apply where the employer is a company.

However, it is possible that, if they only work part time, the salary that must be paid to them will still be within the typical optimal amounts of £9,100 or £12,570.

Chapter 39

Is My Salary Tax Deductible?

One of the benefits of getting your company to pay you a salary is that the amount will normally be a tax-deductible expense and reduce the company's Corporation Tax bill.

There is no automatic right to Corporation Tax relief. The amount paid has to be justified by the work carried out for the business and the individual's level of responsibility.

While this may not be an important issue for company owners who work full time in the business and pay themselves a small salary, it may be important if you start paying salaries to other family members, in particular those who only work part time.

The question of whether your employment income will attract Corporation Tax relief may also become an issue if you decide to pay yourself a large one-off bonus, or if you are following the large salary method we looked at in Chapter 21. Factors that may determine whether a salary or bonus payment is tax deductible include:

- The number of hours worked in the business
- The individual's legal obligations and responsibilities (e.g. directors' duties)
- The pay received by the company's other employees
- The pay received by employees at other companies performing similar roles
- The company's performance and ability to pay salaries/bonuses.

In the case of large one-off bonus payments made only to the company's director/shareholders it may be necessary to document the commercial rationale for the payment to show the payment is justifiable. This can be done in the minutes of a directors' board meeting. It may also be advisable to record the approval of any bonus in the minutes of a shareholders' meeting.

Chapter 40

Salary vs Dividends: Non-Tax Factors

Most of this guide focuses on choosing the most tax efficient *level* of income and the most tax efficient *mix* of income (i.e. salary versus dividends).

However, when it comes to withdrawing money from your company there are lots of other non-tax factors that may need to be considered. This chapter provides a short overview of some of the issues but is not definitive.

Cashflow and Working Capital Needs
When deciding how much income you withdraw from your company you must consider the cashflow and working capital requirements of the business.

It would naturally be irresponsible to pay yourself a large bonus or dividend if this affects the company's ability to carry on its business.

If you prefer to retain the cash in your company, it may be possible for a dividend to be declared but not paid out. The dividend can simply be credited to the director's loan account and withdrawn at a later date when it is more convenient.

Income Tax will still be payable on any dividends declared but not paid.

Dividends & Company Insolvency
Dividends should not be declared when the company is insolvent or if the payment of those dividends will render the company insolvent.

Dividends that are deemed illegal may have to be repaid, even if this results in the director being made bankrupt or being forced into an individual voluntary arrangement (IVA).

Director's Ability to Borrow
If you take a small salary and the rest of your income as dividends there is a possibility this will affect your ability to borrow money personally.

Some lenders may only be interested in the level of your salary and ignore your dividends, being unfamiliar with this sort of pay structuring. Others, on the other hand, will look at the complete picture and will look at your recent tax returns and the company's most recent accounts when assessing your ability to repay a loan.

Effect on Share Value
The value of a company is usually based on a multiple of its after-tax profits. A small minority shareholder's stake, however, is often valued according to the dividend history of the company. A consistent or steadily increasing annual dividend may enhance the value of the shares.

Company's Profitability
The payment of a large salary or bonus will depress the company's profits. This may affect the company's ability to borrow.

It could also affect the amount received in the event of a sale of the company or its underlying business: although more sophisticated buyers will generally discount actual payments to directors and substitute a market rate when valuing the company's shares or business goodwill.

Government Support
It's worth remembering that during the covid pandemic, one of the groups that received very little support from the government was small company directors paying themselves a small salary.

While sole traders and business partners were able to claim grants and regular employees could get most of their pay, all a small company director could claim was a proportion of their salary and then *only if* they stopped work in their business. Those following the small salary/large dividend route received very little support. Perhaps this was the Government's revenge for years of tax savings.

There is always the risk of something similar happening again one day, so it's worth remembering what happened last time!

Chapter 41

Paying Salaries & Dividends: Profits & Paperwork

Real Time Information

Employers have to report salary payments to HMRC under the Real Time Information (RTI) regime. Under real time information, employers are required to submit a Full Payment Submission (FPS) to HMRC at the same time or before each payment is made to a director or employee.

The idea is to make sure the right amount of tax is paid at the right time. Under the previous system, employers generally only had to report payroll information to HMRC at the end of the year.

Under RTI, the directors' own salaries could result in additional payroll costs (for example, in small 'husband and wife' companies or 'one man band' companies, where the only salaries paid are those of the directors themselves).

Where the directors receive small salaries, it may be cheaper and easier to register with HMRC as an annual scheme and pay salaries as a single annual lump sum (for example, in March just before the end of the tax year).

With annual schemes an FPS is only expected in the month of payment and HMRC only has to be paid once a year. However, it is only possible to register as an annual scheme if all employees are paid annually at the same time.

Once a business is registered as an annual scheme, an Employer Payment Summary (EPS) is not required for the 11 months of the tax year where no payments are made to the directors. Schemes not registered as annual schemes have to make monthly submissions, even if no salaries are paid.

Overdrawn Loan Accounts

An additional problem may arise where directors withdraw cash from their companies and only later decide how these payments are to be treated (for example, as salaries or dividends).

Where the director's loan account is overdrawn, an amount withdrawn and subsequently designated as salary could result in a late filing penalty under RTI.

When directors withdraw money from their companies, it is essential to decide up front the nature of the payment (salary, loan, dividend, reimbursement of expenses, etc) and to have evidence supporting that decision.

For example, where a director borrows money from the company, the terms of the loan should be set out in writing. Withdrawals by directors that cannot be categorised might be treated as earnings by HMRC unless the company can prove otherwise.

Loan Accounts in Credit

The exception to these stringent requirements is where the director is simply drawing from a director's loan account that is in credit (the company owes them money). In these cases, withdrawals can usually be safely debited to the loan account (provided it does not then become overdrawn) and then a salary, dividend, etc, might later be declared and credited to the loan account to re-establish the balance. The supporting evidence still has to be there, but there is a little more time to sort things out.

Dividends

Distributable Profits

Under the Companies Act, a company cannot legally pay a dividend unless it has sufficient distributable profits to cover it.

A company's distributable profits are its accumulated realised profits, less accumulated realised losses. This information can generally be found in the company's most recent annual accounts.

It is not necessary for the company to actually make a profit in the year the dividend is paid, as long as there are sufficient accumulated profits (after tax) from previous years.

So, all is not necessarily lost if your company has been experiencing difficult trading conditions in recent times. As long as there are sufficient distributable profits from previous years, it may be possible to continue paying dividends.

Where the most recent annual accounts do not show sufficient profits, interim or management accounts can be prepared with more up to date information. This may be useful if business conditions have improved since the last accounts were prepared.

It's also important to remember directors have a duty to promote the company's success, protect its assets, and take reasonable action to ensure the company can pay its debts.

If future trading losses are expected, this is a factor that should be taken into account when considering the cash flow implications of any proposed dividend.

Thus, even if the most recent set of accounts show there are sufficient distributable profits, the directors must take account of any change in the company's financial position since the accounts date and consider whether the company will remain solvent after any proposed dividend is paid. The key point is that directors must act honestly and reasonably at all times.

Before paying any dividends, it is probably wise to speak to your accountant to check whether the company does indeed have sufficient distributable profits.

If the company does not have sufficient distributable profits to cover its dividend payments, the dividends will be illegal and the shareholder will be liable to repay the company. While this is seldom enforced unless the company becomes insolvent, it is important to be aware of the legal position and wise to 'play it safe' by avoiding any illegal dividends.

Dividend Formalities & Paperwork

If the proper formalities are not observed, it is possible HMRC will try to tax dividends as employment income. To help avoid any such challenge it is essential to ensure dividends are properly declared and you have the supporting paperwork to prove it. This includes:

- Holding a directors' board meeting to recommend the dividend payment (with written minutes to prove the meeting took place)
- Holding a general meeting of the company's members (i.e. shareholders) to approve the dividend payment (with written minutes to prove the meeting took place).
- Issuing a dividend confirmation to each shareholder.

See Appendix A for sample documentation.

Some commentators also argue it is not advisable to declare dividends monthly because this will look more like salary income, especially if the above formalities are neglected.

A better alternative would be an infrequent dividend credited to the director's loan account which can then be drawn down throughout the year.

Paying a dividend towards the end of the tax year, when it may be easier to work out how much Income Tax will be payable, is possibly best in timing terms. If a dividend is paid at the beginning of the year and income from other sources (for example, rental income) turns out to be higher than expected, the company owner could end up paying tax at a higher rate on their dividend income.

Interim versus Final Dividends
A final dividend must be recommended by the directors and endorsed by a shareholders' meeting. For tax purposes, the dividend is treated as paid on that date (unless a later date is specified).

Interim dividends can be authorised at the discretion of directors and are recognised for tax purposes only when they are paid, for example by crediting the director's loan account.

Chapter 42

Dividends Taxed as Earnings and Other Potential Dangers

Back in 2013, HMRC managed to get something called the general anti-abuse rule (GAAR) onto the statute books. As the name implies, the rule is aimed at blocking abusive tax arrangements. An arrangement is considered abusive if it cannot reasonably be regarded as a reasonable course of action: commonly referred to as the double reasonableness test.

Clearly this is very subjective, but HMRC has sought to reassure us there is a high threshold for showing that tax arrangements are abusive:

"In respect of any particular arrangement there might be a range of views as to whether it was a reasonable course of action: it is possible that there could be a reasonably held view that the tax arrangements were a reasonable course of action, and also a reasonably held view that the arrangement is not a reasonable course of action. In such circumstances the tax arrangements will not be abusive for the purposes of the GAAR."

An indicator that tax arrangements are not abusive is if they were established practice when entered into and HMRC indicated its acceptance of that practice at the time.

On the other hand, tax arrangements may be abusive if, for example, the tax result is different to the real economic result, such as tax deductions or tax losses significantly greater than actual expenses or real economic losses.

If you think all of the above is a bit vague, you are not alone. Even the best tax brains in the land don't know what this test means in practice. When legislation contains words like 'reasonable' and 'abusive' you know you have to be on your guard!

The question for us in this guide is: could the anti-abuse rule ever be used to attack 'normal' or 'mainstream' tax planning carried out by small company owners, such as taking small salaries and large dividends?

Thankfully, most tax experts are confident that well-established, conventional tax planning will not be attacked by HMRC using the GAAR. Instead the focus is on 'aggressive' or 'artificial' tax avoidance schemes.

This view is backed up by HMRC guidance, which says the following about small company dividends:

"Just as it is essential to understand what the GAAR is targeted at, so it is equally essential to understand what it is not targeted at. To take an obvious example, a taxpayer deciding to carry on a trade can do so either as a sole trader or through a limited company whose shares he or she owns and where he or she works as an employee. Such a choice is completely outside the target area of the GAAR, and once such a company starts to earn profits a decision to accumulate most of the profits to be paid out in the future by way of dividend, rather than immediately paying a larger salary, is again something that should in any normal trading circumstances be outside the target area of the GAAR."

Phew! So, routine tax planning carried out by small company owners when extracting money from their company as tax efficiently as possible is safe from the GAAR... but what about case law?

There have been some tax cases which demonstrate there is a potential danger that dividends paid to a director/shareholder could, in some circumstances, be vulnerable to a National Insurance liability and possibly a full PAYE charge.

It is unlikely these decisions will ever affect small family companies with simple share structures, but it's worth us taking a look at them as they illustrate the courts' attitude to this area of tax planning.

P A Holdings: PA Holdings switched from a conventional bonus arrangement to a more intricate structure whereby an employee benefit trust was funded by the company, which in turn awarded preference shares to employees. These preference shares duly paid a dividend after which they were redeemed.

The company and its employees argued the dividends should be taxed as dividends using dividend tax rates and without any PAYE or National Insurance implications.

By contrast, HMRC took the view that the dividends simply amounted to earnings and the normal PAYE and National Insurance payments should have been deducted from them and accounted for to HMRC.

The Court of Appeal decided the dividends were indeed earnings for employment and should therefore suffer deductions of Income Tax at source through PAYE. Both employers' and employees' National Insurance deductions should also have been made. PA Holdings initially decided to appeal to the Supreme Court but later threw in the towel.

Uniplex (UK) Ltd: Uniplex was sold a scheme aimed at giving employees dividend income instead of remuneration, issuing different classes of share to each employee. This type of arrangement is generally known as alphabet shares.

The scheme failed as it was not implemented as planned. However, the First Tier Tribunal judge added that the scheme, even if implemented correctly, might still have failed.

Practical Implications
The practical implications of these cases relate to the boundary between normal dividend payments and those which, under the PA Holdings/Uniplex principles, would be treated as employment earnings and hence attract Income Tax and National Insurance deductions through PAYE. For instance, in PA Holdings the First Tier Tribunal said:

"if something is paid out as a distribution by a company to an investing shareholder then the issue of derivation may arise if the shareholder is also an employee. The facts may show that the derivation of a dividend from a share may not be related to earnings because the acquisition and ownership of the share was not related to earnings or more generally to the status of the individual as an employee of the company"

In Uniplex, the First Tier Tribunal said:

"The PA Holdings case is authority for the proposition that payments from a party other than the employer can be from an employee's employment" and *"It may well have still been the case that the full amount would have been taxable because employees had given no consideration for the payment other than their services"*

What all this demonstrates is there can come a point where dividends paid to an employee-shareholder could be vulnerable to a National Insurance liability, and possibly a full PAYE charge.

However, both these cases involved complex tax avoidance schemes: a million miles from the normal, routine tax planning whereby a small company owner structures the payments they take from their company in the most tax efficient way.

Most tax advisers would argue the aggressive tax planning undertaken by PA Holdings (trying to change bonuses into dividends for a large number of employees) is entirely different to the profit extraction model of most small companies.

As yet, the simple salary versus dividend planning we have examined throughout most of this guide, where we are concerned only with payments to one or more director/shareholders, each of whom holds a sizeable stake in a company with only one class of share capital, would not appear to be threatened by the decisions in the more complex cases examined above.

Nonetheless, there is a fear among some more cautious advisers that cases like these might one day be seized upon by HMRC as having created a wider precedent they can apply to any employer that pays dividends to its staff.

The most vulnerable are those who use tax planning HMRC may view as aggressive. We already know some of their main targets. Those we would class as *'Close to Extinction'* include:

- Large scale contrived arrangements where dividends are created for tax avoidance purposes (as in *PA Holdings*).
- 'Alphabet' share arrangements, where different classes of shares (A, B, C, etc) have no substantive rights other than to dividends and are used to share profits in a way that relates to the amount of work carried out in the business (by substituting dividends for salaries or bonuses).

These contrived arrangements have probably had their day and there is a strong risk that dividends paid under these circumstances will be taxed as employment income. In short, we wouldn't touch these types of schemes with a bargepole.

Beyond these, there are other arrangements that we would view as being on the *'Endangered Species'* list, including:

- Alphabet share arrangements or other shares that have no capital or voting rights, used to divert income to spouses/partners or other family members with lower Income Tax rates. These arrangements are highly likely to fall foul of the settlements legislation.
- Directors' loans written off and taxed as dividends.
- Dividend waivers used to divert income to other shareholders, for example where a director waives their own dividends so that their spouse/partner can receive more income. HMRC succeeded in challenging dividend waivers in the case of *Donovan & McLaren v HMRC*.
- Situations where previous salaries paid to minority shareholders have been reduced in favour of dividends.

While these arrangements might still work in some cases, we would urge anyone considering using them to proceed with extreme caution and to seek independent professional advice (independent of whoever is recommending them to you).

Back to Normal

The sixty-four thousand dollar question is: where does all this leave the average small company owner taking a small salary and the rest of their income as dividends?

At the time of writing, it would appear the vast majority of small companies are not under any threat of attack, but this state of affairs could change in the future. The small salary/big dividend tax planning technique may not continue to produce the same savings company owners are currently able to enjoy indefinitely. There is a danger, no matter how small, that HMRC may try to tax your dividends as earnings at some point in the future.

Some tax advisers recommend taking a salary slightly larger than the 'optimal' amounts, so that at least some Income Tax and National Insurance is paid by the director. Some even argue that if you are currently taking a salary larger than the 'optimal' amounts listed in Chapter 9 you should not reduce it.

However, there are still many tax advisers who are content to continue with the current, long-standing tax planning technique, where the most optimal salary is taken each year, until such time as there is an actual change in the law that puts a stop to it.

Remember, HMRC do not make tax law, they only administer it. It's only judges and politicians who can change the law: now isn't that comforting!

Chapter 43

Personal Service Companies

If your company is classed as a personal service company, many of the tax planning opportunities available to other company owners may not be available, for example, the ability to take dividends that are free from National Insurance.

Personal service companies often have to operate the infamous 'IR35' regime, which means the company may be forced to calculate a notional salary for the director/shareholder. This deemed income will be subject to PAYE and National Insurance.

Essentially, HMRC may ignore the company set up and treat most of the company's income as employment income.

Which Companies Are Affected by IR35?
This is where it all becomes a bit of a grey area (which is why professional advice is essential!)

A personal service company is, generally speaking, a firm that receives all or most of its income from services provided by the director/shareholder personally.

Often the work will be carried out for just one client, often for a long period of time, and the client will probably only want the personal services of the company owner (hence IR35 often applies to 'one man band' companies).

Essentially HMRC is looking for cases of 'disguised employment'. In other words, ignoring the fact that there is an intermediary company, the relationship is more like that of an employer and employee rather than the kind of relationship that exists between independent self-employed business owners and their clients.

Where such 'disguised employment' exists, the company must generally apply the IR35 regime to the payments received from that client: effectively treating most of those payments as if they were salary paid to the director/shareholder.

A typical situation that might be caught under the IR35 rules is where the individual resigns as an employee and then goes back to the same job, but working through their own personal service company.

However, it's all very subjective with a long line of legal cases adding to the confusion.

Personal service companies can be found in many different business sectors: the most cited example is IT consultants. They have also come under the media spotlight in recent times, such as when it was disclosed that some BBC presenters had been operating as 'freelancers' via personal service companies, when many would argue they are in fact nothing but employees of the BBC.

Off-Payroll Rules

The 'off-payroll' legislation has applied to employers in the public sector since 2017 and to larger *private sector* employers since 2021.

Under these rules, the onus is on the employer to assess the contractor's employment status and pay Income Tax and National Insurance where there appears to be an employment relationship.

Small organisations are exempt from this legislation. Where small businesses take on contractors through an intermediary, the responsibility for applying the IR35 rules stays with the contractor.

A business will generally be treated as small if it satisfies two or more of the following requirements:

- Annual turnover does not exceed £10.2 million
- Assets not more than £5.1 million
- No more than 50 employees

IR35 and the off-payroll legislation are beyond the scope of this guide.

Part 8

More Tax Planning Ideas

Chapter 44

How to Pay Less CGT by Postponing Dividends

The main Capital Gains Tax (CGT) rates are currently:

- 10% for basic rate taxpayers
- 20% for higher or additional rate taxpayers

Rates of 18% and 24% respectively apply to gains arising on disposals of *residential* property.

Where the individual is entitled to business asset disposal relief, the gain is taxed at 10%. This relief is generally only available when you sell or wind up a trading business (furnished holiday letting businesses may also qualify until 5th April 2025).

Another relief, called investor's relief, also applies a 10% tax rate to certain share disposals. It does not apply to director/shareholders selling their own company, however.

In other cases, the CGT rate depends on how much income you've earned during the tax year.

The basic-rate band is £37,700 which means you can have up to £37,700 of capital gains taxed at the lower rates this year.

The maximum CGT saving that can be achieved by reducing your income and freeing up your basic-rate band is currently as follows:

£37,700 x 6% = £2,262 Residential property (18% instead of 24%)
£37,700 x 10% = £3,770 Most other assets (10% instead of 20%)

Postponing Dividends
If you expect to realise a large capital gain, for example by disposing of a buy-to-let property, you may be able to save some tax by making sure the disposal takes place during a tax year in which your taxable income is quite low.

In this respect, company owners can manipulate their incomes more easily than regular employees, sole traders, or business partners. The company itself can keep trading and generating profits, but the company owner can make sure very little of these profits are extracted and taxed in his or her hands.

Example: Richard, a company owner, sells his second home in March 2025, realising a gain of £40,700 after deducting all buying and selling costs. Deducting his annual CGT exemption of £3,000 leaves a taxable gain of £37,700.

Richard hasn't paid himself any dividends during the current tax year and decides to postpone paying any so that his £37,700 capital gain is taxed at 18% instead of 24%. This simple piece of planning saves Richard £2,262 in CGT.

Note that Richard can still pay himself a tax-free salary of £12,570, or a salary of £9,100 plus dividends of £3,470, to utilise his Income Tax personal allowance. The Income Tax personal allowance does not interfere with the CGT calculation.

Limitations
Although postponing dividends could help you pay less CGT, it's probably not worth doing this unless you can withdraw the postponed dividends in a future tax year and pay no more than 8.75% tax. If you take a bigger dividend in a later tax year, and end up paying 33.75% Income Tax, you may end up worse off overall.

Example continued: In the above example Richard postponed taking a dividend of £37,700 to free up his basic rate band and pay 18% CGT.

If during 2025/26 he takes an additional dividend of £37,700, on top of his usual salary and maximum dividend taxed at 8.75%, he will pay additional Income Tax of £12,724 (£37,700 x 33.75%). If he had taken that income in 2024/25, however, he would have paid Income Tax of £3,255: so he ends up paying £9,469 more Income Tax.

He saved £2,262 in CGT in 2024/25, but pays an additional £9,469 in Income Tax in 2025/26. Overall Richard is £7,207 worse off.

Chapter 45

Emigrating to Save Tax

Possibly the most drastic step you can take to save tax is leave the country. By becoming non-UK resident, you may be able to avoid both CGT (when you sell your company) and Income Tax (if you want to withdraw big dividends).

Capital Gains Tax

In the past it was possible to go and live in certain countries for just one year and completely avoid CGT. This was a fantastic loophole, especially when CGT was levied at rates of up to 40%.

Unfortunately, that loophole was closed and most UK taxpayers who move abroad temporarily to avoid CGT will be taxed when they return if their period of non-UK residence lasts less than five years.

With a CGT rate of just 10% applying to many company sales (where business asset disposal relief applies), many company owners would be unwilling to exile themselves from the UK for five years just to increase their bank accounts by 10%.

Moving abroad is an expensive and time-consuming business and these costs would eat into your tax savings.

Having said this, the reduction in the lifetime allowance for business asset disposal relief from £10 million to just £1 million of gains means many business owners will now pay the higher 20% CGT rate when they sell their companies.

If you plan to emigrate one day anyway, this is all academic. You may be able to live in the country of your dreams **and** reduce your tax bill at the same time.

However, emigration isn't always what it used to be. UK CGT may still be charged on all or part of the gain on the sale of your company after you become non-UK resident if UK property (land and buildings) accounts for 75% or more of the company's total gross asset value. The charge applies to the increase in value arising after 5th April 2019. For further details, see the Taxcafe guide *Using a Property Company to Save Tax*.

Income Tax

Where a company has built up significant distributable profits it was possible in the past to withdraw these profits as tax-free dividends during a short period of non-UK residence.

This tax planning opportunity is no longer available following the introduction of some anti-avoidance rules.

Income from 'closely controlled companies' (most small companies) will be taxed if the recipient becomes UK resident again after a temporary period of non-residence of five years or less.

This anti-avoidance rule does not apply to dividends paid out of post-departure profits, i.e. profits built up while you are non-UK resident.

It is not meant to apply to employment and self-employment earnings or regular investment income, e.g. dividends from stock market companies and bank interest.

Furthermore, the anti-avoidance rule will only apply where an individual has been UK resident in at least four out of the seven tax years prior to the tax year in which they become non-resident.

While it may no longer be possible to avoid Income Tax by becoming non-UK resident for a short period, this tax planning strategy may still work for genuine emigrants who decide to leave the UK permanently.

Becoming Non-UK Resident

It used to be the case that you could generally establish, or maintain non-UK resident status by making sure you never spent more than 90 days in the UK in any tax year. That's still a reasonable rule of thumb in many cases, but there is now far more that needs to be considered.

A statutory residence test is now used to determine whether or not you are UK resident in any particular tax year.

The test is complex to say the least and includes rules which can seem quite arbitrary at times. For example, I once had to tell my step-daughter that she couldn't stay at her mother's house (my ex-partner) beyond a certain date as she would then lose her non-UK resident status and be liable for UK Income Tax on the salary she had earned in Dubai earlier in the same tax year. Honestly, I'm not making this up!

Anyway, suffice to say, if you intend to emigrate to avoid or reduce UK taxes, it's essential to get professional advice.

Professional advice should also be obtained in your new intended country of residence, as becoming resident in another country will expose you to their taxes: you don't want to end up 'jumping out of the frying pan and into the fire!'

Sample Dividend Documentation

1. Directors' Board Meeting Minute

BOARD MINUTE

Minutes of a Meeting of Directors of Winging It Ltd held at 13 Fluky Road, Charmedtown, ZZ1 1AA on 31st March 2025.

Present: Mr AB Happy – Director
    Mrs CD Go – Director
    Mr EF Lucky – Director

In attendance: Mr G Downcast – Company Secretary

Motions:
1) The directors noted the company's excellent trading results for the year ended 31st December 2024.
2) It was recommended that the company pay a dividend of £2.50 per ordinary share out of the profits for the year ended 31st December 2024, to be paid on 1st April 2025.
3) No other motions.

Signed _____ Date _____
   (Mr AB Happy)

Notes (Not Part of the Minute)
The minutes of a directors' board meeting should:
 a) Show who is present.
 b) Include enough information to show how directors reasonably came to reasonable decisions.
 c) Include details of any conflicts of interest or abstention from voting.
 d) Be signed by a director present at the meeting.
 e) Be retained with the company's statutory records.

Regarding point (a) above, a quorum may need to be present for the meeting to be valid. This depends on the company's constitution as set out in its Articles of Association.

2. Member's General Meeting Minute

GENERAL MEETING OF MEMBERS

Minutes of an Extraordinary General Meeting of the Ordinary Shareholders of Winging It Ltd held at 13 Fluky Road, Charmedtown, ZZ1 1AA on 31st March 2025.

Present: Mr AB Happy – Ordinary Shareholder
                Mrs CD Go – Ordinary Shareholder
                Mr EF Lucky – Ordinary Shareholder

In attendance: Mr G Downcast – Company Secretary

Motions:
1) The members, all being present, agreed to accept the short notice period for the meeting.
2) The members approved the recommendation of the directors that the company pay a dividend of £2.50 per ordinary share for the year ended 31st December 2024. Payment to be made on 1st April 2025.
3) No other motions.

Signed _____   Date _____
      (Mr AB Happy)

3. Dividend Confirmation

Dividend Confirmation

Winging It Limited
13 Fluky Road, Charmedtown, ZZ1 1AA

Ordinary shares of £1 each

Mr AB Happy   1st April 2025
1 Blessed Street
Charmedtown
ZZ2 1XY

Payment of the final dividend in respect of the year ended 31st December 2024, at the rate of £2.50 per share on the ordinary shares registered in your name on 31st March 2025 is enclosed herewith.

G. Downcast, Company Secretary

Shareholding	Dividend Payable	Payment Number
10,000	£25,000.00	12

This dividend confirmation should be kept with your tax records.

Notes (Not Part of the Document)
If payment is made electronically (as is more common these days), the words 'has been made directly into your bank account' can be substituted for 'is enclosed herewith'.

Alternatively, if no actual payment is made, the words 'has been credited to your director's loan account' can be used instead.

Appendix B

Connected Persons

The concept of 'connected persons' is important for a number of the issues discussed in this guide. The exact definition of 'connected persons' differs slightly from one area of UK tax law to another, so it is always important to get professional advice on this issue. Generally, however, an individual's connected persons include the following:

i)   Their husband, wife or civil partner
ii)   The following relatives:
        o   Mother, father or remoter ancestor
        o   Son, daughter or remoter descendant
        o   Brother or sister
iii)   Relatives under (ii) above of the individual's spouse or civil partner
iv)   Spouses or civil partners of the individual's relatives under (ii) above
v)   Spouses or civil partners of an individual under (iii) above
vi)   The individual's business partners
vii)   Trusts where the individual is:
        o   The settlor (the person who set up the trust or transferred property, other assets, or funds into it), or
        o   A person 'connected' (as defined in this appendix) with the settlor
viii)   Companies under the control of the individual, either alone, or together with persons under (i) to (vii) above